The NEW Meaning of Educational Change

THIRD EDITION

The NEW Meaning of Educational Change

THIRD EDITION

MICHAEL FULLAN

Teachers College, Columbia University
New York and London

RoutledgeFalmer
London

Published simultaneously by Teachers College Press, 1234 Amsterdam Avenue, New York, NY 10027 and by RoutledgeFalmer, 11 New Fetter Lane, London, EC4P 4EE.

RoutledgeFalmer is an imprint of the Taylor and Francis Group.

Library of Congress Cataloging-in-Publication Data

Fullan, Michael.
    The new meaning of educational change / Michael G. Fullan — 3rd ed.
      p. cm.
    Includes bibliographical references and index.
    ISBN 0-8077-4070-5 (cloth) — ISBN 0-8077-4069-1 (pbk. : alk. paper)
     1. Educational change—Canada.   2. Educational change—United States.
  3. Education and state—Canada.   4. Education and state—United States.
    I. Title.
    LA412 .F85   2001
    370'.971—dc21   00-066317

ISBN 0-8077-4069-1 (paper)
ISBN 0-8077-4070-5 (cloth)

RoutledgeFalmer ISBN 0-415-26019-1 (cloth)
RoutledgeFalmer ISBN 0-415-26020-5 (paper)

Printed on acid-free paper
Manufactured in the United States of America

08   07   06   05   04   03   8   7   6   5   4   3

And Conor makes five

Contents

PART III:
EDUCATIONAL CHANGE
AT THE REGIONAL AND NATIONAL LEVELS

Preface

This is the third edition of *The Meaning of Educational Change*. An enormous amount has happened in the decade since the last edition. If anything, "the meaning hypothesis" has become deeply confirmed. As we shall see, advances in cognitive science make meaning the foundation for the new pedagogy of constructivism. Chaos or complexity theory leads us inevitably to the conclusion that working on "coherence" is the key to dealing with the nonlinear fragmented demands of overloaded reform agendas.

Fortunately, the interest in educational reform has reached new heights as we enter the 21st century. Grappling with the problem of achieving large-scale reform grounded in local ownership has become the new challenge—overtaking the false choice between local innovation and macro, superficial reform. There are a great many new examples of initiatives and corresponding lessons of change to be mined.

These new lessons of reform enable us to become much more precise about the inner workings of educational change processes. To do this we have to understand both the small and big pictures. We have to know what change feels like from the point of view of the teacher, student, parent, and administrator if we are to understand the actions and reactions of individuals; and if we are to comprehend the big picture, we must combine the aggregate knowledge of these individual situations with an understanding of organization and institutional factors that influence the process of change as governments, teacher unions, school systems, and communities interact.

One of the most promising features of this new knowledge about change is that it makes sense. Indeed, rendering complexity understandable and amenable to productive action is the theme of this book. This doesn't mean that it is easy. When you have a good idea and you are facing an urgent problem it is easy to ignore the process of change. Resisting the urge to bulldoze ahead is counterintuitive.

I have written this book for individuals at all levels of the educational system. All key players will find a chapter on their own roles, as well as chapters on other roles and agencies with whom they must interact. Part I—Understanding Educational Change—provides an overview of the history, sources, processes, and outcomes of change and the implications for dealing with it. Part II contains chapters on each of the main roles at the local level, examining the daily reality people face. In Part III, I return to the larger scene to consider the role of governments, the evolution of the teaching profession, and the future of educational change. Each of the 16 chapters can be read and understood on its own, although the underlying theme and total picture depend on the combined chapters.

I contend that the "knowledge base" of change is becoming more profound, and that it is absolutely indispensable to dealing with the relentless ubiquity of innovation and reform. It isn't that people resist change as much as they don't know how to cope with it. The answer is for individuals, especially in interaction with others, to arm themselves with knowledge of the change process and to refine it continually through reflective action, and to test what they know against the increasingly available knowledge in the literature on change.

There is not much jargon in the book: one cannot claim that meaning is the answer and then proceed to write an abstruse treatise on the subject. The main findings are amply referenced. For the student of change who wishes to delve into the topic, the reference section contains some 250 items, many of which are new. For those less interested in the research base, the chapters can be read without attention to the references. In short, the book is intended for professionals (policymakers and practitioners) at all levels of the system, as well as for professors and university students seeking a textbook on theories and practices of educational change.

Dissatisfaction with and interest in educational reform is a worldwide phenomenon. Although most of the material I draw on comes from North America, any discussion with those involved in educational innovation and reform in other countries quickly reveals that the nature of problems and the principles of success and failure are common around the world. The fact that our books on educational change have been translated into almost a dozen languages attests to the wide relevance of the ideas.

It is also important to acknowledge that the best insights into the change process come from our association with practice. While Kurt Lewin was right in saying that "there is nothing so practical as good theory," it is equally true that "there is nothing so theoretical as good practice." This is especially so when it comes to change theory. In this sense, I have learned most from the work we have been directly involved in locally and around the world. Many of these ideas have been developed in our Learning Consortium partnership with school districts in the Toronto region, and with my colleagues at the University of Toronto where we have been engaged in our own laboratory reform of higher education including a massive merger involving almost 200 professors, 3,500 students, 300 administrative staff, and two lab schools coming together in 1996 from two different cultures. I have been privileged to learn about change with my colleagues at the University of Toronto on a day-to-day basis.

Other long-term projects we are involved in fuel the fire: policy developments in Ontario concerning the Ministry of Education and Training, the Education Quality and Accountability Office, and the Ontario College of Teachers; the Manitoba School Improvement Program; the Assessment Literacy Initiative in Edmonton; the Consortium on Educational Change in Illinois; the Center for Development in Louisiana; the Guilford County Leadership Development Initiative in North Carolina; the partnership with the Aga Khan University in Pakistan; the work with the Soros Foundation in Eastern Europe; the exchanges with the World Bank on reform projects in many countries; and the fascinating evaluation of the National Literacy and Numeracy Strategy in England in which targeted improvements are being attempted in 20,000 schools simultaneously.

In other words, I have benefited enormously from these action projects working with large international groups of students and doers of change. These include the thousands of teachers, principals, superintendents, teacher union leaders, and others who have participated in our workshops. Conducting workshops on managing change is one of the better ways of learning about it. In these sessions, there is no shortage of wrenching practical questions constantly causing one to go back to the drawing board.

It is now impossible to thank by name the hundreds of co-change agents working on educational improvement who so generously give of their time and ideas. I can only say that they know who they are and I thank them sincerely.

Producing the manuscript was a massive task. It had to be done well, and it had to be done quickly. Claudia Cuttress was able to pull all of it together in short order because of her knowledge of the various projects and sources, and because she works with amazing speed and quality. My heartfelt thanks for her tremendous contribution.

On the home front, Wendy, Bailey, and Conor have been great and fun supporters throughout. They know that *The New Meaning of Educational Change* is a special book. While it would be a stretch to call it a family project, my family has been closely associated with its history over the almost 25 years of development to the present edition.

To all these people, I hope the final product contributes some sense of new meaning and value commensurate with at least a fraction of the support I have received. Thank you all.

PART I

UNDERSTANDING EDUCATIONAL CHANGE

CHAPTER 1

A Brief History of Educational Change

*Everything must change at one time or another or else
a static society will evolve.*
> —Anonymous first-year university student
> on an English language proficiency test

One person claims that schools are being bombarded by change;
another observes that there is nothing new under the sun. A policy-
maker charges that teachers are resistant to change; a teacher complains that administrators introduce change for their own self-
aggrandizement and that they neither know what is needed nor
understand the classroom. A parent is bewildered by a new practice
in reading and by the relevance of education to future jobs. Some
argue that restructuring schools is the only answer, while others
decry that this too is just a pipe dream diverting our attention
from the core curriculum changes that are desperately needed. One
university professor is convinced that schools are only a reflection
of society and cannot be expected to bring about change; another
professor is equally convinced that schools would be all right if only
superintendents and principals had more "vision" as educational
leaders, and teachers were more motivated to learn new approaches
to improving the curriculum. A governor works hard to get major
new legislation passed to reform education; a principal thinks, "this
too shall pass." Charter schools are hailed simultaneously as saving
the day and destroying the public education system. Commercial
entities take over school districts and claim that they can do a
better job. States pass dramatic legislation to serve notice to "failing
schools" and "failing school districts" with corresponding invasive

interventions intended to make things right. Standards-based reform is held up as the answer to our woes.

Amidst all this turmoil, agents at all levels wonder how to get
more and more programs institutionalized, while teachers think
that it is these same promoters of change who should be institutionalized, not their programs. Students are too distracted by a host
of other matters to pay much attention to all the uproar.

What are we learning from these mostly aborted and confused
attempts at reform? Remarkably, the history of intensive educational change is less than half a century old. I won't say much
about the 1950s. It was relatively quiet for most of the decade. The
big initial development, as Miles (1993) has noted, was the National
Training Laboratories' (NTL) training in group skills, shared reflection, diagnosis, and action. For the most part these experiences
were laboratory-based, detached from the day-to-day instructional
issues and function of schools.

To say that NTL and related projects had limited impact is
not to say that they were on the wrong track. Today, for example,
it is abundantly clear that one of the keys to successful change is
the *improvement of relationships* (Fullan, 2001)—precisely the focus
of group development. In any case, as it turned out, these early
attempts represented mere tinkering. There were much larger fish
to fry if education was to play a leading role in societal development.

THE FIRST ATTEMPT FALLS FLAT

One doesn't have to believe that Sputnik was the literal cause of
large-scale reform in the United States post-1957, or that all new
ideas started in the 1960s, or that the United States was the only
country engaged in national educational reform, to know that something very different was in the air in the 1960s. Elmore (1995) stated
earlier in describing the pre-1950s "progressive period":

> What is most interesting about the progressive period, as com-
> pared with other periods of educational reform, is that its aims
> included explicit attempts to change pedagogy, coupled with a
> relatively strong intellectual and practical base. Noted intellectu-

als—John Dewey, in particular—developed ideas about how schools might be different. (p. 7)

Progressive reformers believed, according to Elmore, that for the most part "good ideas would travel of their own volition" into schools and classrooms (p. 18). The strategy, noted Elmore, "turned inward, toward the creation of exemplary settings" (p. 11), particularly over time. The result:

> We can produce many examples of how educational practice could look different, but we can produce few, if any, examples of large numbers of teachers engaging in these practices in large scale institutions designed to deliver education to most children. (Elmore, 1995, p. 11)

Despite these failures, and indeed ignoring their lessons, the U.S. federal government launched a large-scale national curriculum reform series of initiatives in the late 1950s and throughout the 1960s. I have previously labeled this the "adoption era" of reform because the goal was to get innovations out there, as if flooding the system with external ideas would bring about desired improvements. Huge sums of money were poured into major curriculum reforms like PSSC Physics, BSCC Biology, and MACOS Social Sciences, and organizational innovations such as open plan schools, flexible scheduling, and team teaching.

By the early 1970s there was mounting evidence that the yield was minuscule, confined to isolated examples. Goodlad, Klein and associates' (1970) *Behind the Classroom Door*, Sarason's (1971) *The Culture of the School and the Problem of Change*, and Gross, Gianquinta, and Bernstein's (1971) *Implementing Organizational Innovations* all attested to the absence of change at the level of the classroom. The term "implementation" (or more accurately, "failed implementation") came into the vocabulary of reform, and in the first major review of research, Fullan and Pomfret (1977) documented the massive failure of reform. Putting ideas into practice was a far more complex process than people realized.

Elmore summarized that what these models missed

> was the complex process by which local curricular decisions get made, the entrenched and institutionalized political and com-

mercial relationships that support existing textbook-driven curricula, the weak incentives operating on teachers to change their
practices in their daily work routines, and the extraordinary costs
of making large scale, long-standing changes of a fundamental
kind in how knowledge is constructed in classrooms. (1995,
p. 15)

There was actually great pressure and incentives to become
innovative, and this resulted in many schools adopting reforms for
which they did not have the capacity (individually or organizationally) to put into practice. Thus, innovations were adopted on the
surface with some of the language and structures becoming altered,
but not the practice of teaching.

Another major force for reform around the Western world
in the 1960s was the various forms of civil rights movements,
pinpointing scores of inequities. Numerous national initiatives across
the world focused on the disadvantaged. The education system
was thought to be one of the major societal vehicles for reducing
social inequality. To the intrinsic complexity of changing one's
practice was added the enormous difficulty of tackling the existing
power structure and overcoming the prejudice and ignorance of
ethnic, class, gender, and special differences of all kinds. Nor is
there much evidence that the lives of the disadvantaged have improved, even in cases where sincere efforts to do so are in evidence
(Oakes et al., 1999). And where gains have been achieved, it has
been in isolated cases, seemingly guaranteed not to go to scale.

Not much progress has been made since the 1960s, despite
renewed interest in large-scale reform in the 1980s focusing on
accountability. The *pressure* for reform has increased, but not yet
the reality. The good news is that there is a growing sense of
urgency about the need for large-scale reform, more appreciation
of the complexity of achieving it, and even some examples of partial
success.

The urgent reasons for reform are now familiar. The global
society is increasingly complex, requiring educated citizens who
can learn continuously, and who can work with diversity, locally
and internationally. Although the source of blame varies, it is now
an undeniable conclusion that the educational system and its partners have failed to produce citizens who can contribute to and

benefit from a world that offers enormous opportunity, and equally complex difficulty of finding your way in it. Rohlen (1999) makes this case convincingly in his analysis of "social software for a learning society," in which he argues:

> In essence, the message is that our schools need to teach learning processes that better fit the way work is evolving. Above all, this means teaching the skills and habits of mind that are essential to problem-solving, especially where many minds need to interact. (pp. 251–252)

For these reasons we have witnessed a growing intensity in the efforts at large-scale reform in the 1990s. We can now accurately conclude, as I will illustrate throughout this book, that large-scale reform has returned. We are now less naive than the last time we had such an opportunity, while society, and therefore the problem of reform, is more complex.

The forces reinforcing the status quo are systemic. The current system is held together in many different crosscutting ways. Confronting the isolationism and privatism of educational systems is a tall order. It requires intensive action sustained over several years to make it possible both physically and attitudinally for teachers to work naturally together in joint planning; observation of each other's practice; and seeking, testing, and revising teaching strategies on a continuous basis. Reform is not just putting into place the latest policy. It means changing the cultures of the classrooms, the schools, the districts, the universities, and so on. There is much more to educational reform than most people realize. This book honors that complexity but also identifies the most powerful levers for reform at our disposal. These levers must have the strength to influence complex webs of factors, while having the virtue of clarity, if not simplicity. We need powerful usable strategies for powerful recognizable change.

If a healthy respect for and mastery of the change process does not become a priority, even well-intentioned change initiatives will continue to create havoc among those who are on the firing line. Careful attention to a small number of key details during the change process can result in the experience of success, new commitments, and the excitement and energizing satisfaction of accomplishing something that is important. More fundamentally, reducing the number of failures and realizing new successes can lead to the revitalization of teaching and learning that is so desperately needed in the lives of educators and students today.

The problem of meaning is central to making sense of educational change. In order to achieve greater meaning, we must come to understand both the small and the big pictures. The small picture concerns the subjective meaning or lack of meaning for individuals at all levels of the educational system. Neglect of the phenomenology of change—that is, how people actually experience change as distinct from how it might have been intended—is at the heart of the spectacular lack of success of most social reforms. It is also necessary to build and understand the big picture, because educational change, after all, is a sociopolitical process. This book will have succeeded or failed to the extent that people who are involved in education can read the account and conclude that it makes sense of their individual context, enables them to understand the broader social forces influencing change and—above all—points to some action that they and others around them can take to improve their immediate situation.

In the process of examining the individual and collective settings, it is necessary to contend with both the "what" of change and the "how" of change. Meaning must be accomplished in relation to both these aspects. It is possible to be crystal clear about what one wants and be totally inept at achieving it. Or to be skilled at managing change but empty-headed about which changes are most needed. To make matters more difficult, we often do not know what we want, or do not know the actual consequences of a particular direction, until we try to get there. Thus, on the one hand, we need to keep in mind the values and goals and the consequences associated with specific educational changes; and on the other hand, we need to comprehend the dynamics of educational change as a sociopolitical process involving all kinds of individual, classroom, school, local, regional, and national factors at work in interactive ways. The problem of meaning is one of how those involved in change can come to understand what it is that should change, and how it can be best accomplished, while realizing that the what and how constantly interact and reshape each other.

We are not only dealing with a moving and changing target; we are also playing this out in social settings. Solutions must come through the development of *shared meaning*. The interface between individual and collective meaning and action in everyday situations is where change stands or falls.

THE PLAN OF THE BOOK

I do not attempt to survey the content or substance of all the latest educational innovations and reforms. I do, however, use a wide range of specific innovations to explain the practical meaning of educational change. Included in the studies on which I draw are changes in various curriculum areas (e.g., reading, mathematics, science, social studies), computers, cooperative learning, special education, school restructuring, teacher education, schoolwide innovations, district reform, state and national policies, and so on. Locally initiated changes are well represented along with those sponsored at the provincial/state and national levels.

The book is divided into three main parts. Part I, Understanding Educational Change (Chapters 1 through 6), provides a detailed overview of how educational change works. Chapter 2 addresses the issues regarding what are the main sources and purposes of educational change. It raises questions about who benefits from what types of changes, and about the bases on which decisions to change are made. Evidence is analyzed that leads to the conclusion that many decisions about the kinds of educational innovations introduced in school districts are poorly thought out and unconnected to the stated purposes of education. The sources of innovation and the quality of decisions made indicate that change is not necessarily progress. Change must always be viewed in relation to the particular values, goals, and outcomes it serves. This is frequently difficult to assess in education, because rhetoric differs from reality, and consequences cannot easily be determined or measured. Chapter 2 also concludes that there is an increasingly rich source of innovative ideas "out there." The main difficulty is how to achieve coherence in this sea of potentially valuable clutter.

Whether or not the sources of change are suspect, what does it mean to change? Chapter 3 deals with the subjective reality of coping with change, both involuntary and desired change, and makes explicit the objective reality of what we mean when we refer to something as having changed. This chapter defines what change is. Combined with Chapter 2, we see overwhelming possibilities and thus the problem of achieving meaning.

Chapter 4 identifies the main factors that relate to adoption or decisions to initiate change. There are a variety of reasons why individuals or groups decide to embark on a change—personal prestige, bureaucratic self-interest, political responsiveness, and concern for solving an unmet need. This chapter raises questions about how and why decisions about particular educational changes are made. The way in which these decisions are made strongly influences what will happen at the follow-up or implementation stage.

Implementation and continuation (or the extent to which change actually occurs and is sustained) are the focus of Chapter 5. Since implementation refers to what really happens in practice (as distinct from what was supposed to happen), it is a central theme that runs through the whole book. The history of implementation research is not pleasant. It shows that planned change attempts rarely succeed as intended. As some old sayings go, "There's many a slip 'twixt the cup and the lip," "the proof is in the pudding," and "the road to hell is paved with good intentions." Honorable motives are even more problematic when we attempt to get others to heaven as well as ourselves—when social rather than individual change is at stake. In fact, I will show that, ironically, in many ways the more committed an individual is to a specific form of change, the less effective he or she will be in getting others to implement it. While the above sayings have been around a long time, it is only in the last 30 years that educators have come to realize that "the proof is in the 'putting'": the way in which change is put into practice determines to a large extent how well it fares. As we shall see, some of the most recent evidence indicates that we may be getting better at planning and implementing not only specific innovations, but also more complex policy reforms. Certainly there is greater clarity about what factors need to be addressed and how to address them.

Chapters 4 and 5 cover the process of change: from how changes become initiated to how or whether they get put into practice and become institutionalized. What happens at one stage has powerful consequences for subsequent stages. In the final analysis, Chapter 5 provides an overview of the dynamics of how educational changes get implemented/nonimplemented and institutionalized/discontinued.

It is one thing to know the events and situations that cause change or prevent change from happening; it is an entirely different question to know what to do about it. Chapter 6 delves into the complex issues of planning and coping with educational change. It addresses the perplexing question of "the pathways problem" —knowing what constitutes success is not the same thing as achieving it in a new situation. Many attempts at change fail because no distinction is made between theories of change (what causes change) and theories of changing (how to influence those causes). And when solutions are attempted, they often create their own problems, which are more severe than the original ones. Chapter 6 contains examples of both failure and success at planned change. At a minimum this knowledge offers certain psychological and practical advantages simply by allowing us to become more clear about the process and meaning of change and more realistic about what can be accomplished. By making explicit the problems of planning and coping with change, we gain further understanding of why certain plans fail and others succeed. I also identify guidelines for how change can be approached or coped with more effectively.

Part I, then, provides the overall framework for thinking about and doing something about educational change. It shows, incidentally, that "rationally planned" strategies are not that rational when it comes to dealing with people and the problem of meaning. Part I does not differentiate in detail what it all means for the everyday teacher, principal, parent, and so on. This is the purpose of Part II, "Educational Change at the Local Level," which consists of six chapters (7 through 12) in which I examine what is known about the role of people in different positions at the local school and school-district levels. In each case, I bring to bear the body of research knowledge (particularly concrete, experiential evidence) on a given role in order to address two sets of questions. The first set concerns the meaning of change for people in the role under discussion—what their experience is in relation to the process of educational change. Then, when we have some understanding of the meaning of change for given role incumbents, the second set of questions is directed at generating ideas for what they could or should do about it. These guidelines will range from general suggestions to specific steps to be taken, depending on the circumstances.

The six chapters in Part II are designed so that individuals within these roles can gain greater understanding of their place in the context of changes around them. These chapters also enable individuals in one role to gain an understanding of the realities of participants in other roles and thereby a clearer view of the sociology of educational change in the society as a whole.

Chapters 7 to 9 examine change within the school by analyzing the roles of key participants and their organizational relationships. As implementation is the essence of change, it follows that the teacher as implementer is central. Chapter 7 examines the concrete situation of the teacher and shows that change is only one among many problems the teacher faces—in fact, that the conditions for change as well as strategies employed by central policymakers and administrators provide many more disincentives than benefits. Sociologically speaking, few of us, if placed in the current situation of teachers, would be motivated or able to engage in effective change. Obvious strategies do not seem to work. Professional development of teachers has been ineffective and wasteful more times than not. Building on earlier chapters, Chapter 7 explains why many approaches to change do not work for teachers and suggests some remedies. There have been great new advances in knowledge in the last few years in understanding professional learning communities and the role they play in "reculturing" the teachers' role in improvement.

More lip service than mind service has been given to the pivotal role of the principal as gatekeeper or facilitator of change. However, the research evidence is mounting, and we have much to go on in sorting out the role of school leadership. Chapter 8 describes the situation of the principal and his or her current role in facilitating or inhibiting change. As before, to understand what is, we examine specific evidence and situations. It is only through specificity that we can go beyond the generalities of leadership qualities found in much of the literature. In deriving implications for what the role of the principal could or should be, the emphasis will be on the formulation of specific guidelines that deal with the total reality faced by the principal. The principal is absolutely key when it comes to developing the "school capacity" to manage change.

People think of students as the potential beneficiaries of change. They think of achievement results, skills, attitudes, and the need for various improvements for the good of the children. They rarely think of students as *participants* in a process of change. Consequently, there is little evidence regarding what students think about changes and their role regarding them. It is interesting and worthwhile to attempt to develop the theme of what the role of students is and what it could be. Naturally there will be differences according to the age of students, but Chapter 9 will elaborate on the possible meaning of change for children and adolescents. Fortunately, there is growing attention being paid to the "voice" and participation of students in school reform.

The remaining three chapters of Part II address the immediate local environment of the school—district administrators, consultants or resource people, and the parents, community, and school board. A considerable amount of evidence exists that the superintendent and other district administrators are as crucial for determining change within the district as is the principal within the school. Again it will be necessary to examine evidence that will allow us to determine in which ways this is specifically true. What is it that the district administrator does? What is the actual process of events, and what are the results? As interest in large-scale reform has increased, the role of districts has received greater attention. The goal is to engage *all* schools in the district in ongoing reform, not just a few. Case studies of school districts doing this are discussed in Chapter 10.

There are many different consultants in education, variously called curriculum coordinators or consultants, resource teachers, internal change agents, external agents, staff developers, organization development specialists, disseminators, linking agents, and so on. Chapter 11 considers the role of consultants. The intricacies of being a consultant are considerable: the consultant needs to combine subject-matter knowledge, interpersonal skills in working with individuals and groups, and planned change skills for designing and implementing larger change efforts. Evidence from major studies in recent years combined with the framework for understanding educational change enables us to draw some conclusions about how and why some consultants are effective and others are not and how the roles of consultants can be better conceptualized and practiced.

In Chapter 12 the roles of parents, communities, and school boards are examined. The problem of meaning is especially acute for these groups, which are vitally concerned about and responsible for educational decisions but which often have limited knowledge. Case-study materials and other research evidence will be used to clarify what communities do vis-à-vis questions of initiating, rejecting, supporting, or blocking particular changes in their schools, and will illustrate the dilemma that schools face about whether or not to involve parents in decisions about change. I will especially take up questions regarding the role of the individual parent in instruction, decision making, and otherwise relating to the school and to the education of his or her child.

As Part II analyzes what happens at the local level, the four chapters in Part III turn to the regional and national levels. If we are to understand the realities of change at the local level, we must discover how societal agencies, for better or worse, influence change in schools. The role of government agencies represents another dilemma for understanding educational change. On the one hand, important social reforms would not be launched without federal or state/provincial impetus. On the other hand, external reforms frequently are not successful and are seen as interfering with local autonomy. We now have enough evidence from governmental change efforts since 1960 to understand why this source of reform is necessary, why it often doesn't work, and what the implications are for altering the approach. Common principles and research findings will be used to analyze how national and state agencies function in the realm of education. Chapter 13 assesses these issues and formulates guidelines for governmental action.

In Chapters 14 and 15 the education and continuing professional development of school personnel are examined. Nothing is more central to reform than the selection and development of teachers and administrators. The initial preparation of teachers, including induction, is the purview of Chapter 14. Attention is currently being riveted on teacher education as a major strategy for improvement. The preservice education of teachers has not prepared them at all for the complexities of educational change. And until recently, the plight and the potential of the beginning teacher have been ignored. While reversal of these traditions is not yet in evidence, I will present considerable data to demonstrate that teacher education is finally receiving the critical attention it deserves.

Career-long professional development for teachers and administrators, which I take up in Chapter 15, has not fared much better. In-service education or ongoing staff development explicitly directed at change has failed, in most cases, because it is ad hoc, discontinuous, and unconnected to any plan for change that addresses the set of factors I have identified in earlier chapters. Factors affecting change function in interaction and must be treated as such; solutions directed at any one factor in isolation will have minimal impact. Nevertheless, if there is a premier strategy for reform it would involve the continuum of teacher and administrator selection and development, and its link to school improvement. Fortunately, some of the best and most recent research and practice are in this very area of professional preparation and continuous professional development. Chapters 14 and 15 analyze these developments in some detail, demonstrating that success hinges on how well these new potentialities are realized.

In the final chapter of the book (Chapter 16) I reflect on the problem of change in the context of future trends and expectations for educational change. In many ways we now know what works. Unfortunately this formulation itself is partly a theory of change rather than of changing—to know what works in some situations does not mean we can get it to work in other situations. The basis for hope, however, lies somewhere among the naivete of the 1960s, the cynicism of the 1970s, the partial successes of the 1980s, and the more informed large-scale reforms of the 1990s. Going beyond hope, this book will identify and point to action steps that each and every one of us can take to bring about significant improvements.

PROSPECTS FOR REFORM

In the 1991 edition of *The New Meaning of Educational Change*, Chapter 1 contained the following paragraph:

> As we approach the 1990s we are in the midst of an educational reform movement the likes of which we have never before seen. This time reform efforts are more comprehensive *and* backed up by more resources and follow-through. We should find out over the course of the next decade whether our now considerable knowledge about the do's and don'ts of implementing educational improvements can be put to good use. (Fullan, 1991, p. 13, emphasis in original)

Well, the next decade has just passed. And we do know more, much more. These lessons will be highlighted throughout the book.

I have argued in the *Change Forces* trilogy (Fullan, 1993, 1999, forthcoming) that teachers are "moral change agents"—that the moral purpose of schools is to make a difference in the lives of students and that making a difference is literally to make changes that matter. This raises the larger question concerning the relationship between public schools and democracy. In many ways this represents the unfinished legacy of John Dewey. Cohen (1998) argues that Dewey was not child-centered as an end in itself, but rather for the purpose of developing a new system of curriculum and instruction rooted in scientific and social problem-solving through the development of new, more democratic social relations. Schools were to become counter-cultural agencies that would "correct the human and social devastation of industrial capitalism" (Cohen, 1998, p. 427). Need I say that the problem of potential human destruction (and growth) has become compounded in the chaotic conditions of postmodern society?

As Cohen says, Dewey never addressed the problem of how such a public school system could develop let alone thrive in a society that it was to help make over. And we do know that, as it has turned out so far, schools are a much more conservative agency for the status quo than a revolutionary force for transformation.

For starters, developing the capacity for schools to serve as "moral change agents" means understanding the relationship between democracy and the public school system. In Galbraith's (1996, p. 17) *Good Society*:

> Education not only makes democracy possible; it also makes it essential. Education not only brings into existence a population with an understanding of the public tasks; it also creates their demand to be heard.

Similarly, Saul (1995) says that a primary purpose of education is "to show individuals how they can function *together* in a society" (p. 138, emphasis in original).

In modern society the relationship between democracy and schooling has always been too abstract, or perhaps taken for granted and thereby often neglected. It should no longer be. As Andy Hargreaves and I said in *What's Worth Fighting for Out There?*: "Teachers and parents observe democracy deteriorating every time the gap between the privileged and the underprivileged learner widens" (Hargreaves & Fullan, 1998, p. 15). Public schools need to develop what Coleman (1990) termed "social capital"—to help produce citizens who have the commitment, skills, and disposition to foster norms of civility, compassion, fairness, trust, collaborative engagement, and constructive critiques under conditions of great social diversity. Schools also need to develop intellectual capital— problem-solving skills in a technological world—so that all students can learn. This too is a moral purpose. To become committed to the development of social and intellectual capital is to understand the goal of moral purpose; to address it productively is to delve into the intricacies of complexity and change.

We have learned over the past decade that the process of educational reform is much more complex than had been anticipated. Even apparent successes have fundamental flaws. For example, in our development work we have been interested in how long it takes to turn around a poor performing school or district to become a good or better performing system. Our current conclusion is that you can turn around an elementary school in about 3 years, a high school in about 6 years, and a school district (depending on size) in about 8 years (Fullan, 1999, 2000b).

As valid as these general conclusions are, there are three problems. First, the time lines are too long. Given the sense of urgency,

people rightly ask: Can these time lines be accelerated? Say, reduced by half? Incidentally, all these successes have involved "the
use of the change knowledge" documented in this book. The question is: By *more intensive and more thorough* use of the change knowledge, can we accelerate the process of successful change? The answer is yes, which we will see does not solve the problem.

Second, the number of examples of turnaround is small. There
is only a minority of elementary schools, and fewer high schools
and school districts, that are engaged in this manner. In other
words, we have not nearly gone to scale where the majority of
schools improve. It is not enough to have a handful of successful
cases.

Third, and most revealing, it takes 3, 6, 8 years of hard work
to produce improvement, but the results are fragile. One or two
key people leave and the success can be undone almost overnight.
Thus, from the point of view of "sustaining change," even in those
small number of success cases, there are serious problems.

The main reason that change fails to occur in the first place on
any scale, and does not get sustained when it does, is that the
infrastructure is weak, unhelpful, or working at cross purposes.
By the infrastructure I mean the next layers above whatever unit
we are focusing on. In terms of successive levels, for example, a
teacher cannot sustain change if he or she is working in a negative
school culture; similarly, a school can initiate and implement successful change, but cannot sustain it if it is operating in a less than
helpful district; a district cannot keep going if it works in a state
which is not helping to sustain reform.

In other words, we have our work cut out. At the individual
level we must carve out a niche of meaning and effectiveness despite
a less than helpful system. At the same time we must join others in
helping to change local cultures and contexts so that those making
improvements are rewarded, and those who are complacent are
both understood and end up feeling less and less comfortable with
the status quo. Finally, more and more people must address "the big
picture," exploiting the current underutilized potential for reform
while strengthening the infrastructure of policies and resources.
The agenda for the next decade is to "transform the system" by
improving the overall infrastructure in a way that reinforces and

extends local innovation in some cases, and helps to cause local development in others.

This is not a race to see who can become the most innovative. The key words are meaning, coherence, connectedness, synergy, alignment, and capacity for continuous improvement. Paradoxically, if meaning is easy to come by it is less likely to be powerful. Simple systems are more meaningful, but less deep. Complex systems generate overload and confusion, but also contain more power and energy. Our task is to realize that finding meaning in complex systems is as difficult as it is rewarding.

CHAPTER 2

Sources of Educational Change

Entrepreneurs exploit innovation.
—Peter Drucker (1985)

The main problem is not the absence of innovation in schools, but rather the presence of too many disconnected, episodic, fragmented, superficially adorned projects. Bryk and associates (1998) in the Chicago evaluation called this the "Christmas tree" problem. Schools that take on or are forced to take on every policy and innovation that comes along may look innovative at a distance but actually have a severe case of "projectitis" or meaninglessness.

At the same time there is a growing abundance of innovative ideas around the world. The goal is to appreciate the necessity and richness of external knowledge, but not to become victimized by it.

This chapter has two purposes. One is to give some idea of the sheer volume of innovations, policies, and demands that are "out there." The second is to show how schools, more times than not, are indeed victimized by innovation overload. This establishes the case up front that working on new meaning and program coherence is job one.

I start with the second purpose because working backward from the subjective reality of reform is more revealing of the problem of wasted effort.

INNOVATION OVERLOAD

The biggest problem facing schools is fragmentation and overload. It is worse for schools than for business firms. Both are facing turbulent, uncertain environments, but only schools are suffering the additional burden of having a torrent of unwanted, uncoordinated policies and innovations raining down on them from hierarchical bureaucracies.

Hatch's (2000) study of innovation on the ground is instructive:

> The list of reforms suggested or attempted since 1983 encompasses almost everything from higher standards and new tests for student performance to merit pay and school-based management. . . . And it is not uncommon now to find school districts in which vastly different approaches to educational reform are being attempted at the same time. . . . In fact, in a study of 57 different districts from 1992–1995, Hess (1999) reports that the typical urban district pursued more than eleven "significant initiatives" in basic areas such as rescheduling, curriculum, assessment, professional development and school management. (pp. 1–2)

Further,

> As a result, rather than contributing to substantial improvements, adopting improvement programs may also add to the endless cycle of initiatives that seem to sap the strength and spirit of schools and their communities. (Hatch, 2000, p. 4)

In a survey of schools in districts in California and Texas, Hatch reports that 66% of the schools were engaged with three or more improvement programs, 22% with six or more; and in one district, 19% of the "schools were working with nine or more different improvement programs simultaneously" (p. 9).

The result, according to one associate superintendent, is that

> frustration and anger at the school level have never been higher. When attempting to garner new funds or develop new programs, over and over again, he [the associate superintendent] hears from principals and teachers "we don't want anything else. We're over our heads." (Hatch, 2000, p. 10)

One external provider reported: "We work in schools that have seven, eight, nine affiliations with outside organizations all purporting to have something to do with reform" (p. 25).

In short, we have a classic case of the helping hand striking again! The effect is that "multiple innovations collide" (Hatch, 2000).

The answer, apparently, is not just to narrow and standardize the curriculum. In a detailed study in Texas, McNeil demonstrates the links between standardized policy reform and what happens at the classroom level. As she states:

> The sound bites that seduce policymakers always emphasize claims of benefits, not the actual costs. As documented in this book, the costs are great: a decline in the quality of what is taught and a new form of discrimination in the education of poor and minority kids. But perhaps the worst effect is the silencing of two voices most important in understanding the real effects of standardization: the teachers and the children. (McNeil, 2000, xxi–xxii)

The current accountability system in Texas, says McNeil, bases assessment of schools on a single state test with hidden, devastating consequences. It is:

> A system of education that . . . uses those scores for such high stakes decisions as grade promotion and high school graduation [and] rules out the possibility of discussing student learning in terms of cognitive and intellectual development, in terms of growth, in terms of social awareness and social conscience, in terms of social and emotional development. It is as if the "whole child" has become a stick figure. (McNeil, 2000, p. 733)

McNeil cites Haney's (forthcoming) longitudinal study of high school graduation rates in Texas from 1978 to the present. In 1978, about 70% of Whites graduated, compared to 60% of Blacks and Latinos. By 1999, the percentage of Whites graduating was still at 75% while the rate for Latinos and Blacks was below 50%. Later, we will see that schools and districts with greater capacity can take advantage of state initiatives, but many schools remain at the mercy of top-down reforms.

Even apparently "virtuous" reforms with considerable resources and multiyear commitments founder. Oakes and her colleagues (1999) conducted a decade-long study of school reform in 16 middle schools that implemented the Carnegie Council on Adolescent Development's (1989) *Turning Points*.

The eight main recommendations in *Turning Points* are directed at:

- Creating small, respectful communities for learning
- Teaching a core of academic knowledge
- Ensuring success for all students
- Empowering teachers and administrators
- Preparing teachers for the middle grades
- Fostering adolescents' health and fitness
- Reengaging families in the education of young adolescents
- Connecting schools with communities

Despite great efforts and pockets of success, Oakes and associates observe:

> So much in the culture of these schools and their districts worked against reform. The . . . schools had to respond to a glaring spotlight of local public attention, district office skepticism, and jealousy from other building administrators. Sometimes even those who were at the core of the reform—in the state projects, for example—could act in ways that slowed or obstructed the reform. Policies, technical support, and resources frequently carried unanticipated and unhelpful consequences. (Oakes, Quartz, Ryan, & Lipton, 1999, pp. 14–15)

The point of all this is not to conclude that nothing good is happening. Subsequent chapters provide case examples of success at the school, district, and state levels. However, these successes are *in the minority*. They are happening despite the current system, and are unlikely to be sustained because of the current system. The experiences of the vast majority of people are closer to what Hatch describes. Innovations—even promising-looking ones— turn out to be burdens in disguise. But let us take another look at the potentially positive side.

INNOVATIONS ABOUND

In a recent article, I argued that for the first time since the 1960s we are witnessing "The Return of Large Scale Reform" (Fullan,

2000a). The evidence is overwhelming. Witness, for example, whole school models of reform, districtwide reform, and state or national initiatives. Over one half of the improvement programs listed in the *Catalogue of School Reform Models* (Northwest Regional Education Laboratory, 1998) in the United States have been created since 1983. In a related resource, *The American Institutes for Research* (1999) reviewed 24 schoolwide models including, for example, Direct Instruction, High Schools that Work, Success for All, School Development Program, and more. Supporting many of these initiatives is the federal government's 1998 legislation on the *Comprehensive School Reform Demonstration Program* which in the year 2000 has an annual budget of $220 million dollars.

Also related to these initiatives is the New American Schools (NAS), which was founded in 1991 by business leaders using private funds. NAS is a private, nonprofit organization "dedicated to supporting the development, testing, and scale-up of designed-based comprehensive school programs" (Bodilly & Berends, 1999, p. 111). Seven design teams are working with over 1,000 schools to implement the models.

Charter schools are also expanding a pace. There are charter laws in 36 states involving over 1,700 charter schools and 350,000 students (Manno, Finn, & Vanourek, 2000). Manno and associates offer a concise definition of charter schools: "An independent public school of choice, freed from rules but accountable for results" (p. 737).

Similar action is happening at the school district level, the most noteworthy example being the Annenberg Challenge, which derives from a $500 million dollar gift to public education announced by Walter Annenberg in 1993. The focus is on school and community development in whole school districts, that is, including *all* schools in the district. The initial $500 million is being matched by an equal amount in local funds involving more than a thousand local partners including businesses, foundations, and numerous other agencies. By 1999 there were 18 Annenberg Challenge Projects involving some 2,400 schools in 400 districts, in 40 states.

At the state level there has been a burgeoning of effort and resources (and imposition) of large-scale reform. Most states have invested heavily in educational reform in the past few years. One of the most prominent state-level examples is the National Literacy and Numeracy Strategy (NLNS) in England, which we are evaluating—a strategy that involves all children in the country up to the age of 11 in 20,000 schools. The government has publicly and explicitly committed to raising the literacy and numeracy performance over a 5-year period from 1997–2002 (see Chapter 13). In the NLNS initiative, the annual budget of new money for curriculum resources and professional development is £74 million and £167 million for 1998 and 1999, with even greater allocations for 2000 and beyond.

It is not just the action by schools, districts, and governments that count. Remember we are talking about *sources* of innovation. And this is, after all, the *knowledge society*. One must not leave out the fundamental revolution in what we are "learning about learning." Bransford and associates (1999) devote over 300 pages to the new breakthroughs in cognitive science:

> In the last 30 years, research has generated new conceptions of learning in five areas. As a result of the accumulation of new kinds of information about human learning, views of how effective learning proceeds have shifted from the benefits of diligent drill and practice to focus on students' understanding and application of knowledge. [The five areas pertain to]:
>
> 1. Memory and structure of knowledge
> 2. Analysis of problem-solving and reasoning
> 3. Early foundations
> 4. Metacognitive processes and self-regulatory capabilities
> 5. Cultural experience and community participation (Bransford, Brown, & Cocking, 1999, xi–xii)
>
> These five assumptions have guided the development of numerous specific designs that are being developed within classrooms. Similarly, the National Research Council (NRC) (1999) has taken up the cause, stressing four key interrelated components:
>
> 1. Teaching that builds on students' prior learning
> 2. Teaching for deep understanding
> 3. Effective transfer of knowledge to new situations
> 4. Building an environment that supports learning (NRC, 1999, 24–28)

What can we conclude about the sources of innovation? First, there is an abundance of ideas out there, and if anything they will continue to expand. Second, policies and programs are often imposed on schools in multiple disconnected ways. Third, even if there is choice, schools and school districts do not have the capacity to sort out which programs to pursue, or even the capacity to say no in the face of innovation overload. Fourth, only a minority of schools and districts are tapping into the more powerful teaching and learning ideas that are beginning to emerge from cognitive science.

If there was ever a problem of meaning, it is amply demonstrated by the miasma of innovations and their sources. The challenge is to replace superficial adoption and disjointed cycles of change with program coherence and deep meaning—a journey we embark on in Chapter 3.

The Meaning of
Educational Change

If there is no meaning in it, that saves a world of trouble, you know, as we needn't try to find any.
—King of Hearts in *Alice in Wonderland*, after
reading the nonsensical poem of the White Rabbit

We have become so accustomed to the presence of change that we rarely stop to think what change really means as we are experiencing it at the personal level. More important, we almost never stop to think what it means for others around us who might be in change situations. The crux of change is how individuals come to grips with this reality. We vastly underestimate both what change is (the topic of this chapter) and the factors and processes that account for it (to be discussed in Chapters 4 and 5). In answering the former question, let us put aside for the moment the problem of the reliability of the sources and the purpose of change (Chapter 2) and treat change for what it is—a fact of life. The clarification process that I propose to follow has four parts. The first task is to consider the more general problem of the meaning of individual change in society at large, not as confined to education. Second, I elaborate on the *subjective* meaning of change for individuals in education. Third, I organize these ideas more comprehensively to arrive at a description of the *objective* meaning of change, which more formally attempts to make sense of the components of educational change. The test of the validity of this objective description will indeed be whether it orders and makes sense of the confusion and complexity of educators' subjective realities. Fourth, and as a forward link to much of the rest of the book, I take up the critical related issues of shared meaning and program coherence. Finally, let me stress at the outset that meaning has both moral and intellectual dimensions. Making a difference in the lives of students requires care, commitment, and passion as well as the intellectual know-how to do something about it.

THE GENERAL PROBLEM OF THE MEANING OF CHANGE

The titles of some of the more general accounts of individual change and reality in modern society provide us with as succinct an introduction to the problem as any—*Loss and Change* (Marris, 1975), *Beyond the Stable State* (Schön, 1971), *The Social Construction of Reality* (Berger & Luckmann, 1967), *Thriving on Chaos* (Peters, 1987), *Riding the Waves of Change* (Morgan, 1989), *The Fifth Discipline* (Senge, 1990), *Only the Paranoid Survive* (Grove, 1996), and *Competing on the Edge* (Brown & Eisenhardt, 1998).

While there is a difference between voluntary and imposed change, Marris (1975) makes the case that *all* real change involves loss, anxiety, and struggle. Failure to recognize this phenomenon as natural and inevitable has meant that we tend to ignore important aspects of change and misinterpret others. As Marris states early in his book, "Once the anxieties of loss were understood, both the tenacity of conservatism and the ambivalence of transitional institutions became clearer" (p. 2).

According to Marris, "Whether the change is sought or resisted, and happens by chance or design; whether we look at it from the standpoint of reformers or those they manipulate, of individuals or institutions, the response is characteristically ambivalent" (p. 7). New experiences are always initially reacted to in the context of some "familiar, reliable construction of reality" in which people must be able to attach personal meaning to the experiences regardless of how meaningful they might be to others. Marris does not see this "conservative impulse" as incompatible with growth: "It seeks to consolidate skills and attachments, whose secure possession provides the assurance to master something new" (p. 22).

Change may come about either because it is imposed on us (by natural events or deliberate reform) or because we voluntarily participate in or even initiate change when we find dissatisfaction, inconsistency, or intolerability in our current situation. In either case, the meaning of change will rarely be clear at the outset, and ambivalence will pervade the transition. Any innovation "cannot be assimilated unless its *meaning is* shared" (Marris, 1975, p. 121, emphasis added).

I quote at some length a passage from Marris (1975) that is most revealing and fundamental to our theme.

> No one can resolve the crisis of reintegration on behalf of another. Every attempt to pre-empt conflict, argument, protest by rational planning, can only be abortive: however reasonable the proposed changes, the process of implementing them must still allow the impulse of rejection to play itself out. When those who have power to manipulate changes act as if they have only to explain, and when their explanations are not at once accepted, shrug off opposition as ignorance or prejudice, they express a profound contempt for the meaning of lives other than their own. For the reformers have already assimilated these changes to their purposes, and worked out a reformulation which makes sense to them, perhaps through months or years of analysis and debate. If they deny others the chance to do the same, they treat them as puppets dangling by the threads of their own conceptions. (p. 166)

Schön (1971) has developed essentially the same theme. All real change involves "passing through the zones of uncertainty . . . the situation of being at sea, of being lost, of confronting more information than you can handle" (p. 12). "Dynamic conservatism" in both Marris's and Schön's formulation is not simply an individual but a social phenomenon. Individuals (e.g., teachers) are members of social systems (e.g., schools) that have shared senses of meaning:

> Dynamic conservatism is by no means always attributable to the stupidity of individuals within social systems, although their stupidity is frequently invoked by those seeking to introduce change. . . . The power of social systems over individuals becomes understandable, I think, only if we see that social systems provide . . . a framework of theory, values and related technology which enables individuals to make sense of their lives.

Threats to the social system threaten this framework. (Marris, 1975, p. 51)

The implications of the principles and ideas described by Marris and others are profound in relation to our understanding of educational change in two senses—one concerning the meaning of change, and the other regarding the process of change. In the rest of this chapter, I will begin to apply these principles to specific examples of the meaning of educational change by introducing concepts pertaining to different dimensions and degrees of change. In Chapters 4 through 6 the implications for the management of change will be documented in an examination of a large body of evidence on the causes and processes of change.

Real change, then, whether desired or not, represents a serious personal and collective experience characterized by ambivalence and uncertainty; and if the change works out it can result in a sense of mastery, accomplishment, and professional growth. The anxieties of uncertainty and the joys of mastery are central to the subjective meaning of educational change, and to success or failure thereof—facts that have not been recognized or appreciated in most attempts at reform.

THE SUBJECTIVE MEANING OF EDUCATIONAL CHANGE

The details of the multiple phenomenologies of the different roles engaged in the educational enterprise will be taken up in each of the relevant chapters in Parts II and III. In this section, my purpose is to establish the importance and meaning of the subjective reality of change. For illustration I will use examples taken from the world of the teacher, but the reader should refer to Chapter 7 for a more complete treatment of the teacher's situation, and to other chapters for the various relevant realities of other participants.

The daily subjective reality of teachers is very well described by Huberman (1983), Lortie (1975), Rosenholtz (1989), Ball and Cohen (1999), and Stigler and Hiebert (1999). The picture is one of limited development of technical culture: Teachers are uncertain about how to influence students, and even about whether they are having an influence; they experience students as individuals in specific circumstances who are being influenced by multiple and differing forces for which generalizations are not possible; teaching decisions are often made on pragmatic trial-and-error grounds with little chance for reflection or thinking through the rationale; teachers must deal with constant daily disruptions, both within the classroom such as managing discipline and interpersonal conflicts, and from outside the classroom such as collecting money for school events, making announcements, dealing with the principal, parents, and central office staff; they must get through the daily grind; the rewards are having a few good days, covering the curriculum, getting a lesson across, having an impact on one or two individual students (success stories); and they constantly feel the critical shortage of time.

Based on his own investigations and reviews of other research, Huberman summarizes the "classroom press" that exerts daily influences on teachers:

- The press for *immediacy and concreteness*: Teachers engage in an estimated 200,000 interchanges a year, most of them spontaneous and requiring action.
- The press for *multidimensionality and simultaneity*: Teachers must carry out a range of operations simultaneously, providing materials, interacting with one pupil and monitoring the others, assessing progress, attending to needs and behavior.
- The press for *adapting to ever-changing conditions or unpredictability*: Anything can happen. Schools are reactive partly because they must deal with unstable input—classes have different "personalities" from year to year; a well-planned lesson may fall flat; what works with one child is ineffective for another; what works one day may not work the next.
- The press for *personal involvement with students*: Teachers discover that they need to develop and maintain personal relationships and that for most students meaningful interaction is a precursor to academic learning. (Huberman, 1983, pp. 482–483)

This "classroom press," according to Huberman, affects teachers in a number of different ways: It draws their focus to *day-to-day effects* or a short-term perspective; it *isolates them from other adults*, especially meaningful interaction with colleagues; it *exhausts their energy*; and it *limits their opportunities for sustained reflection*.

In addition to these day-to-day factors that inhibit learning on the part of teachers, most strategies for reform focus on structures, formal requirements, and event-based activities involving, for example, professional development sessions. They do not struggle directly with existing cultures and which new values and practices may be required. As I have said elsewhere (Fullan, 1993, 1999), *restructuring* (which can be done by fiat) occurs time and time again, whereas *reculturing* (how teachers come to question and change their beliefs and habits) is what is needed.

Three recent studies, among many I could have selected, show that going deeper into reculturing is proving far more difficult than previously realized (Ball & Cohen, 1999; Oakes et al., 1999; Stigler & Hiebert, 1999).

Ball and Cohen (1999) talk about the persistent superficiality of teacher learning:

> Although a good deal of money is spent on staff development in the United States, most is spent on sessions and workshops that are often intellectually superficial, disconnected from deep issues of curriculum and learning, fragmented and noncumulative. (Ball & Cohen, 1999, pp. 3–4)

Teachers do not fare much better on the job, argue Ball and Cohen:

> Teacher learning . . . is usually seen as either something that just happens as a matter of course from experience or as the product of training in particular methods or curricula. (p. 4)

The result is lack of consistency and coherence, with few opportunities for what Ball and Cohen call practice-based inquiry and teaching for understanding—a topic we will return to in Chapter 7.

Stigler and Hiebert's (1999) *The Teaching Gap* is even more revealing as it is based on videotapes of an international sample of eighth grade mathematics teachers. Mathematics lessons were videotaped in 231 classrooms: 100 in Germany, 50 in Japan, and 81 in the United States. Mathematical content was examined with regard to its potential for helping students understand mathematics as judged in a blind test by experienced mathematicians and mathematics teachers. The results showed that 89% of U.S. lessons contained low-level content, compared to 34% in Germany and 11% in Japan. Looking further into U.S. classrooms, Stigler and Hiebert found that a very large percentage of U.S. teachers said that they were familiar with the National Council of Teachers of Mathematics's (NCTM) *Professional Standards for Teaching Mathematics* (which is a well-developed vision of how teaching of mathematics should change in order to raise student understanding of math). Despite apparent familiarity with the NCTM *Standards*, Stigler and Hiebert report:

> When we looked at the videos, we found little evidence of reform, at least as intended by those who had proposed the reforms . . . [moreover] reform teaching, as interpreted by some teachers, might actually be worse than what they were doing previously in their classrooms . . . Teachers can misinterpret reform and change surface features—for example, they include more group work; use more manipulatives, calculators, and real-world problem scenarios; or include writing in the lesson—but fail to alter their basic approach in teaching mathematics. (Stigler & Hiebert, 1999, pp. 106–107)

Third, in Chapter 2, I referred to Oakes and associates' study of middle schools implementing Carnegie's *Turning Points* agenda to create caring, intellectually productive schools for young adolescents. Oakes observes that educators often rush to adopt new structures and strategies without considering their deeper implications. As one local leader observed:

> People jump on the practices. [They say], "*Turning Points* is having teams." Well, why are we having teams? What is the purpose of teams? "Well it's just having teams." Interdisciplinary curriculum? "Ok, let's do interdisciplinary curriculum." But why are we doing it? What are the purposes of it? What is our belief system about why we have interdisciplinary [curriculum]? They'll never have those discussions unless you've got somebody asking questions to prompt that dialogue. They haven't had an inquiry approach to making decisions. I think that we've said, "These are the good practices for middle grades." So everybody

kind of jumps on the bandwagon and does them without really thinking about the process of change and how do we make that change happen? And then some people think that because they've changed the structure, they're there. (Oakes et al., 1999, p. 242)

All of this is less a criticism of teachers and more a problem of the way in which change is introduced, and especially the lack of opportunity for teachers to engage in deeper questioning and sustained learning. As a result, *meaningful* reform escapes the typical teacher, in favor of superficial, episodic reform that makes matters worse. Enter the multiplicity of reforms that was discussed in Chapter 2 and the possibilities for achieving meaning under current circumstances become nearly impossible.

In short, there is no reason for teachers to believe in the value of proposed changes, and few incentives (and large costs) to find out whether a given change will turn out to be worthwhile. House's (1974) observation over a quarter of a century ago still holds:

The personal costs of trying new innovations are often high . . . and seldom is there any indication that innovations are worth the investment. Innovations are acts of faith. They require that one believe that they will ultimately bear fruit and be worth the personal investment, often without the hope of immediate return. Costs are also high. The amount of energy and time required to learn the new skills or roles associated with the new innovation is a useful index to the magnitude of resistance. (p. 73)

Predictably, "rational" solutions to the above problems have backfired because they ignore the culture of the school (Sarason, 1982). Two of the most popular, but in themselves superficial, solutions consist of the use of general goals (on the assumption that teachers should specify the change according to their own situation), and in more recent times specifying standardized requirements in great detail. The result has been that the more things change, the more they remain the same. As to the former, Goodlad, Klein, and associates (1970) comment on the presence of educational reforms (e.g., team teaching, individualization) in 158 classrooms that they examined across the United States. They found:

A very subjective but nonetheless general impression of those who gathered and those who studied the data was that some of the highly recommended and publicized innovations of the past decade or so were dimly conceived, and, at best, partially implemented in the schools claiming them. The novel features seemed to be blunted in the effort to twist the innovation into familiar conceptual frames or established patterns of schooling. For example, team teaching more often than not was some form of departmentalization. . . . Similarly, the new content of curriculum projects tended to be conveyed into the baggage of traditional methodology. . . . [Principals and teachers] claimed individualization of instruction, use of a wide range of instructional materials, a sense of purpose, group processes, and inductive or discovery methods when our records showed little or no evidence of them. (pp. 72–73)

Other studies of attempted change show that not all teachers experience even the comfort of false clarity. Gross and associates (1971) and Huberman and Miles (1984) both found that abstract goals combined with a mandate for teachers to operationalize them resulted in confusion, frustration, anxiety, and abandonment of the effort. Thus, false clarity occurs when people *think* that they have changed but have only assimilated the superficial trappings of the new practice. Painful unclarity is experienced when unclear innovations are attempted under conditions that do not support the development of the subjective meaning of the change.

Standards-based reform is more complicated. On the one hand, witness McNeil's devastating account of the consequences of standardized testing in Texas to which I referred in Chapter 2. On the other hand, we will discuss in subsequent chapters the new potential of standards-based (not standardized) reform (see Barber, 2000; Elmore, 2000; Hill & Crévola, 1999). We will conclude that standards-based reform, whether applied to student learning or teacher development, is an essential strategy for achieving meaning and coherence.

In any case, at this stage I draw two basic conclusions. First, change will always fail until we find some way of developing infrastructures and processes that engage teachers in developing new understandings. Second, it turns out that we are talking not about surface meaning, but rather deep meaning about new approaches to teaching and learning. Meaning will not be easy to come by given this goal and existing cultures and conditions.

THE OBJECTIVE REALITY OF EDUCATIONAL CHANGE

People do not understand the nature or ramifications of most educational changes. They become involved in change voluntarily or involuntarily and in either case experience ambivalence about its meaning, form, or consequences. I have implied that there are a number of things at stake—changes in goals, skills, philosophy or beliefs, behavior, etc. Subjectively these different aspects are experienced in a diffuse, incoherent manner. Change often is not conceived of as being *multidimensional*. Objectively, it is possible to clarify the meaning of an educational change by identifying and describing its main separate dimensions. Ignorance of these dimensions explains a number of interesting phenomena in the field of educational change: for example, why some people accept an innovation they do not understand; why some aspects of a change are implemented and others not; and why strategies for change neglect certain essential components.

The concept of objective reality is tricky (see Berger & Luckmann, 1967). Reality is always defined by individuals and groups. But individuals and groups interact to produce social phenomena (constitutions, laws, policies, educational change programs), which exist outside any given individual. There is also the danger that the objective reality is only the reflection of the producers of change and thus simply a glorified version of *their* subjective conceptions. As Berger and Luckmann (1967) put it, we can minimize this problem by following the practice of posing double questions: "What is the existing conception of reality on a given issue?" Followed quickly by "Says who?" (p. 116). With this caution in mind, I would now like to turn to the possibility of defining educational change.

What Is Change in Practice?

The implementation of educational change involves "change in practice." But what exactly does this mean? Although change in practice can occur at many levels—for example, the teacher, the school, the school district—I will use as an illustration the classroom or teacher level because this level is closest to instruction and learning. When we ask which aspects of current practice would be altered, if given educational changes were to be implemented, the complexity of defining and accomplishing actual change begins to surface. The difficulty is that educational change is not a single entity even if we keep the analysis at the simplest level of an innovation in a classroom. Innovation is *multidimensional*. There are at least three components or dimensions at stake in implementing any new program or policy: (1) the possible use of new or revised *materials* (instructional resources such as curriculum materials or technologies), (2) the possible use of new *teaching approaches* (i.e., new teaching strategies or activities), and (3) the possible alteration of *beliefs* (e.g., pedagogical assumptions and theories underlying particular new policies or programs).

All three aspects of change are necessary because together they represent the means of achieving a particular educational goal or set of goals. Whether or not they do achieve the goal is another question depending on the quality and appropriateness of the change for the task at hand. My point is the logical one that the change has to *occur in practice* along the three dimensions in order for it to have a chance of affecting the outcome. As Charters and Jones (1973) observe, if we do not pay careful attention to whether change in practice has actually occurred, we run "the risk of appraising non-events."

It is clear that any individual may implement none, one, two, or all three dimensions. A teacher could use new curriculum materials or technologies without altering the teaching approach. Or a teacher could use the materials and alter some teaching behaviors without coming to grips with the conceptions or beliefs underlying the change.

Before we turn to some illustrations of the dimensions, three difficulties should be noted. First, in identifying the three aspects of change, there is no assumption about who develops the materials, defines the teaching approaches, and decides on the beliefs. Whether these are done by researchers, an external curriculum developer, or a group of teachers is an open question (see Chapters 4 and 5). Second, and partly related, there is a dilemma and tension running through the educational change literature in which two different emphases or perspectives are evident: the fidelity perspective and the mutual-adaptation or evolutionary perspective. The fidelity approach to change, as the label indicates, is based on the assumption that an already developed innovation exists and the task is to get individuals and groups of individuals to implement it faithfully in practice—that is, to use it as it is "supposed to be used," as intended by the developer. The mutual-adaptation or evolutionary perspective stresses that change often is (and should be) a result of adaptations and decisions made by users as they work with particular new policies or programs, with the policy or program and the user's situation mutually determining the outcome. Third, we can see that it is very difficult to define once and for all exactly what the objective dimensions of change are with respect to materials, teaching approach, and beliefs, because they may get transformed, further developed, or otherwise altered during implementation. Nonetheless, there is value in conceptualizing change (in order to define it over time) in terms of the three dimensions. Some examples illustrate this point.

In considering examples, it should be recognized that individual innovations or programs vary in terms of whether they entail significant change on the three dimensions in relation to the current practices of particular groups of individuals; but I suggest that the majority of educational innovations extant in the field involve substantial changes with regard to these criteria. In fact, innovations that do not include changes on these dimensions are probably not significant changes at all. For example, the use of a new textbook or materials without any alteration in teaching strategies is a minor change at best. Put in terms of the theme of this book, real change involves changes in conceptions and role behavior, which is why it is so difficult to achieve.

Numerous examples could be used to illustrate the objective reality of the dimensions of change. I will draw on three examples—one on a provincewide curriculum for language arts, one on open education, and one pertaining to new developments in cognitive science. Considering these innovations in the light of the dimensions puts us in a better position to argue the desirability of the content of change because we can argue concretely.

Simms (1978) conducted a detailed study in one of the provinces in Canada on the use of an elementary language arts program. A few of the main objectives of the program are stated as follows:

- developing students' competencies in receiving information (critically) through listening, reading, viewing, touching, tasting, smelling;
- understanding the communication process as well as their role as receivers, processors or expressers in that process. (quoted in Simms, 1978, p. 96)

The three dimensions of potential change can be illustrated by reference to the basic document. For example, implications for pedagogical *beliefs* are contained in the following passage:

> The basic focus is on the child as a flexible user of language. If language is to be truly useful (functional) we must begin with the present experience and competence of the child and fit our teaching into the natural language situation, which is an integrated, whole situation. It should be emphasized that the developing philosophy is one of total integration of all aspects of language arts. In this sense, integration refers to the treatment of all the communication skills as closely interrelated. (Simms, 1978, pp. 90–91)

References to possible alterations in *teaching approaches* are stated throughout the document. Recommended teaching methodologies include providing opportunities for active involvement of the child, using a variety of resources and techniques (viewing, reading, speaking, informal drama, mime, photography, etc.), and using "the inductive method . . . frequently in small groups and individual teaching situations" (pp. 366–377). We need not describe the content of *curriculum materials and resources*—the third dimension—but the difficulties of clarifying and accomplishing changes in practice involving the interrelationship of beliefs, teaching approaches, and resources should be clear.

By employing the distinction between surface curriculum and deep structure in analyzing open education, Bussis, Chittenden, and Amarel (1976) have played right into our theme. They found that open-education teachers differed fundamentally in their use of open-education dimensions. Some teachers operated at the level of surface curriculum, focusing on materials and seeing that students were "busy." They tried to address open-education goals *literally*, but they did not comprehend the underlying purpose. For example, they wanted to ensure that children were "learning to share materials, to take turns, to respect the property of others, and so on—with the focus of concern being the manifestation of these behaviors rather than concomitant attitudes and understanding" (Bussis et al., 1976, p. 59). It was these teachers who reacted to the problem of ambiguity by requesting further guidance on "what exactly has to be covered." Other teachers had developed a basic understanding of the principles of open education and concrete activities that reflected them. They were "able to move back and forth between classroom activities and organizing priorities, using a specific encounter to illustrate a broader concern and relating broader priorities back to specific instances" (p. 61). Reflectivity, purposefulness, and awareness characterized these teachers, but not in a linear way; for example, they would do something out of intuition and then reflect on its meaning in relation to overall purpose. Assumptions about and orientations to children varied similarly. Teachers ranged from those who felt that children's ability to choose was unreliable and idiosyncratic (some could, others couldn't) to those who assumed and experienced that *all* children have interests and who were able to relate individualized interests to common educational goals across the curriculum (pp. 95–98).

In the pages of quotes from teachers and in their own analysis, Bussis and associates clearly demonstrate (although not using the same words) the nature of the dimensions of change at work. Some examples: teachers who saw open education as literally covering subject content but who had no underlying rationale (p. 57); those "who were reasonably articulate in indicating priorities for children [but] were more vague in describing concrete connections between these priorities and classroom activities" (p. 69); still others who "may provide the classroom with rich materials *on the faith* that they will promote certain learning priorities" (p. 74, emphasis in original).

In the words of our dimensions, it is possible to change "on the surface" by endorsing certain goals, using specific materials, and even imitating the behavior *without specifically understanding* the principles and rationale of the change. Moreover, with reference to beliefs, it is possible to value and even be articulate about the goals of the change without understanding their implications for practice: " . . . action based on valuing and faith is not very likely to lead to an enlargement or strengthening of the teacher's own understanding. The potential informational support available in feedback to the teacher is not received because it is not recognized" (Bussis et al., 1976, p. 74).

The third example concerns the deep and expanding work in cognitive science. We have seen earlier in this chapter that the conditions for teachers coming to grip with this new knowledge are severely constrained (Ball & Cohen, 1999; Stigler & Hiebert, 1999). The best single source of these new theories are the companion volumes published by the National Research Council under the title *How People Learn* (Bransford et al., 1999; Donovan, Bransford, & Pellegrino, 1999). Donovan and associates (1999, pp. 10–17) summarize the key findings with respect to students and teachers. With respect to students:

1. Students come to the classroom with preconceptions about how the world works. If their initial understanding is not engaged, they may fail to grasp the new concepts and information that are taught, or they may learn them for purposes of a test but revert to their preconceptions outside the classroom.
2. To develop competence in an area of inquiry, students must: (a) have a deep foundation of factual knowledge, (b) understand facts and ideas in the context of a conceptual framework, and (c) organize knowledge in ways that facilitate retrieval and application.
3. A "metacognitive" approach to instruction can help students learn to take control of their own learning by defining learning goals and monitoring their progress in achieving them.

Concerning teachers:

1. Teachers must draw out and work with the preexisting understandings that their students bring with them.
2. Teachers must teach some subject matter in depth, providing

many examples in which the same concept is at work and providing a firm foundation of factual knowledge.
3. The teaching of metacognitive skills should be integrated into the curriculum in a variety of subject areas.

Needless to say, the implications for sorting out the beliefs, pedagogical practices, and learning materials from a meaning perspective are absolutely staggering given our starting point.

We could take other educational changes to illustrate the significance of the different dimensions of change. Virtually every program change states or implies all three aspects, whether we refer to literacy, science, school-work programs, technology, early childhood, special education, restructuring, standards-based reform, etc. Working on the meaning and definition of change is all the more important these days because larger scale and more complex reforms are being attempted, thus more is at stake. The point is that educational change programs have an objective reality that may be more or less definable in terms of which beliefs, teaching practices, and resources they encompass.

Why worry about all three aspects of change? Why not be content to develop quality innovations and provide access to them? The answer is simply that such an approach does not adequately recognize how individuals come to confront or avoid behavioral and conceptual implications of change. The new policy or innovation as a set of materials and resources is the most visible aspect of change, and the easiest to employ, but only literally. Change in teaching approach or style in using new materials presents greater difficulty if new skills must be acquired and new ways of conducting instructional activities established. Changes in beliefs are even more difficult: they challenge the core values held by individuals regarding the purposes of education; moreover, beliefs are often not explicit, discussed, or understood, but rather are buried at the level of unstated assumptions. And the development of new understandings is essential because it provides a set of criteria for overall planning and a screen for sifting valuable from not-so-valuable learning opportunities. The ultimate question, of course, is how essential are all three dimensions of change. The use of new materials by themselves may accomplish certain educational objectives, but it seems obvious that developing new teaching skills and approaches and understanding conceptually what and why something should be done, and to what end, represents much more fundamental change, and as such will take longer to achieve but will have a greater impact once accomplished.

McLaughlin and Mitra (2000) draw a similar conclusion based on their study of three innovations in which they were concerned about what it would take to achieve "deep" reform:

> The experiences of these three theory-based reforms underscore the point that the relevant "it" that needs to be embedded in practice is not the particular activity structures, materials, or routines of a reform but rather the first principles. The problem for implementation then, is not only teachers "learning how to do it," but teachers learning the theoretical project . . . absent knowledge about *why* they are doing what they're doing; implementation will be superficial only, and teachers will lack the understanding they will need to deepen their practice or to sustain new practices in the face of changing context. (p. 10, emphasis in original)

In other words, changes in beliefs and understanding (first principles) are the foundation of achieving lasting reform. Put differently, the changes referred to by Ball and Cohen, the National Research Council, Stigler and Hiebert, and McLaughlin and Mitra are revolutionary because they are based on fundamental changes in conception, which in turn relate to skills and materials. I will leave the whole matter of strategies of change until later chapters. How best to deal with conceptions (e.g., beliefs) and behavior (e.g., teaching approaches) is complicated, but some of the implications include the need for addressing them on a *continuous* basis through communities of practice and the possibility that beliefs can be most effectively discussed *after* people have had at least some behavioral experience in attempting new practices.

In summary, the purpose of acknowledging the objective reality of change lies in the recognition that there are new policies and programs "out there" and that they may be more or less specific in terms of what they imply for changes in materials, teaching practices, and beliefs. The real crunch comes in the relationships between these new programs or policies and the thousands of subjective realities embedded in people's individual and organizational contexts and their personal histories. How these subjective realities are addressed or ignored is crucial for whether potential changes become meaningful at the level of individual use and effectiveness. It is perhaps worth repeating that changes in actual practice along the three dimensions—in materials, teaching approaches, and beliefs, in what *people do and think*—are essential if the intended outcome is to be achieved.

SHARED MEANING AND PROGRAM COHERENCE

So far I have understated the collective and organizational requirements related to meaning. Acquiring meaning, of course, is an individual act but its real value for student learning is when *shared* meaning is achieved across a group of people working in concert.

We have long known about the value of collaboration and the debilitating effects of isolation (see Fullan & Hargreaves, 1992). Rosenholtz's (1989) study of teachers' workplace is a good case in point. Rosenholtz studied 78 schools in eight districts in the state of Tennessee. She classified the schools as "stuck," "in-between," or "moving." Rosenholtz describes teachers' subjective construction of reality as part and parcel of their everyday activities. Her study indicates that schools in which teachers have a shared consensus about the goals and organization of their work are more likely to incorporate new ideas directed to student learning. In contrast, teachers that worked in "low-consensus schools" more commonly "skirted the edge of catastrophe alone," learning the lesson that they must shoulder classroom burdens by themselves, not imposing on one another. In Rosenholtz's study, "shared meaning" among teachers and others characterized those schools that were continually improving.

Oakes and associates (1999) remind us that teacher exchanges are likely to be weak unless they are coupled with moral commitments. Many teachers in her study welcomed opportunities to share ideas about students:

> But unless they were bound together by a moral commitment to growth, empathy, and shared responsibility, teachers were as likely to replicate the prevailing school culture as to change it. Unless they applied their collaboration to educative, caring, socially just, and participatory activities they continued to closely guard their classroom autonomy, be suspicious of the capacity of teaming to divide and balkanize their faculty, and distrust collaboration with those outside the school. (Oakes et al., 1999, p. 285)

In addition to shared moral commitment, the pursuit of meaning involves constantly refining knowledge. Nonaka and Takeuchi (1995) talk about the critical importance of knowledge creation in successful organizations. They found that collaborative cultures constantly convert tacit knowledge into shared knowledge through interaction. We will also see in explicit detail in Chapters 7 and 8 how teachers and principals in some elementary and secondary schools go about creating and acting on best knowledge through the development of professional learning communities.

Finally, I return to the matter of how multiple, fragmented initiatives compound the problem of meaning. Organizationally speaking, schools must figure out how to achieve *program coherence* among many pieces. I address this vexing issue later at the school (Chapter 8), district (Chapter 10), and state (Chapter 13) levels.

What I have been saying has nothing to do with the *intentions* of promoters of change. No matter how honorable the motives, each and every individual who is necessary for effective implementation will experience some concerns about the meaning of new practices, goals, beliefs, and means of implementation. Clear statements at the outset may help, but do not eliminate the problem; the psychological process of learning and understanding something new does not happen in a flash. The presence or absence of mechanisms to address the ongoing problem of meaning—at the beginning and as people try out ideas—is crucial for success, because it is at the individual level that change does or does not occur. Of course, in saying that change occurs at the individual level, it should be recognized that organizational changes are often necessary to provide supportive or stimulating conditions to foster change in practice.

Perhaps the most important conclusion of this chapter is the realization that finding moral and intellectual meaning is not just to make teachers feel better. It is fundamentally related to whether teachers are likely to find the considerable energy required to transform the status quo. Meaning fuels motivation; know-how feeds on itself to produce ongoing problem-solving. Their opposites—confusion, overload, and low sense of efficacy—deplete energy at the very time that it is sorely needed.

So far I have dwelt on the problem of meaning in relation to the content of innovations. I have suggested that individuals and groups working together have to become clear about new educational practices that they wish (and/or someone else wishes them) to implement. This is meaning, if you will, about the content and theory of educational practice. Affecting the likelihood of obtaining meaning about the desirability and workability of specific educational practices is the question of *how* new practices are introduced. The latter concerns the theory of change as a complex social process in which people have just as many problems understanding what is happening and why. I mentioned in Chapter 1 that educational change involves two main aspects: what changes to implement (theories of education) and how to implement them (theories of change). There are dangers in separating these two aspects, because they interact and shape each other. But it is helpful to realize this distinction in planning or analyzing specific reform efforts. In short, we have to understand *both* the change and the change process.

I start in Chapter 4 near the beginning of the process, with how educational changes get decided on or initiated in the first place.

CHAPTER 4

The Causes and Processes
of Initiation

*The pressures [for change] seem to subside with the
act of adoption followed by the appearance of implementation.*
          —Berman & McLaughlin et al. (1979, p. 1)

There is no shortage of recommendations about how the ills of
education *should* be rectified. But the remedies remain pie in the
sky as long as competing "shoulds" fight it out without an understanding of how to get started and how to keep going. The next
two chapters contain a description of the educational change process and an explanation of why it works as it does.

The number and dynamics of factors that interact and affect
the process of educational change are too overwhelming to compute
in anything resembling a fully determined way. We do know more
about the processes of change as a result of research of the past 30
years, which has shown that there are no hard-and-fast rules, but
rather a set of suggestions or implications given the contingencies
specific to local situations. In fact, Clark, Lotto, and Astuto (1984);
Huberman and Miles (1984); Fullan (1999); and others suggest that
the uniqueness of the individual setting is a critical factor—what
works in one situation may or may not work in another. This is
not to say that there are not guidelines, and we will get to them.
Research findings on the change process should be used less as
instruments of "application" and more as means of helping practitioners and planners "make sense" of planning, implementation
strategies, and monitoring. It is also important to say that this is
a possible task: "Schools, classrooms, and school systems can and

do improve and the factors facilitating improvement are neither so exotic, unusual, or expensive that they are beyond the grasp of . . . ordinary schools" (Clark, Lotto, & Astuto, 1984, pp. 59, 66).

Most researchers now see three broad phases to the change process. Phase I—variously labeled initiation, mobilization, or adoption—consists of the process that leads up to and includes a decision to adopt or proceed with a change. Phase II—implementation or initial use (usually the first two or three years of use)—involves the first experiences of attempting to put an idea or reform into practice. Phase III—called continuation, incorporation, routinization, or institutionalization—refers to whether the change gets built in as an ongoing part of the system or disappears by way of a decision to discard or through attrition (see Berman & McLaughlin, 1977; Huberman & Miles, 1984). Figure 4.1 depicts the three phases in relation to outcomes, especially whether or not student learning is enhanced, and whether or not experiences with change increase subsequent capacity to deal with future changes.

In simple terms, someone or some group for whatever reasons initiates or promotes a certain program or direction of change. The direction of change, which may be more or less defined at the early stages, moves to a phase of attempted use (implementation), which can be more or less effective. Continuation is an extension of the implementation phase in that the new program is sustained beyond the first year or two (or whatever time frame is chosen). Outcome, depending on the objectives, can refer to several different types of results and can be thought of generally as the degree of school improvement in relation to given criteria. Results could include, for example, improved student learning and attitudes; new skills, attitudes, or satisfaction on the part of teachers and other school personnel; or improved problem-solving capacity of the school as an organization.

Figure 4.1 presents only the general image of a much more detailed and snarled process. First, there are numerous factors operating at each phase. Second, as the two-way arrows imply, it is not a linear process but rather one in which events at one phase can feed back to alter decisions made at previous stages, which then proceed to work their way through in a continuous interactive way. For example, a decision at the initiation phase to use a specific

FIGURE 4.1 A simplified overview of the change process.

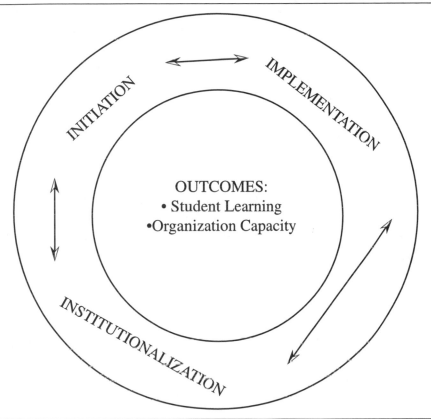

program may be substantially modified during implementation, and so on.

The third set of variables, which are unspecified in Figure 4.1, concerns the scope of change and the question of who develops and initiates the change. The scope can range from large-scale externally developed innovations to locally produced ones. In either of these cases the teacher may or may not be centrally involved in development and/or decisions to proceed. Thus, the concept of "initiation" leaves open the question of who develops or initiates the change. The question is taken up at various places in the rest of this chapter and in relevant chapters on particular roles.

The fourth complication in Figure 4.1 is that the total time perspective as well as subphases cannot be precisely demarcated. The initiation phase may be in the works for years, but even later specific decision making and preimplementation planning activities can be lengthy. Implementation for most changes takes 2 or more years; only then can we consider that the change has really had a chance to become implemented. The line between implementation and continuation is somewhat hazy and arbitrary. Outcomes can be assessed in the relatively short run, but we would not expect many results until the change had had a chance to become implemented. In this sense implementation is the *means* to achieving certain outcomes; evaluations have limited value and can be misleading if they provide information on outcomes only.

The total time frame from initiation to institutionalization is lengthy; even moderately complex changes take from 3 to 5 years, while larger scale efforts can take 5 to 10 years with sustaining improvements still being problematic. The single most important idea arising from Figure 4.1 is that *change is a process, not an event*—a lesson learned the hard way by those who put all their energies into developing an innovation or passing a piece of legislation without thinking through what would have to happen beyond that point.

So far we have been talking as if schools adopt one innovation at a time. This single innovation perspective can be useful for examining individual innovations, but the broader reality, of course, is that schools are in the business of contending simultaneously with *multiple innovations* or innovation overload, as I called it in Chapter 2. Thus, when we identify factors affecting successful initiation and implementation, we should think of these factors operating across many innovations—and many levels of the system (classroom, school, district, state, nation). This multiplicity perspective inevitably leads one to look for solutions at the level of individual roles and groups, which I do in the chapters in Part II. This is so because it is only at the individual and small group level that the inevitable demands of overload can be prioritized and integrated. At the same time, we should try to achieve greater policy alignment at the state level (see Chapter 13), but won't hold our breath waiting for it to occur.

What happens at one stage of the change process strongly affects subsequent stages, but new determinants also appear. Because the processes are so entangled, I will endeavor to identify a list of the main factors and to describe their influence at each stage. The ideas in this chapter and Chapter 5 will be used to help explain why the processes of initiation, implementation, and continuation function as they do. It should also be understood that all three phases should be considered at the outset. As one goes about the initiation of change, implementation planning must already be underway. Put another way, the moment that initiating begins is the moment that the stage is being set for implementation and continuation.

FACTORS AFFECTING INITIATION

Initiation is the process leading up to and including the decision to proceed with implementation. It can take many different forms, ranging from a decision by a single authority to a broad-based mandate. At a general level, we might assume that specific educational changes are introduced because they are desirable according to certain educational values and meet a given need better than existing practices. As we have seen, however, this is not the way it always or even usually happens.

There are countless variables potentially influencing whether a change program is started. Figure 4.2 depicts eight sources affecting initiation, which have been derived from recent literature. I make no claim that the list is exhaustive, only that there is evidence of support across many studies. The order is not important, although different combinations are. For example, community pressure combined with a problem-solving orientation will have quite different consequences than community pressure combined with a bureaucratic orientation. The main point is that innovations get initiated from many different sources and for different reasons. The matter of the need for change can be embedded in any one or several of the factors, depending on whose viewpoint one takes.

Figure 4.2. Factors associated with initiation.

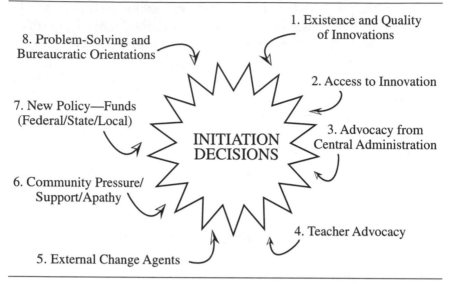

Existence and Quality of Innovations

Educational innovations exist in plentiful numbers. The question is what innovations are out there. It is well beyond the scope of this study to investigate the world of invention and development. Therefore, it will be impossible to draw systematic data-based conclusions about the content of available changes. The answer probably is that there are all kinds of innovations in existence, which could address a wide range of values, as we would expect in any pluralistic or heterogeneous society. And this number is rapidly and constantly expanding in an increasingly sophisticated technologically driven knowledge society.

Since 1983 the struggle between standardization and restructuring has produced changes that both limit (or focus, depending on your viewpoint) and liberate change possibilities. Relative to the former, for example, many states have begun to prescribe textbooks and link them to standardized state tests (McNeil, 2000; Wise, 1988). Restructuring initiatives have also resulted in numerous local efforts as well as several high-profile national projects in the United States, including Success for All, the Coalition of Essential Schools

School Development Program, and many more (see American Institutes of Research, 1999; Bodilly, 1998).

Along with the question of what innovations are available is the issue of the quality of new programs. Program clarity and quality have been a major problem since the innovation boom of the 1960s. The situation has improved immensely over the past decade. A good example is in the area of what has come to be known as schoolwide reform models. The American Institutes of Research (AIR) reviewed the research on 24 models that they assessed. The results were that three demonstrated strong evidence of "positive effects" on student achievement (Direct Instruction, High Schools that Work, and Success for All); five showed "promising effects" (Community for Learning, Core Knowledge, Different Ways of Knowing, Expeditionary Learning Outward Bound, and School Development Program); another six indicated "marginal effects" (Accelerated Schools, High/Scope, League for Professional Schools, Onward to Excellence, Roots and Wings, and Talent Development High School). The other ten programs, including Coalition of Essential Schools, Atlas Communities, and Paideia, among others, provided weak or no evidence of impact.

The AIR report is more of a compendium or guide. It describes the nature of the model, the cost, and the support required, but provides little analytical discussion of the ins and outs of implementation. It is intended as a consumers' guide to the field.

Nonetheless, taking the field as a whole, there is some evidence that projects with greater definition and more specific implementation support strategies do better at impacting student achievement. Slavin's "Success for All" model is a good case in point. As described in American Institutes of Research (AIR) (1999), the model has nine components:

- A reading curriculum designed to provide at least 90 minutes of daily instruction in classes, in groups across age lines according to reading performance;
- Continual assessment of student progress (at least once every 8 weeks);
- One-to-one reading tutors;

- An Early Learning Program for prekindergarten and kinder-garten that emphasizes language development and reading;
- An emphasis on cooperative learning as a key teaching strategy;
- A family support team to encourage parental support and involvement as well as to address problems at home;
- A local facilitator to provide mentoring, counseling, and sup-port to the school as needed;
- Staff support teams that assist teachers during the implemen-tation process; and
- Training and technical assistance provided by Success for All staff on such topics as reading assessment, classroom management, and cooperative learning.

The central components of implementation include: (1) organi-zational change, staffing, and administrative support, (2) a focus on curriculum and instruction, (3) supplies and materials, (4) sched-uling and grouping, (5) monitoring of student progress and perfor-mance, and (6) family and community support. Slavin has also set down five mandatory preimplementation requirements:

- District and schools staff are encouraged to examine Success for All materials and visit Success for All schools to become familiar with the approach.
- A secret ballot must be taken, in which at least 80% of school staff vote to adopt the approach.
- A full-time facilitator must be provided.
- At least one certified teacher tutor and three other tutors must be provided.
- Staff for the Family Support Team must be provided. (Slavin & Madden, 1998)

Success for All is a predefined program that has been adopted in over 1,100 schools in 300 districts in 44 states in the United States, not to mention its expansion internationally to England, Australia, and other countries.

A second good example of well-designed programs is Hill and Crévola's description of the standards-based reform in Victoria,

Australia focusing on literacy, in which they claim that improvement requires all of the critical elements of the school and of the school system, working out what needs to change in order for them to operate effectively and in alignment with all other elements, and then redesigning them accordingly (Hill & Crévola, 1999, p. 122). Their model encompasses:

- Standards and targets
- Monitoring and assessment
- Classroom teaching programs
- Professional learning teams
- School and class organization
- Intervention and special assistance
- Home, school, and community partnerships
- Leadership and coordination

The point here is not to say that Success for All, well-designed standards-based reforms, and similar programs provide the solution (see the concluding section of this chapter, on initiation dilemmas), but that the design quality of innovations has improved dramatically over the past few years. And this in turn affects the likelihood that innovations will be adopted in the first place.

Access to Information

A second factor related to initiation is the selectivity that occurs as a result of differential access to information. The primacy of personal contact in the diffusion of innovations has been known for years (Katz, Lewin, & Hamilton, 1963), and its importance in education is concisely summarized by House (1974, chap. 1). District administrators and other central office personnel such as coordinators and consultants spend large amounts of time at conferences and workshops within ongoing professional networks of communication among their peers. Part and parcel of the development of innovations has been the proliferation of networks, partnerships, collaboratives, and other agencies that have transformed the infrastructure of opportunities to access and work interactively with others on common themes over a period of years. Without doubt, in recent years *availability* of innovative networks has grown in leaps and bounds, which is not to say that enough schools take advantage of them, or that they implement programs well when they do.

Beyond schools, parents and communities, especially those whose members have limited formal education, are at a double disadvantage: They are unfamiliar with and not confident about technical matters, and they have almost no personal contact (or time and energy to develop contact) with even a small part of the educational universe. School boards have more direct responsibility in this realm but also are dependent on central administrators. (This does not mean that boards are unable to put pressure on administrators.) Finally, access to innovations, as is obvious but rarely emphasized, depends on an infrastructure of communication—ease of transportation, resources, and density of population and ideas in the geographical area. In this respect, urban school districts and large school districts enjoy favorable conditions; rural and small school districts do not.

In sum, there is no doubt that the development of innovations will continue to grow dramatically in the world, and access will become more and more available. The remaining problem—the theme of this book—will be whether individuals and institutions have the capacity to operate effectively in this complex, messy system.

Advocacy from Central and/or School Administrators

Initiation of change rarely occurs without an advocate, and one of the most powerful is the chief district administrator, with his or her staff, especially in combination with school board support or mandate. In some circumstances, the district administration may not be interested in innovation, and little may happen. But when there is an interest, for whatever reason—mandate from a board, or a reform-minded or career-oriented administrator—it is the superintendent and central staff who combine access, internal authority, and resources necessary to seek out external funds for a particular change program and/or to obtain board support. Numerous studies have found this to be the case: the Rand Change Agent study (Berman & McLaughlin, 1977); Berman, McLaughlin, and

associates' (1979) more intensive study of 5 school districts; Huberman and Miles's (1984) case studies of 12 districts; LaRocque and
Coleman's (1989) study of district ethos in British Columbia; and
Elmore and Burney's (1999) study of District 2 in New York City.
All of these studies show that the chief district administrator and
central district staff are an extremely important source of advocacy,
support, and initiation of new programs.

For example, Huberman and Miles (1984) found that "central
office administrators were at the locus of decision-making in 11
of the 12 cases" (p. 55). Hidden in these findings is the message
that district administrators are often an important source of
districtwide changes that favor groups that might otherwise be
neglected. In Chapter 10 we will also see, in the case of District 2,
that the superintendent is crucial in maintaining a focus on
which innovative directions to pursue (namely, those that were
aligned and tuned to sustained instructional improvement for all
schools in the system). At the same time, superintendents can be
a source of overload if they take on too many disconnected innovations.

Meanwhile, at the school level, the principal has become
increasingly important. The principal has always been the "gatekeeper" of change, often determining the fate of innovations coming
from the outside or from teacher initiatives on the inside. With the
advent of site-based management across the world, more and more
onus for initiative has landed at the principal's doorstep. Principals
are now expected to lead change, and thus they have become a
critical source of initiation.

Teacher Advocacy

While teachers as a group have less opportunity to come into
contact with new ideas and less time and energy to follow through
on those that they do become aware of, most teachers do innovate.
In fact, the "innovation paradigm," which in effect traces the development and implementation of *formally* initiated innovations, is
biased because it misses the thousands of small innovations that
individual and small groups of teachers engage in every day. There
is a strong body of evidence that indicates that other teachers are

often the preferred source of ideas. On the other hand, the evidence is equally strong that opportunities to interact with other teachers are limited, and that when good ideas do get initiated by one or more teachers, the support of others is required if the ideas are to go anywhere.

When schools establish "professional learning communities" teachers constantly search for new ways of making improvements. Rosenholtz (1989), as we saw, found this to be the case in her study involving 78 schools, as did Newmann and Wehlage (1995), McLaughlin and Talbert (2001), and many others. All these re-searchers, however, also conclude that the working conditions of teachers in the vast majority of schools are not conducive to sus-tained teacher innovation.

On a larger scale, national, state, and local teacher unions in some cases are becoming strong advocates of reform (see Consor-tium of Educational Change, 2000; Shanker, 1990). Indeed, a teach-ers' union in Toronto is the initiator and sponsor of our *What's Worth Fighting For* trilogy (Fullan, 1997; Fullan & Hargreaves, 1992; Hargreaves & Fullan, 1998). While it is true that most teacher unions in the public's eye are known more for what reforms they are against, rather than what they favor, teacher unions can be powerful initiators when they do decide to lead reform.

These findings taken together indicate that many teachers are willing to adopt change at the individual classroom level and will do so under the right conditions (e.g., an innovation that is clear and practical, a supportive district administration and princi-pal, opportunity to interact with other teachers, advocacy from the union, and outside resource help). There are several qualifiers: Most teachers do not have adequate information, access, time, or energy; and the innovations they do adopt are often individualistic and on a small scale and are unlikely to spread to other teachers.

External Change Agents

Change agents or facilitators external to the district—that is, in regional, state, or national roles—play an important part in initiat-ing change projects (see Chapter 11). Many roles at these levels are formally charged with the responsibility of stimulating and supporting change. The importance of these roles, especially at the initiation stage, has been documented over a number of years. What is new in the past decade is the enormous presence on a large scale of not-for-profit foundations and business partnerships. Much of the innovative money and opportunities for large-scale reform are made possible through foundations.

Community Pressure/Support/Opposition/Apathy

Since communities vary and characteristics of school districts differ greatly, different combinations of factors will result in various initiation patterns—a perennial problem in understanding change processes. But when some of the main combinations are examined, we can make sense of the paradox that some communities support innovation, others block it, most are apathetic, and even more are all of those things at one time or another.

In general terms, and depending on the circumstances, communities can either (1) put pressure on district administrators (directly or through school boards) to "do something" about a problem, (2) oppose certain potential adoptions about which they become aware, or (3) do nothing (passive support or apathy). The meaning of these patterns is clarified by considering some evidence.

The most predictable initial pressure for change from the community is likely to come as a result of population shifts. The Berman, McLaughlin, and associates (1979) study of five school districts demonstrates that major demographic changes (rapid growth in population, or a change in composition that results in different social-class and cultural mixes) lead to the development of community efforts and demands for change. How the demands are handled depends very much on the problem-solving versus bureaucratic orientations to be discussed below. In other words, demands may or may not result in initiation, depending on a combination of factors. But the point is that communities can instigate educational change. (In one of the Berman and McLaughlin cases, for example, population growth led to community activism in a previously stagnant school system; the election of new board members; the hiring of an innovative superintendent; and the facilitation of change by other central staff, principals, teachers, and so forth.)

Schaffarzick's study of 34 San Francisco Bay Area districts is also very revealing. He found that 62% of the curriculum decision cases in his sample did not involve lay participation (cited in Boyd, 1978, p. 613). Community apathy and indifference characterized these decisions. However, in the 19 cases that involved conflict and bargaining, the community groups nearly always prevailed. Concerning the selective role of communities, Daft and Becker (1978) found that highly educated ones correlated substantially with the adoption of innovations for college-bound students, but less-well-educated communities did *not* correlate with the greater likelihood of programs of benefit to high school terminating students. Bridge (1976, p. 370) makes a similar point: "It is easier to organize parents, particularly lower class parents, to resist perceived threats than it is to organize them to achieve long term positive goals."

In putting these findings together, we can conclude that the role of the community in the initiation process is not straightforward, but it is understandable when we break it down into the following components:

1. Major demographic changes create turbulence in the environment, which may lead to initiation of change or irreconcilable conflict, depending on the presence of other factors listed in Figure 4.2.
2. Most communities do not actively participate in change decisions about educational programs.
3. More highly educated communities seem to put general pressure on their schools to adopt high-quality, academic-oriented changes. They also can react strongly and effectively against proposed changes that they do not like.
4. Less-well-educated communities are not as likely to initiate change or put effective pressure on educators to initiate changes on their behalf. They are also less likely to oppose changes because of lack of knowledge, but once activated, they too can become effective.

New Policy and Funds

Most federal projects in the United States are voluntary, but we need to distinguish these projects from new legislation or policy that *mandates* adoption at the local district level. Increasingly, state and provincial governments are mandating new requirements, especially standards-based reforms. Since we are talking just about "causes of adoption," we need make only two points. First, state and federal policymakers initiate many new social change programs that would otherwise never be formally adopted. Many major educational initiatives are generated through government policymaking and legislation in areas in the greatest need of reform, such as special needs, desegregation, literacy and numeracy initiatives, teacher education, and the like.

The second point is more of a dilemma. On the one hand, policies are often left ambiguous and general; it is easier in this case for local districts to adopt policies in principle without actually implementing them to any substantial degree. On the other hand, policies have became increasingly prescriptive in many states, which results in resistance, superficial and/or narrow forms of implementation (McNeil, 2000; Wise, 1988).

In any case, new policies, especially if accompanied by funds, stimulate and sometimes require initiation of change at the local level. One major example of the influence of state policy and resources, which we will examine in more detail in Chapter 13, is England's National Literacy and Numeracy Strategy, which involves all 20,000 schools in the country (Barber, 2000).

Problem-Solving and Bureaucratic Orientations

The orientation that school districts take to external policy and funds is another story. Berman and McLaughlin (1977) discovered almost a quarter of a century ago that adoption decisions of school districts were characterized by either an opportunistic (bureaucratic) or a problem-solving orientation. Districts welcome external funds and/or policies either as an opportunity to obtain extra resources (which they use for other purposes and/or which represent a symbolic act of appearing to respond to a given need) or as a chance to solve particular local problems. Nothing much has changed in this regard. Many schools and districts are, in Bryk, Sebring, Kerbuw, Rollow, and Easton's (1998) words, "Christmas tree" organizations in which acquiring new projects is the name of the game.

We do not know the proportions of problem solvers and bu-
reaucrats in the school districts of North America. Pincus (1974)
would have us believe that the properties of public school systems
qua systems make them more bureaucratic than problem oriented.
Pincus claims that compared with competitive firms:

1. public schools are less motivated to adopt cost-reducing innovations unless the funds so saved become available for other purposes in the district;
2. they are less likely to adopt innovations that change the resource
   mix or the accustomed authority roles (e.g., that involve behavioral
   changes in role); and
3. they are more likely to adopt new instructional processes that do
   not significantly change structure, or to adopt new wrinkles in
   administrative management, because such innovations help to sat-
   isfy the demands of the public without exacting heavy costs. (1974,
   pp. 117–118)

That is, in terms of the multidimensionality of implementation
(see Chapter 3), schools are more likely to implement superficial
changes in content, objectives, and structure than changes in culture, role behavior, and conceptions of teaching.

Three factors favorable to adoption are identified by Pincus:

1. *bureaucratic safety*, as when innovations add resources without
   requiring behavioral change;
2. *response to external pressure* (in which "adoption" may ease the
   pressure); and
3. *approval of peer elites* (in the absence of clearly defined output
   criteria, whatever is popular among leading professional peers is
   sometimes the determining criterion). (1974, p. 120)

In other words, "schools tend voluntarily to adopt innovations
which promote the schools' self-image" as "up-to-date . . . efficient
. . . professional . . . responsive" (p. 122). Stated differently again, it
is relatively easy for schools to *adopt* complex, vague, inefficient,
and costly (especially if someone else is paying) innovations as
long as they do not have to *implement* them.

Bureaucratically speaking, then, the political and symbolic
value of initiation of change for schools is often of greater signifi-

cance than the educational merit and the time and cost necessary for implementation follow-through. However, the symbolic value is not unimportant. Such decisions may be necessary for political survival, may be needed first steps that set the preconditions for real change in practice, or may represent the only change possible in certain situations.

While the tendency to adopt and not implement is still the predominant pattern, there are two trends that are putting pressure on systems to act differently. One is the standards-based reform strategies that are intensifying pressure and support with the goal of maximizing follow-through, that is, these strategies assume that adoption is only the beginning. The other is the capacity-building stances of local entities in which initiation begins at the grassroots level and reaches out to exploit state policies. In other words, the goal is to build capacities at the school and district levels so that schools and districts act in a problem-solving rather than a bureaucratic manner.

THE DILEMMAS OF INITIATION

We have presented an amalgam of different factors that influence the initiation of change projects. The first message is that change is and will always be initiated from a variety of different sources and combination of sources. This presents constant opportunity for pursuing innovations, or for the imposition of change, depending on the innovation and one's role in the setting. The second matter, which we have not teased out, is what we know about the *initiation process*—that is, what happens by way of mobilization, and planning to prepare for change. In particular, what do we know about *successful* initiation; that is, what do we know about startups that have a better chance of mobilizing people and resources toward the implementation of desired change?

There is no easy answer as to what represents successful initiation because, as with so many aspects of the change process, those contemplating change are faced with a series of dilemmas. Should we have a short or long time period for starting? Should we go for internal development or import external innovations? Should we work with volunteers or a more representative group? Should we go with large numbers or small numbers? Should we focus on instruction or on the organization, or on both? Should we try major change or start with minor change? Should we have lots of participation at the early stages or not?

The main leadership dilemma at the initiation stage is whether to seek majority agreement before proceeding versus being assertive at the beginning. The fact is that there is a great deal of inertia in social systems, requiring high energy to overcome.

We know that top-down change doesn't work. But we are also finding out that bottom-up initiatives either fail to result in much, or when they do get off to a promising start, often fail to connect to the authority structure.

Even when there is a requirement of "buy in" by teachers, agreement can be superficial and uninformed. In Datnow and Stringfield's (2000) review of innovative programs, the authors observe:

> In several of our studies we found that educators adopted reform models without thinking through how the model would suit their school's goals, culture, teachers or student ... even when opportunities to gather information were available, educators seldom made well-informed choices about reform designs. . . .
>
> Policy and political decisions at state and district levels also often influenced schools' adoption of external reform designs, which also caused some local educators to adopt models quickly and without careful consideration of "fit." (p. 191)

Similarly, Hatch (2000) observes that agreement may be more likely to reflect how effective the campaigns for and against a proposed program have been rather than to demonstrate whether or not a school actually has learned enough about a program to make an informed choice or to embark on successful implementation (p. 38).

And what about poor performing schools that fail to do anything or explicitly reject potentially effective innovations, so that no new initiatives are undertaken? Clearly they cannot be allowed to continue their inaction on the grounds that grassroots decisions are the only way to go.

Our temporary answer to this dilemma is this: Ideally, local capacity is developed at the school level (see Chapters 7 and 8) to the point that these schools actually do know how to go about sorting out and acting on required improvements. Some schools— a minority—currently are this good. Less than ideally, but necessary in cases of persistently poor performing or otherwise stuck schools, assertive leadership (including teacher leaders) is required. To put it one way, you can get away with top-down or assertive leadership as a principal or superintendent under two conditions: first, in situations where it turns out you have a good idea; and second, when assertive initiation is combined with empowerment and choices as the process unfolds. The criterion here is *eventual* motivation to put energy into the reform direction—ownership, if you like. But note that ownership is something that develops over time if the ideas are good and if people have the capacity and opportunity to make informed judgments, which they may not be able to do early on.

In other words, initiation of change does represent difficult dilemmas. The relationship between initiation and implementation is loosely coupled and interactive. The process of initiation can generate meaning or confusion, commitment or alienation, or simply ignorance on the part of participants and others affected by the change. Poor beginnings can be turned into successes depending on what is done during implementation. Promising startups can be squandered by what happens afterward.

At this point we know that initiation decisions occur all the time and come through a variety of sources. We have some inkling that, depending on the sources, the process followed, and the combination of contextual conditions in the situation, what happens after the initiation phase will be all over the map. We can now turn to the next critical phase in the process. Implementation is where the action is. The two key questions are: What is the relationship between the initiation process and subsequent implementation? What other factors emerge during implementation that determine which changes in practice actually occur?

CHAPTER 5

Causes/Processes of Implementation and Continuation

Well, the hard work is done. We have the policy
passed; now all you have to do is implement it.
   —Outgoing deputy minister of education to colleague

Educational change is technically simple and socially complex. While the simplicity of the technical aspect is no doubt overstated, anyone who has been involved in a major change effort will intuitively grasp the meaning of and concur with the complexity of the social dimension. A large part of the problem of educational change may be less a question of dogmatic resistance and bad intentions (although there is certainly some of both) and more a question of the difficulties related to planning and coordinating a multilevel social process involving thousands of people.

As I described in Chapter 4, a great majority of policies and innovations over the past 25 years did not get implemented even where implementation was desired. Implementation consists of the process of putting into practice an idea, program, or set of activities and structures new to the people attempting or expected to change. The change may be externally imposed or voluntarily sought; explicitly defined in detail in advance or developed and adapted incrementally through use; designed to be used uniformly or deliberately planned so that users can make modifications according to their perceptions of the needs of the situation.

In this chapter I identify those factors that affect whether or not an initiated or decided-upon change happens in practice. The processes beyond adoption are more intricate, because they involve more people, and real change (as distinct from verbal or "on-paper" decisions) is at stake. Many attempts at policy and program change have concentrated on product development, legislation, and other on-paper changes in a way that ignored the fact that what people did and did not do was the crucial variable. This neglect is understandable, for people are much more unpredictable and difficult to deal with than things. They are also essential for success.

The positive side is that the persistence of people-related problems in educational change has forged greater knowledge about what makes for success. If we constantly remind ourselves that educational change is a *learning experience for the adults involved* (teachers, administrators, parents, etc.) as well as for children, we will be going a long way in understanding the dynamics of the factors of change described in this chapter.

We must start by restating where implementation fits and why it is important. The simple implementation question is: What types of things would have changed if an innovation or a reform were to become fully implemented? As discussed in Chapter 3, several definable aspects of classroom or school life would be altered. Sticking with the classroom for the sake of simplicity, we suggested that changes would likely occur in (1) curriculum materials, (2) teaching practices, and (3) beliefs or understandings about the curriculum and learning practices. Implementation is critical for the simple reason that it is the *means* of accomplishing desired objectives. Recalling Charters and Jones's (1973) concern about the risk of appraising "nonevents," implementation may turn out to be nonexistent (i.e., no real change in the desired direction), superficial, partial, thorough, and so on. In a word, implementation is a variable, and if the change is a potentially good one, success (such as improved student learning or increased skills on the part of teachers) will depend on the degree and quality of change in actual practice.

It is not quite that simple, but the logic of the change process depicted earlier, in Figure 4.1, is essentially straightforward. However changes get initiated, they proceed or not to some form of implementation and continuation, resulting in some intended and/ or unintended outcomes. In this chapter we are interested in the factors and processes that affect implementation and continuation.

Our goal is to identify the critical factors that commonly influence change in practice, and to obtain insights into how the implementation process works.

FACTORS AFFECTING IMPLEMENTATION

The idea of implementation and of the factors affecting actual use seems simple enough, but the concept has proven to be exceedingly elusive. Examples of successful improvement described in the research of the last 30 years seem to make common sense. More and more, the evidence points to a small number of key variables, although as we shall see, the question of what to do remains exceedingly complex. Intrinsic dilemmas in the change process, coupled with the intractability of some factors and the uniqueness of individual settings, make successful change a highly complex and subtle social process. Effective approaches to managing change call for combining and balancing factors that do not apparently go together—simultaneous simplicity-complexity, looseness-tightness, strong leadership participation (or simultaneous bottom-up/top-downness), fidelity-adaptivity, and evaluation-nonevaluation. More than anything else, effective strategies for improvement require an understanding of the process, a way of thinking that cannot be captured in any list of steps or phases to be followed (Fullan, 1985, p. 399; see also the *Change Forces* series, Fullan, 1993, 1999).

We should keep in mind that we are interested in factors to the extent that they causally influence implementation (or more specifically, the extent to which teachers and students change their practices, beliefs, use of new materials, and corresponding learning outcomes) in the direction of some sought-after change. If any one or more factors are working against implementation, the process will be less effective. To put it positively, the more factors supporting implementation, the more change in practice will be accomplished. Finally, we should avoid thinking of sets of factors in isolation from each other. They form a *system of variables* that interact to determine success or failure. Above all, educational change is a dynamic process involving interacting variables over time, regardless of whether the mode of analysis is factors or themes.

KEY FACTORS IN THE IMPLEMENTATION PROCESS

Figure 5.1 lists nine critical factors organized into three main categories relating to (1) the characteristics of the innovation or change project, (2) local roles, and (3) external factors. In describing the roles, I have tried to emphasize aspects that can be altered rather than those that are fixed or givens. The list is necessarily oversimplified. Each factor could be "unpacked" into several subvariables, as I do in later chapters. At this time the goal is to obtain an overview and feel for the main dynamics in the change process.

Before discussing the factors in Figure 5.1, it is useful to summarize a few of the most recent studies of implementation in order to get a more holistic view of the change process. The Education Commission of the States (ECS, 1999), for example, undertook to

Figure 5.1. Interactive factors affecting implementation.

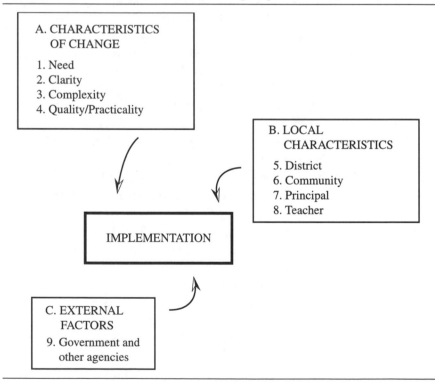

draw together lessons learned from implementing whole school reform models. Their five lessons and subthemes are:

1. Comprehensive school reform changes the way schools, districts, and states do business (transform schools to focus on learning; district support is essential);
2. Legislative leadership sets the tone (provides a strong voice, builds coalitions, allocates resources);
3. State education department support is key for long-term success (schools in need are not necessarily schools that can succeed on their own);
4. Teachers make comprehensive reform possible (professional development is key, union support is vital);
5. Evaluation—early and often—is critical (monitor implementation as carefully as gains in student achievement; make results available to all).

Similarly, the Education Trust (1999) examined 366 schools in 21 states, all of which were high-poverty schools that exceeded expectations in student learning. They found that these top-performing high-poverty schools tend to:

1. Use state standards extensively to design curriculum and instruction, assess student work, and evaluate teachers;
2. Increase instructional time in reading and math in order to help students meet standards;
3. Devote a larger proportion of funds to support professional development focused on instructional practice;
4. Implement comprehensive systems to monitor individual student progress and provide extra support to students as soon as it is needed;
5. Focus their efforts to involve parents on helping students meet standards;
6. Have state or district accountability systems in place that have real consequences for adults in the schools.

Datnow and Stringfield (2000) conducted a comprehensive study of 16 projects involving over 300 schools implementing diverse reforms for at-risk students. The study is especially valuable because of its comprehensive, longitudinal design:

All 16 of the studies have involved conducting longitudinal, quantitative case studies of stability and/or change over time, combined in most cases with quantitative studies of student achievement. (Datnow & Stringfield, 2000, p. 190)

Their findings are confirmatory and revealing:

We found that clear, strong district support positively impacted reform implementation, and the lack thereof often negatively impacted implementation . . . schools that sustained reforms had district and state allies that protected reform efforts during periods of transition or crisis and secured resources (money, time, staff and space) essential to reforms . . . schools that failed to sustain reforms were sometimes located in districts that were "infamous for experimenting with new kinds of programs" but did not provide ongoing support for any of them. (Datnow & Stringfield, 2000, pp. 194–195)

Numerous studies document the fact that professional learning communities or collaborative work cultures at the school and ideally at the district level are critical for the implementation of attempted reforms. Leithwood and his colleagues have conducted several multifaceted studies in different parts of Canada focusing on organizational learning at the school level (Leithwood, Leonard, & Sharratt, 2000). Their main findings are that school learning that produces desirable outcomes is a function of several in-school variables (school leadership, vision, culture, structure, strategy, and policy resources) interacting with supportive out-of-school variables (district, community, and government). This is indeed true, and not a bad summary of Figure 5.1.

The Manitoba School Improvement Program also demonstrates clearly that success is generated by a combination of external stimulus (in that case involving the Walter and Duncan Gordon Foundation), external support, and internal school mobilization involving teachers, principals, students, and community members (Earl & Lee, 1999).

I could go on, and I will in later chapters, with more case studies of success, but suffice it to say that the above themes are found in other studies of successful schools (see Chapters 7 and 8, this volume; Newmann & Wehlage, 1995; Newmann, King, &

Youngs, 2000), successful school districts (see Chapter 10, this volume; Bryk et al., 1998; Elmore & Burney, 1999; Ross, Wang, Sanders, Wright, & Stringfield, 1999); and successful states (see Chapter 13, this volume; Barber, 2000; Darling-Hammond, 2000; Earl et al., 2000).

In short, the findings are consistent. They are based on evidence, not just theory. To acknowledge that hidden in these findings are several fundamental "Implementation/Continuation Worries" (which I do in the final section of this chapter) is not to deny the importance of the message. But first, let us briefly comment on the nine factors in Figure 5.1.

Factors Related to Characteristics of the Change

As we return to Figure 5.1, we start with four factors related to the characteristics of innovations themselves; namely, need, clarity, complexity, and quality. We saw in Chapter 4 that these issues cannot be resolved at the initiation stage. This lack of resolution carries over into implementation and becomes much more visible.

Need. As noted earlier, many innovations are attempted without a careful examination of whether or not they address what are perceived to be priority needs. Teachers, for example, frequently do not see the need for an advocated change. Several large-scale studies in the United States confirm the importance of relating need to decisions about innovations or change directions. In the Experimental Schools (ES) project, Rosenblum and Louis (1979) found that "the degree to which there was a formal recognition within the school system of unmet needs" (p. 12) was one of the four "readiness factors" associated with subsequent implementation. The Rand Change Agent study identified problem-solving/ orientation (i.e., identification of a need linked to selection of a program) as strongly related to successful implementation. The question of determining whether needs are agreed upon is not always straightforward. Datnow (2000) talks about one school's adoption of a New American School model:

> [I]n spite of the fact that the majority of teachers voted for the change, this was not a genuine vote, nor was it based on a process

of critical inquiry into current practices at the school and what
might need to change. (pp. 167–168)

Thus, while the importance of perceived or felt need is obvious,
its role is not all that straightforward. There are at least three
complications. First, schools are faced with overloaded improvement agendas. Therefore, it is a question not only of whether a
given need is important, but also of how important it is relative
to other needs. Needless to say, this prioritizing among sets of
desirables is not easy, as people are reluctant to neglect any goals,
even though it may be unrealistic to address them all. Second,
precise needs are often not clear at the beginning, especially with
complex changes. People often become clearer about their needs
only when they start doing things; that is, during implementation
itself. Third, need interacts with the other eight factors to produce
different patterns. Depending on the pattern, need can become
further clarified or obfuscated during the implementation process.

In summary, the "fit" between a new program and district
and/or school needs is essential, but it may not become entirely
clear until implementation is underway (see Bodilly, 1998, and
Bodilly & Berends, 1999 for evaluation of the New American
Schools, which also emphasizes the need for fit). Huberman and
Miles (1984) similarly remind us that by this early implementation
stage, people involved must perceive both that the needs being
addressed are significant *and* that they are making at least some
progress toward meeting them. Early rewards and some tangible
success are critical incentives during implementation.

Clarity. Clarity (about goals and means) is a perennial problem
in the change process. Even when there is agreement that some
kind of change is needed, as when teachers want to improve
some area of the curriculum or improve the school as a whole, the
adopted change may not be at all clear about what teachers should
do differently. Problems related to clarity appear in virtually every
study of change, from the early implementation studies when Gross
and associates (1971) found that the majority of teachers were unable to identify the essential features of the innovation they were
using, to present studies of reform in which finding clarity among

complexity remains a major problem (Fullan, 1999). And the more complex the reform (as is presently the case), the greater the problem of clarity. In short, lack of clarity—diffuse goals and unspecified means of implementation—represents a major problem at the implementation stage; teachers and others find that the change is simply not very clear as to what it means in practice.

There is little doubt that clarity is essential, but its meaning is subtle; too often we are left *with false clarity* instead. False clarity occurs when change is interpreted in an oversimplified way; that is, the proposed change has more to it than people perceive or realize. For example, an approved textbook may easily become *the* curriculum in the classroom, yet fail to incorporate significant features of the policy or goals that it is supposed to address. Reliance on the textbook may distract attention from behaviors and educational beliefs critical to the achievement of desired outcomes. In Canada, new or revised provincial curriculum guidelines may be dismissed by some teachers on the grounds that "we are already doing that"; but this is another illustration of false clarity if the teachers' perception is based only on the more superficial goal and content aspects of the guidelines to the neglect of beliefs and teaching strategies. Similarly, many of the latest curriculum guidelines in Canada contain greater specificity of objectives and content than previous guidelines, with the result that teachers and others welcome them as "finally providing direction"; however, these guidelines may be used in a literal way without the realization that certain teaching strategies and underlying beliefs are essential to implementing the guidelines effectively. Worse still, teachers introducing reforms superficially may actually make matters worse, as Stigler and Hiebert (1999) found in their video analysis of Grade 8 mathematics lessons in three countries.

On the other hand, I have cited evidence above that not everyone experiences the comfort of false clarity. Unclear and unspecified changes can cause great anxiety and frustration to those sincerely trying to implement them. Clarity, of course, cannot be delivered on a platter. Whether or not it is accomplished depends on the *process*. Nor is greater clarity an end in itself: Very simple and insignificant changes can be very clear, while more difficult and worthwhile ones may not be amenable to easy clarification. This brings me directly to the third related factor—complexity.

Complexity. Complexity refers to the difficulty and extent of change required of the individuals responsible for implementation. The actual amount depends on the starting point for any given individual or group, but the main idea is that any change can be examined with regard to difficulty, skill required, and extent of alterations in beliefs, teaching strategies, and use of materials. Many changes, such as open education (Bussis, Chittenden, & Amarel, 1976), teaching mathematics for understanding (Stigler & Hiebert, 1999), breakthroughs in cognitive science (Bransford et al., 1999), effective schools (Sammons, 1999), parent involvement (Chapter 12, this volume), and so on require a sophisticated array of activities, structures, diagnoses, teaching strategies, and philosophical understanding if effective implementation is to be achieved.

While complexity creates problems for implementation, it may result in greater change because more is being attempted. Berman and McLaughlin (1977) found that "ambitious projects were less successful in absolute terms of the percent of the project goals achieved, but they typically stimulated more teacher change than projects attempting less" (p. 88). Those changes that did occur were more thorough as a result of the extra effort that the project required or inspired. As Berman (1980) stated elsewhere, "little ventured, nothing gained." With *The Return of Large Scale Reform*, (Fullan, 2000a), we are seeing even more complex and ambitious reforms, which require a greater understanding of "the big picture" as well as one's place in it. There is more to gain and correspondingly more to lose.

In summary, simple changes may be easier to carry out, but they may not make much of a difference. Complex changes promise to accomplish more, which is good news given the kinds of changes in progress these days, but they also demand more effort, and failure takes a greater toll.

Quality and Practicality of the Program. The last factor associated directly with the nature of change concerns the quality and practicality of the change project—whether it is a new curriculum, a new policy, or a restructured school. The history of the quality of attempted changes relative to the other three variables (need, clarity, complexity) is revealing. To say that the importance of the quality of the change is self-evident is to underestimate how initiation decisions are made. Inadequate quality and even the simple unavailability of materials and other resources can result when adoption decisions are made on the grounds of political necessity, or even on the grounds of perceived need without time for development. Put differently, when adoption is more important than implementation, decisions are frequently made without the follow-up or preparation time necessary to generate adequate materials. Ambitious projects are nearly always politically driven. As a result, the time line between the initiation decision and startup is often too short to attend to matters of quality.

Part and parcel of the return of ambitious reform has been the realization that "large-scale" change requires greater attention to front-end quality. This attention to developing and continually refining "proven" innovations is what has driven Success for All (Slavin & Madden, 1998), the New American Schools (Kearns & Harvey, 2000), and the National Literacy and Numeracy (Barber, 2000; Earl et al., 2000). In many ways the big curriculum projects of the 1960s gave the role of curriculum materials a bad name. Since implementation was neglected, people, including me, concluded that curriculum materials were less important. I now draw a different conclusion:

> To achieve large scale reform you cannot depend on people's capacity to bring about substantial change in the short run, so you need to propel the process with high quality teaching and training materials (print, video, electronic). There is still the problem of superficial implementation when new materials are in use, and even new practices in evidence, without the deeper understanding required for substantial and sustained implementation. But you get farther, faster by producing quality materials and establishing a highly interactive infrastructure of pressure and support. Finally, the materials do not have to be treated as prescriptive. Many judgements can and should be make during implementation as long as they are based on evidence linking teacher practices with student performance. (Fullan, 2000a, pp. 23–24)

In short, it is possible, indeed necessary, to combine ambitious change and quality. I have maintained that it is what people develop in their minds and actions that counts. People do not learn or accomplish complex changes by being told or shown what to do. Deeper meaning and solid change must be born over time. Good change is hard work; yet engaging in a bad change or avoiding needed changes may be even harder on us. The goal, then, is to attempt substantial reform and do it by persistently working on multilevel meaning across the system over time.

Local Factors

This section analyzes the social conditions of change; the organization or setting in which people work; and the planned and unplanned events and activities that influence whether or not given change attempts will be productive. The local school system represents one major set of situational constraints or opportunities for effective change. The same program is often successful in one school system and a disaster in another. Some districts have a track record of continual innovative achievement; others seem to fail at whatever they attempt.

The individual school may be the unit of change, but frequently change is the result of system initiatives that live or die based on the strategies and supports offered by the larger organization. This is especially true of multilevel, complex system-oriented innovations where what is being changed is the organizational culture itself.

The School District. We have seen evidence that adoption decisions are frequently made without adequate follow-through, and that the difficulties (subjective realities) inherent in the process of change are not well understood. Most attempts at collective change in education seem to fail, and failure means frustration, wasted time, feelings of incompetence and lack of support, and disillusionment. Since introducing innovations is a way of life in most school systems, districts build up track records in managing change. Whatever the track record at a given point in time, it represents a significant precondition relative to the next new initiative. The importance of the district's history of innovation attempts can be stated in the form of a proposition: The more that teachers or others have had negative experiences with previous implementation attempts in the district or elsewhere, the more cynical or apathetic they will be about the next change presented, regardless of the merit of the new idea or program. Districts, provinces or states, and countries can develop an incapacity for change as well as a capacity for it.

Nothing is more gratifying psychologically than attempting a change that works and benefits students. Success can beget more success. If the subjective meaning of change is so central, it is worth stressing that people carry meanings from one experience to the next. This psychological history of change is a major determinant of how seriously people try to implement new programs. To predict and to understand individuals' and groups' responses to particular innovative programs, one must know their immediate past history.

The role of the district administration and central staff is the subject of Chapter 10; it will be sufficient here to summarize the main findings. Individual teachers and single schools can bring about change without the support of central administrators, but districtwide change will not happen. Although it has always been said that the superintendent and the principal are critical to educational change, it is only recently that we are beginning to understand more specifically what that means in practice. All of the research cited in this chapter shows that the support of central administrators is critical for change in district practice. It also shows that general support or endorsement of a new program by itself has very little influence on change in practice (e.g., verbal support without implementation follow-through). Teachers and others know enough now, if they didn't 20 years ago, not to take change seriously unless central administrators *demonstrate through actions* that they should. Berman, McLaughlin, and associates (1979, pp. 84–95) give an excellent description of how one new superintendent with a mandate from the board "transformed the organization" by actively supporting new proposals, by visiting schools to see what was happening, by following through on decisions, and so on. Two decades later, Elmore and Burney (1999) provide an even more detailed example in their study of District 2 in New York City.

All major studies show that the local implementation process at the district level is essential if substantial improvement is the goal. The chief executive officer and other key central administrators set the conditions for implementation to the extent that they show specific forms of support and active knowledge and understanding of the realities of attempting to put a change into practice. To state it most forcefully, district administrators affect the quality of implementation to the extent that they understand and help to manage the set of factors and the processes described in this chapter.

Board and Community Characteristics. It is very difficult to generalize about the role of communities and school boards vis-à-vis implementation. Smith and Keith (1971) and Gold and Miles (1981) tell the painful sagas of what happens when middle-class communities do not like the innovations they see in their schools. School boards can indirectly affect implementation by hiring or firing reform-oriented superintendents. Demographic changes often put increasing pressure on schools to adopt, if not implement, new policies. Major conflicts sometimes incapacitate districts in bringing about actual change; in a sense, certain adoption decisions have to be settled before energy can be turned to implementation. In situations where the school board and the district are *actively* working together, substantiated improvements can be achieved, compared to conflictful or uninvolved boards (LaRocque & Coleman, 1989). At the local school level, as we will see in Chapter 12, successful schools in the past decade virtually all have strong parent-school relationships that they have painstakingly developed (Coleman, 1998; Epstein et al., 1997). There is also an increasing number of incident where school boards are taken over by the mayor or the state (see Bryk et al., 1998, with respect to Chicago).

All in all, the role of communities and school boards is quite variable ranging from apathy to active involvement—with the latter varying from conflictful to cooperative modes depending on the conditions. I leave the details of this set of relationships until Chapter 12.

The Principal. As we shift from the district to the school level, the meaning of the phrase "the school is the unit or center of change" will become evident. While we talk about the potential role of students in Chapter 9, the main agents (or blockers) of change are the principals and teachers.

All major research on innovation and school effectiveness shows that the principal strongly influences the likelihood of change, but it also indicates that most principals do not play instructional or change leadership roles. Berman and McLaughlin (1977) found that "projects having the *active* support of the principal were the most likely to fare well" (p. 124, emphasis in original)—a finding replicated time and time again over the past 25 years. Principals' actions serve to legitimate whether a change is to be taken seriously (and not all changes are) and to support teachers both psychologically and with resources. Berman, McLaughlin, and associates (1979, p. 128) note that one of the best indicators of active involvement is whether the principal attends workshop training sessions. If we recall the earlier dimensions of change (beliefs, teaching behavior, curriculum materials), we might speculate that unless the principal gains some understanding of these dimensions (not necessarily as an expert or an instructional leader) he or she will not be able to understand teachers' concerns—that is, will not be able to provide support for implementation. Such understanding requires interaction.

There is an abundance of other new evidence cited in Chapter 8 that describes how and why the principal is necessary for effective implementation. The principal is the person most likely to be in a position to shape the organizational conditions necessary for success, such as the development of shared goals, collaborative work structures and climates, and procedures for monitoring results. The new evidence reveals that effective principals help address the "multiple innovations" by working on program coherence. We also see in Chapter 8 a much better description of the specific strategies that effective school leaders pursue.

The subjective world of principals is such that many of them suffer from the same problem in "implementing a new role as facilitator of change" as do teachers in implementing new teaching roles: What the principal should do *specifically* to manage change at the school level is a complex affair for which the principal has little preparation. The psychological and sociological problems of change that confront the principal are at least as great as those that confront teachers. Without this sociological sympathy, many principals will feel exactly as teachers do: Other people simply do not seem to understand the problems they face.

The Role of Teachers. Both individual teacher characteristics and collective or collegial factors play roles in determining implementation. At the individual level, Huberman (1988) and others have found that the psychological state of a teacher can be more or less predisposed toward considering and acting on improvements. Some teachers, depending on their personality and influenced by their previous experiences and stage of career, are more self-actualized and have a greater sense of efficacy, which leads them to take action and persist in the effort required to bring about successful implementation.

One's psychological state can be a permanent or changeable trait, depending on the individual and on the conditions. Several researchers have found that some schools have a much higher proportion of change-oriented teachers than do others, as we will see in our analysis of professional learning communities in Chapters 7 and 8. Some of this is no doubt through selection, but it also seems to be the case that the culture or climate of the school can shape an individual's psychological state for better or for worse.

In the final analysis it is the actions of the individual that count. Since interaction with others influences what one does, relationships with other teachers is a critical variable. The theory of change that has been evolving in this book clearly points to the importance of peer relationships in the school. Change involves learning to do something new, and interaction is the primary basis for social learning. New meanings, new behaviors, new skills, and new beliefs depend significantly on whether teachers are working as isolated individuals or are exchanging ideas, support, and positive feelings about their work. The quality of working relationships among teachers is strongly related to implementation. Collegiality, open communication, trust, support and help, learning on the job, getting results, and job satisfaction and morale are closely interrelated. There is a vast difference between the "learning-impoverished" schools and the "learning-enriched" schools described by Rosenholtz (1989). Only 13 of the 78 schools in Rosenholtz's sample were classified as learning enriched, but they provide powerful models of work environments that stimulate continuous improvements.

Almost 20 years ago, Little (1981) made the best case for how teachers and principals work together in accomplishing meaningful reform:

> School improvement is most surely and thoroughly achieved when:

Teachers engage in frequent, continuous and increasingly concrete and precise *talk* about teaching practice (as distinct from teacher characteristics and failings, the social lives of teachers, the foibles and failures of students and their families, and the unfortunate demands of society on the school). By such talk, teachers build up a shared language adequate to the complexity of teaching, capable of distinguishing one practice and its virtue from another.

Teachers and administrators frequently *observe* each other teaching, and provide each other with useful (if potentially frightening) evaluations of their teaching. Only such observation and feedback can provide shared *referents* for the shared language of teaching, and both demand and provide the precision and concreteness which makes the talk about teaching useful.

Teachers and administrators plan, design, research, evaluate and prepare teaching materials together. The most prescient observations remain academic ("just theory") without the machinery to act on them. By joint work on materials, teachers and administrators share the considerable burden of development required by long-term improvement, confirm their emerging understanding of their approach, and make rising standards for their work attainable by them and by their students.

Teachers and administrators teach each other the practice of teaching. (pp. 12–13, emphasis in original)

Only two of the six schools in Little's study evidenced a very high percentage of these practices, but no more convincing picture of the conditions for developing *meaning* on the part of individual teachers and administrators could be portrayed than in the passage just quoted. Little's observations were prescient as developing interactive communities of practice has turned out to be one of the leading strategies for reform (see Chapters 7 and 8).

External Factors

The last set of factors that influence implementation places the school or school district in the context of the broader society. In Canada this means primarily the offices of the department or ministry of education of each province, faculties of education, and other regional institutions. In the United States the main authorities consist of state departments of education and federal agencies. Agencies such as regional R&D laboratories and centers, philanthropic foundations, and other external partners also attempt to support educational implementation across the country. The relationship of the school to these various outside agencies is quite complicated, but necessary to analyze in order to understand the forces that impinge on school personnel. This section provides an overview of the influence of this outside set of forces.

I have already discussed the importance of unmet needs at the local level. But what does the larger society think of its educational system? Provincial/state and national priorities for education are set according to the political forces and lobbying of interest groups, government bureaucracies, and elected representatives. Legislation, new policies, and new program initiatives arise from public concerns that the educational system is not doing an adequate job of teaching literacy and mathematics, developing career-relevant skills for the economic system, producing effective citizens, meeting the needs of at-risk children—children of poverty, recent immigrants, special needs children—and so on. These "sources" of reform put pressure on local districts (sometimes to the point of force) and also provide various incentives for changing in the desired direction: New provincial guidelines are established as policy, new federal and state legislation is passed, new nationally sponsored projects are developed. Whether or not implementation occurs will depend on the congruence between the reforms and local needs, and how the changes are introduced and followed through.

Government agencies have been preoccupied with policy and program initiation, and until recently they have vastly underestimated the problems and processes of implementation. We have a classic case of two entirely different worlds—the policymakers on the one hand and the local practitioner on the other hand ("divergent worlds," as Cowden & Cohen, 1979, call them). To the extent that each side is ignorant of the *subjective* world of the other, reform will fail—and the extent is great. The quality of relationships across this gulf is crucial to supporting change efforts when there is agreement, and to reconciling problems when there is conflict among these groups: between provincial ministries and local school boards, administrators, and teachers; between state departments and local districts; and between federal project officers and local authorities.

The most straightforward way of stating the problem is to say that local school systems and external authority agencies have not learned how to establish a *processual* relationship with each other. The relationship is more in the form of episodic events than processes: submission of requests for money, intermittent progress reports on what is being done, external evaluations—paperwork, not people work. More recently, through resource support, standardization, and closer monitoring, departments of education have had some direct influence on accomplishing specific learning outcomes (see Chapter 13). Mostly, however, lack of role clarity, ambiguity about expectations, absence of regular interpersonal forums of communication, ambivalence between authority and support roles of external agencies, and solutions that are worse than the original problems combine to erode the likelihood of implementation.

The difficulties in the relationship between external and internal groups are central to the problem and process of meaning. Not only is meaning hard to come by when two different worlds have limited interaction, but misinterpretation, attribution of motives, feelings of being misunderstood, and disillusionment on both sides are almost guaranteed.

Government agencies have become increasingly aware of the importance and difficulty of implementation and are allocating resources to clarifying standards of practice, to establishing implementation units, to assessing the quality of potential changes, to supporting professional development, to monitoring implementation of policies, and to addressing other factors discussed in this chapter.

In any case, with the increased focus on larger scale reform, some government agencies are becoming more adept at combining "pressure and support" forces in order to stimulate and follow through in achieving greater implementation.

FACTORS AFFECTING CONTINUATION

Implementation is the big hurdle at the level of practice, but the question of the continuation of initiated reforms should be considered in its own right. In a sense, continuation represents another adoption decision, which may be negative, and even if it is positive it may not get implemented. Berman and McLaughlin (1977, pp. 166–183) found that projects that were not implemented effectively were discontinued, as would be expected; but they also found that only a minority of those that were well implemented were continued beyond the period of federal funding. The reasons for lack of continuation were in the main the same ones that influenced implementation, except that their role became more sharply defined. Lack of interest or inability to fund "special projects" out of district funds and lack of money for professional development and staff support for both continuing and new teachers signaled the end of many implemented programs. Lack of interest and support at the central district office (e.g., on the part of those who had taken on the project for opportunistic reasons) was another reason for noncontinuation. Similarly, at the school level:

> The principal was the key to both implementation and continuation. . . . After the end of the federal funding, the principal influenced continuation in . . . direct ways. Often because of turnover in the original cadre of project leaders, projects would have decayed without active efforts by the principal to bring on new staff. . . . It was extremely difficult for teachers to go on using project methods or materials without the principal's explicit support. (Berman & McLaughlin, 1977, p. 188)

Berman and McLaughlin identified a small number of cases in which continuation was sustained. In addition to the specific factors just cited (e.g., active leadership, professional development), the authors noted:

> District officials paid early attention to mobilizing broad-based support for the innovation. And after federal funding ended, mobilization efforts were increased to pave the way for the project's transition from its special status to its incorporation into key areas of district operations: the budget, personnel assignment, curriculum support activities, and the instruction program. In short, the groundwork and planning for sustaining a change agent project had the early, active, and continued attention of school district managers. (Berman & McLaughlin, 1977, p. 20)

The problem of continuation is endemic to all new programs irrespective of whether they arise from external initiative or are internally developed. Huberman and Miles (1984) stress that continuation or institutionalization of innovations depends on whether or not the change gets embedded or built into the structure (through policy, budget, timetable, etc.); has, by the time of the institutionalization phase, generated a critical mass of administrators and teachers who are skilled in and committed to the change; and has established procedures for continuing assistance (such as a trained cadre of assisters), especially relative to supporting new teachers and administrators.

Problems of continuation, even in the face of initial successful implementation, persist to this day. In their longitudinal set of studies, Datnow and Stringfield (2000) talk about the problem of "longevity of reform." In one study of eight schools that had implemented given reform models, only three "had clearly moved toward institutionalizing their reforms" (p. 196). In another study of one district, Datnow and Stringfield (2000) report:

> By the third year of our four-year study, only one of thirteen schools were still continuing to implement their chosen reform designs. Reforms expired in six schools. A significant challenge to the sustainability of reforms . . . was the instability of district leadership and the politics that accompanied it. In 1995–1996 [the] then-superintendent actively, publicly promoted the use of externally developed reforms. During his tenure, the district created an Office of Instructional Leadership to support the designs' implementation. The following year, however, a new district administration eliminated this office, and district support for many of the restructuring schools decreased dramatically. (p. 198)

In another short article I talked about how "Infrastructure is All" (Fullan, 2000b); that is to say, that factors in the wider context can help or usually (unwittingly) hinder sustained reform. As I said earlier, negative school cultures, unstable districts, and uncoordinated state policies all take their toll. These elements of the infrastructure directly affect the likelihood of implementation; they are fateful for sustained reform.

One last caution: we talk about continuation as the third phase in a planned change process, but it should be clear that the process is not simply linear and that all phases must be thought about from the beginning and continually thereafter. For example, one of the most powerful factors known to undermine continuation is staff and administrative turnover. Very few programs plan for the orientation and in-service support for new members who arrive after the program is started. And arrive they do—chipping away, however unintentionally, at what is already a fragile process (or if used positively, they can help establish the critical mass to support new directions).

IMPLEMENTATION/CONTINUATION WORRIES

Despite the consistency of the findings, there remain three fundamental problems. The first is the tendency to oversimplify. Once you think you have a good idea, and you are facing urgent problems, there is a great vulnerability to legislate the solution. These ready-made remedies make matters worse, as they narrow the curriculum and in effect try to control the uncontrollable (see McNeil, 2000).

Second, even if we identify the right set of factors there is a devil of a time getting them in place in new situations. This is the pathways problem. To know what success look like, and even to know how it works in one situation, is not the same thing as getting it in place in another situation. Success is 25% having the right ideas and 75% establishing effective processes that themselves are no guarantee since each situation is unique. We return later to the 25/75% rule.

Third, implementation and continuation are not just technical problems. Even the best technical ideas in the absence of passion and commitment do not go very far. Oakes and associates (1999) are very clear about this point. Schools that had multiyear projects, good technical support, and commitment were not successful over time. Oakes found that

> unless [teachers] were bound together by a moral commitment
> to growth, empathy, and shared responsibility, [they] were as

likely to replicate the prevailing school culture as to change it. (p. 825)

There are four related problems that interact with the three fundamental issues. They pertain to:

- Active initiation and participation
- Pressure and support
- Changes in behavior and beliefs, and
- The problem of ownership

PERSPECTIVES ON THE CHANGE PROCESS

The first issue is how reform can get started when there are large numbers of people involved. There is no single answer, but it is increasingly clear that changes require some impetus to get started. There is no evidence that widespread involvement at the initiation stage is either feasible or effective. It is more likely the case that small groups of people begin and, if successful, build momentum. Active initiation, starting small and thinking big, bias for action, and learning by doing are all aspects of making change more manageable, by getting the process underway in a desirable direction. Participation, initiative-taking, and empowerment are key factors from the beginning, but sometimes do not get activated until a change process has begun. There is also evidence that large-scale startups—think big, start big—focusing on pressure and support may be required if we are to have a chance of achieving major reform (see Chapter 13).

Second, as I have just said, both pressure and support are necessary for success. We usually think of pressure as bad and support as good. But there is a positive role for pressure in change. There are many forces maintaining the status quo. When change occurs it is because some pressure has built up that leads to action. During the change process interaction among implementers serves to integrate both pressure and support. One of the reasons that professional learning communities are so effective is that they combine pressure and support in a seamless way. Successful change projects always include elements of both pressure and support.

Pressure without support leads to resistance and alienation; support without pressure leads to drift or waste of resources. Professional learning communities or collaborative cultures incorporate both support and pressure through lateral accountability as teachers together monitor what they are doing.

Third, the relationship between changes in behavior, on the one hand, and changes in beliefs or understanding, on the other hand, requires careful consideration. Returning to the theme of meaning, it seems that most people do not discover new understandings until they have delved into something. In many cases, changes in behavior precede rather than follow changes in belief. Moreover, when people try something new they often suffer what I call "the implementation dip." Things get worse before they get better and clearer as people grapple with the meaning and skills of change. The relationship between behavioral and belief change is reciprocal and ongoing, with change in doing or behavior a necessary experience on the way to breakthroughs in meaning and understanding.

The role of ownership is the fourth subtlety in the change process. Clearly, shared ownership of something new on the part of large numbers of people is tantamount to real change, but the fact is that ownership is not acquired that easily. And when people are apparently in favor of a particular change, they may not "own it" in the sense of understanding it and being skilled at it; that is, they may not know what they are doing. Ownership in the sense of clarity, skill, and commitment is a progressive process. True ownership is not something that occurs magically at the beginning, but rather is something that comes out the other end of a successful change process.

In summary, the broad implications of the implementation process have several interrelated components. The first is that the crux of change involves the development of meaning in relation to a new idea, program, reform, or set of activities. But it is *individuals* who have to develop new meaning, and these individuals are insignificant parts of a gigantic, loosely organized, complex, messy social system that contains myriad different subjective worlds.

The causes of change also become more easily identifiable and understood once we possess an underlying conception of what constitutes change as a process over time. The factors of implementation and continuation reinforce or undercut each other as an interrelated system. Single-factor theories of change are doomed to failure. Arguments that product quality is more important than teacher attitude, or that external factors are more important than internal ones, or that teachers are more central than administrators, are pointless. Effective implementation depends on the *combination* of all the factors and themes described in this chapter. The characteristics of the nature of the change, the makeup of the local district, the character of individual schools and teachers, and the existence and form of external relationships interact to produce conditions for change or nonchange. It takes a fortunate combination of the right factors—a critical mass—to support and guide the process of relearning, which respects the maintenance needs of individuals and groups and at the same time facilitates, stimulates, and prods people to change through a process of incremental and decremental fits and starts on the way to institutionalizing (or, if appropriate, rejecting) the change in question.

So, now we know why implementation and continuation are so difficult. Datnow and Stringfield (2000, p. 199) summarize:

> Our research has documented that reform adoption, implementation, and sustainability, and school change more generally, are not processes that result from individuals or institutions acting in isolation from one another. Rather, they are the result of the interrelations between and across groups in different contexts, at various points in time. In this way, forces at the state and district levels, at the design team level, and at the school and classroom levels shape the ways in which reforms fail or succeed.

If the theory of change emerging at this point leads us to conclude that we need better implementation plans and planners, we are embarking on the infinite regress that characterizes the pursuit of a theory of "changing." To bring about more effective change, we need to be able to explain not only what causes it but how to influence those causes. To implement and sustain programs successfully, we need better implementation plans; to get better implementation plans, we need to know how to change our planning and follow-through process; to know how to change our planning process, we need to know how to produce better planners and implementers, and on and on. Is it any wonder that the planning, doing, and coping with educational change is the "science of muddling through" (Lindblom, 1959)? But it is a *science*. All of which is another way of saying that Chapter 6 is ready to begin.

Planning, Doing, and Coping with Change

Few, if any, strategies can be purely deliberative, and few can be purely emergent. One suggests no learning, the other, no control.
— Mintzberg (1994, p. 25)

For the growing number of people who have attempted to bring about educational change, "intractability" is becoming a household word. Being ungovernable, however, is not the same as being impervious to influence. And the inability to change *all* situations we would ideally like to reform does not lead to the conclusion that *no* situation can be changed.

The picture of change that has been evolving in the previous chapters needs to be considered from the point of view of what, if anything, can be done about it. To do this, I treat four major aspects of the problem of planning educational change: "Why Planning Fails," "Success Is Possible," "Planning and Coping," and "The Scope of Change."

WHY PLANNING FAILS

We trained hard . . . but it seemed every time we were beginning to form up into teams we were reorganized. I was to learn later in life that we tend to meet any situation by reorganizing, and what a wonderful method it can be for creating the illusion of progress while producing confusion, inefficiency, and demoralization.
— Gaius Petronius, A.D. 66 cited in Gaynor, 1977

Understanding why most attempts at educational reform fail goes far beyond the identification of specific technical problems such as lack of good materials, ineffective professional development, or minimal administrative support. In more fundamental terms, educational change fails partly because of the assumptions of planners, and partly because solving substantial problems is an inherently complex business. These two issues are explored in the next two subsections.

Faulty Assumptions and Ways of Thinking about Change

There are three interrelated reasons why most planning fails. It is hyperrational; it fails to take into account local context and culture; it is dangerously seductive and incomplete. In a word, the assumptions of policymakers are frequently *hyperrational* (Wise, 1977, 1988). One of the initial sources of the problem is the commitment of reformers to see a particular desired change implemented. Commitment to *what should be changed* often varies inversely with knowledge about *how to work through a process of change*. In fact, as I shall claim later, strong commitment to a particular change may be a barrier to setting up an effective process of change, and in any case they are two quite distinct aspects of social change. The adage "Where there's a will there's a way" is not always an apt one for the planning of educational change. There is an abundance of wills, but they are *in* the way rather than pointing the way. As we have seen, a certain amount of vision is required to provide the clarity and energy for promoting specific changes, but vision by itself may get in the way if it results in impatience, failure to listen, etc. Stated in a more balanced way, promoters of change need to be committed and skilled in the *change process* as well as in the change itself.

Lighthall's (1973) incisive critique of Smith and Keith's (1971) famous case study of the failure of a new open-concept elementary school provides strong support for the hypothesis that leadership commitment to a particular version of a change is negatively related to ability to implement it. Lighthall states, as I do throughout this book, that educational change is a process of coming to grips with the *multiple* realities of people, who are the main participants in implementing change. The leader who presupposes what the change should be and acts in ways that preclude others' realities is bound to fail. Lighthall describes Superintendent Spanman's first speech to the Kensington school faculty.

> Spanman's visit to Kensington School was to make a presentation to the 21-member faculty. It was not for the purpose of discussing with them their joint problems of creating a whole new kind of education. His purpose was to express to the faculty parts of his reality; it was not to exchange his for theirs. Inasmuch as it was the faculty who were to carry the educational goals and images of his reality into action—that is, to make much of his reality their realities, too—and inasmuch as no person responds to realities other than his own, Spanman's selection of a one-way form of communication was self-defeating. In order for his reality to become part of theirs he would have to have made part of theirs his (p. 263).

Innovators who are unable to alter their realities of change through exchange with would-be implementers can be as authoritarian as the staunchest defenders of the status quo. This is not to say that innovators should not have deep convictions about the need for reform or should be prepared to abandon their ideas at the first sign of opposition. Rather, for reasons that should be very clear from Chapters 2 through 5, innovators need to be open to the realities of others: sometimes because the ideas of others will lead to alterations for the better in the direction of change, and sometimes because the others' realities will expose the problems of implementation that must be addressed and at the very least will indicate where one should start.

Lighthall documents how the superintendent and principal at Kensington continually imposed only their own realities and how their stance led in a relatively short time to disastrous results. Lighthall (1973) observed: "The tendency is widespread for problem-solvers to try to jump from their private plans to public implementation of these plans without going through the [number of realities] necessary to fashion them in accordance with problems felt by the adult humans whose energy and intelligence are needed to implement the plans" (p. 282). Sarason (1971) states it another

way: "An understandable but unfortunate way of thinking con-
fuses the power (in a legal or organizational chart sense) to effect
change with the process of change" (p. 29). In short, one of the
basic reasons why planning fails is that planners or decision makers
of change are unaware of the situations faced by potential implementers. They introduce changes without providing a means to
identify and confront the situational constraints and without attempting to understand the values, ideas, and experiences of those
who are essential for implementing any changes.

But what is wrong with having a strong belief that a certain
aspect of schooling should be changed? Is it not appropriately
rational to know that a given change is necessary, and to make it
policy, if one is in a position to do so? Aside from the fact that many
new programs do not arise from sound considerations (Chapters 2
and 4), there are other more serious problems. The first problem
is that there are many competing versions of what should be done,
with each set of proponents equally convinced that their version
is the right one. Forceful argument and even the power to make
decisions do not at all address questions related to the process of
implementation. The fallacy of rationalism is the assumption that
the social world can be altered by seemingly logical argument. The
problem, as George Bernard Shaw observed, is that "reformers
have the idea that change can be achieved by brute sanity."

Wise (1977) also describes several examples of excessive ratio-
nalization, as when educational outcomes are thoroughly prescribed (e.g., in competency-based education) without any feasible
plan of how to achieve them. Wise characterizes the behavior of
some policymakers as wishful thinking: "When policy makers require by law that schools achieve a goal which in the past they
have not achieved, they may be engaged in wishful thinking. Here
policy makers behave as though their desires concerning what a
school system should accomplish, will in fact, be accomplished if
the policy makers simply decree it" (p. 45). Wise goes on to argue
that even if rational theories of education were better developed—
with goals clearly stated, means of implementation set out, evaluation procedures stated—they would not have much of an impact,
because schools, like any social organization, do not operate in a
rational vacuum. Some may say that they should, but Wise's point

is that they do not, and wishing them to do so shows a misunderstanding of the existing culture of the school.

The second missing element is the failure of reformers to go to the trouble of treating local context and culture as vital. Micklethwait and Wooldridge (1996) remind us that policymakers often impose ideas without taking into account local context, and that they are very vulnerable to quick fixes:

Senge and associates (1999) make a similar point:

> The fundamental flaw in most innovators' strategies is that they focus on their innovations, on what they are trying to do—rather than on understanding how the larger culture, structures, and norms will react to their efforts. (p. 26)

In *What's Worth Fighting for Out There*, Hargreaves and I (1998) argued that we need to take a very different planning approach to so-called resisters because (1) they may have some good ideas, and (2) you ignore them at your peril if they stay around for implementation. There are, in other words, good technical and political reasons for taking resisters more seriously. In some cases, resistance may be a source of learning. Resisters may be right. They may have "good sense" in seeing through the change as faddish, misdirected, and unworkable (Gitlin & Margonis, 1995). Thus, resistance to change can be instructive. As Maurer (1996) observes:

> Often those who resist have something important to tell us. We can be influenced by them. People resist for what they view as good reasons. They may see alternatives we never dreamed of. They may understand problems about the minutiae of implementation that we never see from our lofty perch atop Mount Olympus. (Maurer, 1996, p. 49)

In a similar vein, according to Heifetz (1994), a counterintuitive rule of thumb is required in order to reject "one's emotional impulse . . . to squash those in the community who raise disturbing questions. Consequently, an authority should protect those whom he [or she] wants to silence. Annoyance is often a signal of opportunity" (p. 271). It is a mistake for principals to go only with like-minded innovators. As Elmore (1995) puts it: "[S]mall groups of

self-selected reformers apparently seldom influence their peers"
(p. 20). They just create an even greater gap between themselves
and others that eventually becomes impossible to bridge.

This is not to say that resistance should carry the day, but
rather that we need more powerful and sensitive strategies to help
instigate the learning and commitment that is necessary for actual
implementation and sustained impact.

A third serious flaw concerns the seductive nature of planning
when one is aching for a clear solution to urgent problems. Our
first guidelines for action for principals (and all leaders) is "steer
clear of false certainty" (Hargreaves & Fullan, 1998, p. 105). In
times of great uncertainty there is an understandable (but dangerous) need to want to know what to do.

Stacey, the "complexity theorist," explains why:

> We respond to the fact that situations are uncertain and conflic-
> tual with a rigid injunction that people be more certain and
> more consensual . . . This denial of uncertainty itself allows us
> to sustain the fantasy of someone up there being in control and,
> perhaps, of things turning out for the best if we simply do what
> we are told, and so it protects us for a while from anxiety.
> However, because that defensive response involves dependency
> and a flight from reality, it hardly ever works. (Stacey, 1996b,
> pp. 7–8)

Management, leadership, and change gurus can bring about
especially seductive kinds of dependency. Their charismatic authority promises people a way out of the chaos that they feel. Gurus
cultivate dependent disciples rather than independent thinkers. In
his study of the guru phenomenon, psychiatrist Anthony Storr
(1997, p. 223) notes that this is because gurus need the reassurance
and sense of certainty that having disciples gives them so they can
cope with and put aside their own inner doubts. What disciples
get out of the relationship is the comfort of someone else taking
responsibility for their decisions. Storr eloquently warns us that
"the charisma of certainty is a snare which entraps the child who
is latent in us all." Disciples of modern gurus, he concludes, are
"looking for what they want in the wrong place." I think this is
also what Peter Drucker was getting at when he allegedly said,

"[P]eople refer to gurus because they don't know how to spell charlatan."

False certainty also occurs when you think you have a good idea, but it turns out that it is incomplete. In Hill and Celio's (1998, pp. 1–10) words, reform theories often have "zones of wishful thinking"; that is, for the reform to be successful certain things have to happen "that the reform needs, but cannot cause." In further work, Hill, Campbell, and Harvey (2000) analyze seven competing reform proposals: standards-based, teacher development, new school designs, decentralization and site-based management, charter schools, school contracting, and vouchers.

In addition to the problem of multiple, disconnected innovation, which we discussed in Chapter 2, Hill, Campbell, & Harvey conclude:

> We learned that there is a plausible case for each of the proposals: each addresses a real problem and would probably cause real changes in public education if fully implemented.
>
> But we also found that none of the proposals was sufficient because none could deliver all of the changes its proponents intended unless other changes which the proposal itself could not deliver, occurred at the same time. For example, reforms based on teacher training do not create incentives to overcome some teachers' reluctance to put in the time and effort to improve their knowledge and skills. In a similar vein, reforms such as vouchers do not in themselves guarantee that there will be a plentiful supply of high-quality independent school providers or that enough teachers and principals to run such schools exist. (p. 23)

We have, of course, now wandered into the next topic—solving today's educational problem is complex; it *is* rocket science.

Complex Problems

Solving complex problems on a continuous basis is enormously difficult because of the sheer number of factors at play. It is further complicated because the *sine qua non* of successful reform is whether *relationships improve*; in fact, we have to learn how to develop relationships with those we might not understand and might not like, and vice versa (Fullan, 2001).

Chaos or complexity theorists put it best:

> Most textbooks focus heavily on techniques and procedures for long-term planning, on the need for visions and missions, on the importance and the means of securing strongly shared cultures, on the equation of success with consensus, consistency, uniformity and order. [However, in complex environments] the real management task is that of coping with and even using unpredictability, clashing counter-cultures, disensus, contention, conflict, and inconsistency. In short, the task that justifies the existence of all managers has to do with instability, irregularity, difference and disorder. (Stacey, 1996a, pp. xix–xx)

Stating the case more fully (and dauntingly), Stacey argues:

> A complexity theory of organization is built on the following propositions:
> - All organizations are webs of nonlinear feedback loops connected to other people and organizations (its environments) by webs of nonlinear feedback loops.
> - Such nonlinear feedback systems are capable of operating in states of stable and unstable equilibrium, or in the borders between these states, that is far-from-equilibrium, in bounded instability at the edge of chaos.
> - All organizations are paradoxes. They are powerfully pulled towards stability by the forces of integration, maintenance controls, human desires for security and certainty, and adaptation to the environment on the one hand. They are also powerfully pulled to the opposite extreme of unstable equilibrium by the forces of division and decentralization, human desires for excitement and innovation, and isolation from the environment.
> - If the organization gives in to the pull to stability it fails because it becomes ossified and cannot change easily. If it gives in to the pull to instability it disintegrates. Success lies in sustaining an organization in the borders between stability and instability. This is a state of chaos, a difficult-to-maintain dissipative structure.
> - The dynamics of the successful organization are therefore those of irregular cycles and discontinuous trends falling within qualitative patterns. Fuzzy but recognizable categories taking the form of archetypes and templates.

- Because of its own internal dynamics, a successful organization faces completely unknowable specific futures.
- Agents within the system cannot be in control of its long-term future, nor can they install specific frameworks to make it success-ful, nor can they apply step-by-step analytical reasoning or plan-ning or ideological controls to long-term development. Agents within the system can only do these things in relation to the short term.
- Long-term development is a spontaneously self-organizing process from which new strategic directions may emerge. Spontaneous self-organization is political interaction and learning in groups. Managers have to use reasoning by analogy.
- In this way managers create and discover their environments and the long-term futures of the organizations. (p. 349)

The positive side, or if you like, the "solution" involves devel-oping learning organizations. In their new field book, Senge and colleagues (2000) argue that fiat or command can never solve com-plex problems; only a learning orientation can:

> This means involving everyone in the system in expressing their aspiration, building their awareness, and developing their capa-bilities together. In a school that's learning, people who tradition-ally may have been suspicious of one another—parents and teachers, educators and local business people, administrators and union members, people inside and outside the school walls, students and adults—recognize their common stake in the future of the school system and the things they can learn from one another. (Senge et al., 2000, p. 5)

Complex indeed! Anything else is tinkering.

SUCCESS IS POSSIBLE

Recognizing the limitations of planning is not the same thing as concluding that effective change is unattainable. But in order to determine if planned educational change is possible, it would not be sufficient to locate situations where change seems to be working. We would need to find examples where a setting has been *deliber-ately transformed* from a previous state to a new one that represents clear improvement. We need to know about the causes and dynamics of how change occurs.

Over the past decade there have been a number of clear examples of how school districts and schools improved the quality of education through a process of deliberate change. The good news is that we have well-documented cases at the school level (see Chapters 7 and 8), at the district level (Chapter 10), and recently at the state level (Chapter 13). The bad news is twofold. First, the successful examples are still in the minority in the sense that only a small proportion of schools, districts, and states have been successful in their attempts. The second worry is more disturbing. There is reason to believe that hard-won successes over a period of 5 to 10 years cannot be sustained under current conditions; furthermore, it appears that the accomplishments are real, but superficial. In other words, even the successful cases cannot be expected to last or to be deep.

Be that as it may, successful change is possible in the real world, even under difficult conditions. And many of the reasons for the achievements can be pinpointed. There are classrooms, schools, communities, districts, and states that have altered the conditions for change in more favorable, workable directions. Not every situation is alterable, especially at certain periods of time; but it is a good bet that major improvements can be accomplished in many more settings than is happening at present.

PLANNING AND COPING

We have come to the most difficult problem of all. What can we actually do to plan for and cope with educational change? This section contains an overview of the assumptions, elements, and guidelines for action. Additional specific implications for particular roles and agencies (e.g., teacher, principal, superintendent, and federal or state/provincial agencies) are left for the appropriate chapters in Parts II and III. First, I introduce the topic by indicating some of the basic issues and by noting that advice will have to vary according to the different situations in which we find ourselves. Second, I provide some advice for those who find that they are forced to respond to and cope with change introduced by others. Third, the bulk of the section is addressed to the question of how to plan and implement change more effectively.

In general, there are four logical types of change situations we could face as individuals. These are depicted in Figure 6.1. There are many different specific roles even within a single cell that cannot be delineated here, but people generally find themselves in one of the four situations depending on whether they are initiating/promoting a change or are on the receiving end, and whether or not they are in authority positions. I start with coping, or being on the receiving end of change (cells III and IV), because this is the most prevalent situation.

Those in situations of having to respond to a particular change should assume neither that it is beneficial nor that it is useless; that much is clear from the previous analysis. The major initial stance should involve *critical assessment*, that is, determining whether the change is desirable in relation to certain goals and whether it is "implementable"—in brief, whether it is worth the effort, because it *will* be an effort if it is at all worthwhile. Several criteria would be applied: Does the change address an unmet need? Is it a priority in relation to other unmet needs? Is it informed by some desirable

Figure 6.1. Change situations according to authority position and relation to the change effort.

		Authority position	
		YES	NO
Relation to change effort	Initiator or promoter	I Planner (e.g., policymaker)	II Planner (e.g., developer)
	Recipient or responder	III Coper (e.g., principal)	IV Coper (e.g., teacher)

sense of vision? Are there adequate (not to say optimal) resources committed to support implementation (such as technical assistance and leadership support)? If the conditions are reasonably favorable, knowledge of the change process outlined in previous chapters could be used to advantage—for example, pushing for technical assistance, opportunities for interaction among teachers, and so on. If the conditions are not favorable or cannot be made favorable, the best coping strategy consists of knowing enough about the process of change so that we can understand why it doesn't work, and therefore not blame ourselves; we can also gain solace by realizing that most other people are in the same situation of nonimplementation. In sum, the problem is one of developing enough meaning vis-à-vis the change so that we are in a position to implement it effectively or reject it, as the case may be.

Those who are confronted with unwanted change and are in authority positions (cell III) will have to develop different coping mechanisms from those in nonauthority positions (cell IV). For the reader who thinks that resisting change represents irresponsible obstinacy, it is worth repeating that nonimplementable programs and reforms probably do more harm than good when they are attempted. The most responsible action may be to reject innovations that are bound to fail and to work earnestly at those that have a chance to succeed. Besides, in some situations resistance may be the only way to maintain sanity and avoid complete cynicism. In the search for meaning in a particular imposed change situation, we may conclude that there is no meaning, or that the problem being addressed is only one (and not the most important or strategic) of many problems that should be confronted. The basic guideline is to work on coherence by selecting and connecting innovations, thereby reducing disjointed overload while increasing focus (see Chapter 8 for how principals can do this, and Chapter 10 for how district administrators do it).

We should feel especially sorry for those in authority positions (middle management in district offices, principals, intermediate government personnel in provincial and state regional offices) who are responsible for leading or seeing to implementation but do not want or do not understand the change—either because it has not been sufficiently developed (and is literally not understandable) or because they themselves have not been involved in deciding on the change or have not received adequate orientation or training. The psychiatrist Ronald Laing captures this situation in what he refers to as a "knot":

There is something I don't know
that I am supposed to know.
I don't know what it is I don't know,
and yet am supposed to know,
And I feel I look stupid
if I seem both not to know it
and not know *what* it is *I* don't know.
Therefore, I pretend I know it.
This is nerve-wracking since I don't
know what I must pretend to know.
Therefore, I pretend I know everything.
—R. D. Laing, *Knots* (1970)

This is a ridiculous stance, to be sure, as painful as it is unsuccessful. It can, of course, be successful in the sense of maintaining the status quo. Depending on one's capacity for self-deception, it can be more or less painful as well. In any case, teachers know when a change is being introduced by or supported by someone who does not believe in it or understand it. Yet this is the position in which many intermediate managers find themselves, or allow themselves to be. Those in authority have a need for meaning, too, if for no other reason than that the change will be unsuccessful if they cannot convey their meaning to others.

Planning and Implementing Change

The implications for those interested in planning and implementing educational change (cells I and II) are very important, because we would all be better off if changes were introduced more effectively. It is useful to consider these implications according to two interrelated sets of issues: What *assumptions* about change should we note? How can we plan and implement change more effectively?

The assumptions we make about change are powerful and frequently subconscious sources of actions. When we begin to understand what change is as people experience it, we begin also to see clearly that assumptions made by planners of change are extremely important determinants of whether the realities of implementation get confronted or ignored. The analysis of change carried out so far leads me to identify ten "do" and "don't" assumptions as basic to a successful approach to educational change.

1. Do not assume that your version of what the change should be is the one that should or could be implemented. On the contrary, assume that one of the main purposes of the process of implementation is to *exchange your reality* of what should be through interaction with implementers and others concerned. Stated another way, assume that successful implementation consists of some transformation or continual development of initial ideas.

2. Assume that any significant innovation, if it is to result in change, requires individual implementers to work out their own meaning. Significant change involves a certain amount of ambiguity, ambivalence, and uncertainty for the individual about the meaning of the change. Thus, effective implementation is a *process of clarification*. It is also important not to spend too much time in the early stages on needs assessment, program development, and problem definition activities—school staff have limited time. Clarification is likely to come in large part through reflective practice.

3. Assume that conflict and disagreement are not only inevitable but fundamental to successful change. Since any group of people possess multiple realities, any collective change attempt will necessarily involve conflict. Assumptions 2 and 3 combine to suggest that all successful efforts of significance, no matter how well planned, will experience an implementation dip in the early stages. Smooth implementation is often a sign that not much is really changing.

4. Assume that people need pressure to change (even in directions that they desire), but it will be effective only under conditions that allow them to react, to form their own position, to interact with other implementers, to obtain technical assistance, etc. It is all right and helpful to express what you value in the form of standards of practice and expectations of accountability, but

only if coupled with capacity-building and problem-solving opportunities.

5. Assume that effective change takes time. It is a process of "development in use." Unrealistic or undefined time lines fail to recognize that implementation occurs developmentally. Significant change in the form of implementing specific innovations can be expected to take a minimum of 2 or 3 years; bringing about institutional reforms can take 5 or 10 years. At the same time, work on changing the infrastructure (policies, incentives, and capacity of agencies at all levels) so that valued gains can be sustained and built upon).

6. Do not assume that the reason for lack of implementation is outright rejection of the values embodied in the change, or hard-core resistance to all change. Assume that there are a number of possible reasons: value rejection, inadequate resources to support implementation, insufficient time elapsed, and the possibility that resisters have some good points to make.

7. Do not expect all or even most people or groups to change. Progress occurs when we take steps (e.g., by following the assumptions listed here) that *increase* the number of people affected. Our reach should exceed our grasp, but not by such a margin that we fall flat on our face. Instead of being discouraged by all that remains to be done, be encouraged by what has been accomplished by way of improvement resulting from your actions.

8. Assume that you will need a *plan* that is based on the above assumptions and that addresses the factors known to affect implementation. Evolutionary planning and problem-coping models based on knowledge of the change process are essential.

9. Assume that no amount of knowledge will ever make it totally clear what action should be taken. Action decisions are a combination of valid knowledge, political considerations, on-the-spot decisions, and intuition. Better knowledge of the change process will improve the mix of resources on which we draw, but it will never and should never represent the sole basis for decision.

10. Assume that changing the culture of institutions is the real agenda, not implementing single innovations. Put another way,

when implementing particular innovations, we should always pay attention to whether each institution and the relationships among institutions and individuals is developing or not.

Finally, do not be seduced into looking for the silver bullet. Given the urgency of problems, there is great vulnerability to off-the-shelf solutions. But most external solutions have failed. The idea is to be a critical consumer of external ideas while working from a base of understanding and altering local context. There is no complete answer "out there."

THE SCOPE OF CHANGE

There are many dilemmas and no clear answers to the question of where to start. The reader who by now has concluded that the theory of educational change is a theory of unanswerable questions will not be too far off the mark. Harry Truman (and later Pierre Trudeau) said, "We need more one-armed economists," because they were frustrated at the advice they kept getting: "On the one hand . . . on the other hand." The same can be said about the scope of educational change efforts. No one knows for sure what is best. We are engaged in a theory of probing and understanding the meaning of multiple dilemmas in attempting to decide what to do.

Sarason (1971) identified many of the underlying issues:

A large percentage of proposals of change are intended to affect all or most of the schools within a system. The assumption seems to be that since the change is considered as an improvement over what exists, it should be spread as wide as possible as soon as possible. The introduction of new curricula is, of course, a clear example of this. What is so strange here is that those who initiate this degree of change are quite aware of two things: that different schools in the system can be depended on differentially to respond to or implement the proposed change, and that they, the sources . . . do not have the time adequately to oversee this degree of change. What is strange is that awareness of these two factors seems to be unconnected with or to have no effect on thinkings about the scope of the change. (pp. 213–214)

In later work Sarason (1990) maintains that we still have not learned to focus our efforts on understanding and working with the culture of local systems:

> Ideas whose time has come are no guarantee that we know how to capitalize on the opportunities, because the process of implementation requires that you understand well the settings in which these ideas have to take root. And that understanding is frequently faulty and incomplete. Good intentions married to good ideas are necessary but not sufficient for action consistent with them. (p. 61)

Above all, planning must consider the preimplementation issues of whether and how to start, and what readiness conditions might be essential prior to commencing. Implementation planning is not a matter of establishing a logical sequence of steps deriving from the innovation or reform at hand.

Two points put the problem of scope in perspective. First, in some situations it may be more timely or compatible with our priorities to concentrate on getting a major policy "on the books," leaving questions of implementation until later. In other words, the first priority is initiation, not implementation. Major new legislation or policies directed at important social reforms often fit this mode—for example, new legislation on desegregation, special education, or restructuring. There is no answer to the question of whether this is more effective than a more gradual approach to legislation, but it should be recognized that implementation is then an immediate problem. Sarason and Doris (1979), in commenting on special education legislation, warn us: "To interpret a decision . . . as a 'victory' is understandable but one should never underestimate how long it can take for the spirit of victory to become appropriately manifested in practice" (p. 358). Much social policy legislation is vague on implementation; some vagueness may be essential in order to get the policy accepted, but nonetheless it means that implementation can be easily evaded. In the face of major value or power resistance, it is probably strategically more effective in the short run to concentrate our energies on establishing new legislation, hoping that in the long run the pressure of the law, the promotion of implementation through incentives and disincentives, and the emergence of new implementers will generate results.

Second, we have reached a stage, face-to-face with urgent need, and equipped with great knowledge of the dynamics of change, where *large-scale reform* must become the agenda—reform which simultaneously focuses on local development and larger system transformation (Fullan, 2000a). In other words, the focus of planning has shifted in recent times, where the most advanced systems are trying to figure out how to coordinate state policy and local development in order to transform large numbers of schools.

We conclude, then, as Mintzberg, Ahlstrand, and Lampei (1998) have, that "strategy formation is complex space":

> Strategy formation is judgmental designing, intuitive reasoning, and emergent learning; it is about transformation as well as perpetuation; it must involve individual cognition and social interaction, cooperation as well as conflict; it has to include analyzing before and programming after as well as negotiating during; and all of this must be in response to what can be a demanding environment. Just try to leave any of this out and watch what happens! (p. 372–373)

It is time now to fill some of this complex space with people. The chapters in Part II portray the social realities and possibilities of those most directly involved and affected by educational reform.

PART II

EDUCATIONAL CHANGE AT THE LOCAL LEVEL

Chapter 7

The Teacher

Low morale, depressed, feeling unfairly blamed for the ills of society? You must be a teacher.
—Times Educational Supplement (1997)

Educational change depends on what teachers do and think—it's as simple and as complex as that. It would all be so easy if we could legislate changes in thinking. Classrooms and schools become effective when (1) quality people are recruited to teaching, and (2) the workplace is organized to energize teachers and reward accomplishments. The two are intimately related. Professionally rewarding workplace conditions attract and retain good people. Using sustained improvement as the criterion, this chapter progresses from the negative—the situation for most teachers—to the positive—conditions where teaching thrives.

The conditions of teaching appear to have deteriorated over the past two decades. Reversing this trend, as I shall argue in this chapter, must be at the heart of any serious reform effort. Leaving aside the question of blame, it is a fact that teachers have become devalued by the community and the public. Teacher stress and alienation are at an all-time high, judging from the increase in work-related illness, and from the numbers of teachers leaving or wanting to leave the profession. The range of educational goals and expectations for schools and the transfer of family and societal problems to the school, coupled with the imposition of multiple, disconnected reform initiatives, present intolerable conditions for sustained educational development and satisfying work experiences.

I start in this chapter with a sketch of where most teachers are. From there I move to the phenomenon of the introduction of change—in nine out of ten cases a gross mismatch, as far as the world of the teacher is concerned. But change is a double-edged sword and in one out of ten cases we will see what makes for success. In the third section I take up the matter of professionalism at the crossroads, for teaching is at a critical juncture in its evolution as a profession.

WHERE TEACHERS ARE

Starting where teachers are means starting with routine, overload, and limits to reform, because this is the situation for most teachers. As we shall see, there are notable exceptions to this modal pattern, which represent glimpses of what could be, but for most teachers daily demands crowd out serious sustained improvements.

It is clearly not possible to describe in a few pages the school lives of 2½ million teachers in diverse settings across North America, let alone across the world. The following, written by a teacher, provides a composite picture that, despite the flamboyance of the language, captures the experience of many high school teachers:

> Teachers routinely have to teach over 140 students daily. On top of that, we have lunch duty, bus duty, hall duty, home room duty. ... We go to parents' meetings, teachers' meetings, in-service meetings, curriculum meetings, department meetings, county-wide teachers' meetings, school board meetings, and state teachers' conferences. We staff the ticket booths and concession stands at football and basketball games. We supervise the production of school plays, annuals, newspapers, dances, sports events, debates, chess tournaments, graduation ceremonies. We go on senior trips. ... We go on field trips to capital buildings, prisons, nature centers, zoos, courtroom trials. We choke down macaroni and cheese and USDA peanut butter at lunch (and have to pay for it). We search lockers during bomb threats. We supervise fire drills and tornado alerts. We write hall passes, notes to the principal, the assistant principal, parents and ourselves. We counsel. We wake up every morning to the realization that the majority of our students would far rather be someplace else. On top of that everyone's yelling at us—state legislatures,

parents, and SAT scores. . . . To add injury to insult, colleges and universities are getting all huffed up and grumpy and indignant over the increasingly poor preparation of the students we're sending them. Well, just who do they think taught us how to teach? How much support and prestige do they accord their own schools of education? (Wigginton, 1986, p. 191)

The situation of elementary school teachers is different, but no more attractive. Most urban teachers in North America, for example, increasingly face ethnic and language diversity, special-needs children, one-parent families, and a bewildering array of social and academic expectations for the classroom. After reviewing the goals of education—mastery of basic skills, intellectual development, career education, interpersonal understandings, citizenship participation, enculturation, moral and ethical character development, emotional and physical well-being, creativity and aesthetic self-expression, and self-realization—Goodlad (1984, chap. 2) concludes *we want it all.*

Teachers all over the world are feeling beleaguered. Teachers in England express their reactions to impending high-stakes inspection of their school, and to the detailed paper accountability that it demands:

Whatever criticism they make, it's going to feel, however stupid it is, that the last 20 years have been for nothing. It's not about what progress schools have made in the last 15 years. It's "Schools fail." "Head (principal) to be removed." "Hit team going in." It doesn't matter what you look at. It's about failure in schools.

I don't want to lose my optimism. People always say that I am optimistic but I am beginning to lose it. I don't want to be negative, for I enjoy some parts, but I'm worrying about the level of support for others I can sustain (as a teacher leader) as I see them suffering more and more . . . We seem to have become (whiners) but that is not really who we are. (Jeffrey & Wood, 1997)

The circumstances of teaching, then, ask a lot of teachers in terms of daily maintenance and student accountability, and give back little in the time needed for planning, constructive discussion, thinking, and just plain rewards and time for composure. The central tendency of these conditions, as I will describe in this section, is decidedly negative in its consequences.

Let us start one quarter of a century ago with one of the most respected and widely quoted studies of what teachers do and think (Lortie, 1975). After reviewing Lortie's conclusions I will then ask, What, if anything, has changed over the past 25 years? Lortie based his study on 94 interviews with a stratified sample of elementary and secondary school teachers in the greater Boston area (called the Five Town sample), questionnaires to almost 6,000 teachers in Dade County, Florida, and various national and local research studies by others. His findings can be best summarized in point form.

1. Teacher training (see also Chapter 14) does not equip teachers for the realities of the classroom. Nor could it be expected to do so in light of the abruptness of the transition. In September, the young teacher (who typically was a student in June) assumes the same responsibility as the 25-year teacher veteran. For both the beginning and experienced teacher, issues of classroom control and discipline are one of the major preoccupations. Lortie claims that for most teachers there is always a tension between the task-oriented controlling aspect of a teacher role and the relational reaching-the-student aspect.
2. The cellular organization of schools means that teachers struggle with their problems and anxieties privately, spending most of their time physically apart from their colleagues.
3. Partly because of the physical isolation and partly because of norms of not sharing, observing, and discussing each other's work, teachers do not develop a common technical culture. The picture is not one of "colleagues who see themselves as sharing a viable, generalized body of knowledge and practice" (Lortie, 1975, p. 79). In many ways student learning is seen as determined either by factors outside the teachers' control (such as family background) or by unpredictable and mysterious influences. According to Lortie, the lack of a technical culture, an analytic orientation, and a serious sharing and reflection among teachers creates ambiguity and ad hocness: "The teacher's craft. . . . is marked by the absence of concrete models for emulation, unclear

lines of influence, multiple and controversial criteria, ambiguity about assessment timing, and instability in the product" (p. 136). A teacher is either a good teacher or a bad one; a teacher has either a good day or a bad one. It all depends.

4. When teachers do get help, the most effective source tends to be fellow teachers, and second, administrators and specialists. Such help is not frequent and is used on a highly selective basis. For example, teachers normally do not relate objectives to principles of instruction and learning outcomes of students. Rather, "they describe the 'tricks of the trade' they picked up— not broader conceptions that underlie classroom practice" (p. 77). As to the frequency of contact, 45% of the Five Town teachers reported "no contact" with other teachers in doing their work, 32% reported "some contact," and 25% reported "much contact" (p. 193). There is some indication that teachers desire more contact with fellow teachers—54% said that a good colleague is someone who is willing to share (p. 194). Again, this refers more to "tricks of the trade" than to underlying principles of teaching and to the relationship of teaching to learning.

5. Effectiveness of teaching is gauged by informal, general observation of students—50% of the teachers in Dade County responded in this vein. The next most frequent choice related to the results of tests—a very distant 13.5%. In short, teachers rely heavily on their own informal observations.

6. The greatest rewards mentioned by teachers were what Lortie labels "psychic rewards": "the times I reached a student or group of students and they have learned" (p. 104). Over 5,000 (86%) of the 5,900 teachers in Dade County mentioned this source of gratification. The next most frequent response—respect from others—was selected by 2,100, or 37% of the sample.

7. Lortie (1975) also found that "striking success with one student" here and one student there was the predominant source of pride (as distinct from raising test scores of the whole group) (p. 121). For secondary school teachers, the success stories often did not become visible until one or more years after graduation, when a former student returned to thank a teacher. In comparing single successes with group results, it is revealing that 64% of the Five Town teachers mentioned the former category, and only 29% mentioned the latter, as a major source of satisfaction.

8. One of the predominant feelings that characterize the psychological state of teachers and teaching is *uncertainty*—teachers are not
   sure whether they have made any difference at all. Intangibility,
   complexity, and remoteness of learning outcomes, along with
   other influences (family, peer, and societal) on the students make
   the teacher's assessment of his or her impact on students endemi-
   cally uncertain (Lortie, 1975, Chap. 6): 64% of the Five Town
   teachers said that they encountered problems in assessing their
   work; two thirds of them said the problem was serious (p. 142).
9. Of particular relevance to innovation, when Lortie asked teachers how they would choose to spend additional work time, if
   they received a gift of 10 hours per week, 91% of the almost
   6,000 teachers in Dade County selected classroom-related activities (more preparation, more teaching with groups of students,
   more counseling). "It is also interesting," writes Lortie, "that 91
   percent of the first choices are *individualistic*; they are all tasks
   which teachers normally perform alone" (p. 164, emphasis
   added). Second, the lack of time and the feeling of not having
   finished one's work is a perennial problem experienced by teachers. Unwanted or unproductive interruptions, Lortie observes,
   "must be particularly galling" (p. 177). Among the Five Town
   teachers, Lortie found that 62 of the 98 reasons for complaints
   given by teachers "dealt with time erosion or the disruption of
   work flow" (p. 178). One can immediately see how unwanted
   innovations can be another source of annoyance.

So, what has changed over the past 25 years? Not much! For
example, a decade later Goodlad (1984) and his colleagues studied
a national sample in the United States of 1,350 teachers and their
classrooms. His conclusions about the modal patterns of classroom
life are not inspiring:

- The dominant pattern of classroom organization is a group to which
  the teacher most frequently relates as a whole.
- Each student essentially works and achieves alone within a group
  setting.
- The teacher is virtually autonomous with respect to classroom
  decisions—selecting materials, determining class organization,
  choosing instructional procedures.

- Most of the time the teacher is engaged in either frontal teaching, monitoring students' seatwork, or conducting quizzes. Relatively rarely are students actively engaged in learning directly from one another or initiating processes of interaction with teachers.
- There is a paucity of praise and correction of students' performance, as well as of teacher guidance in how to do better next time.
- Students generally engage in a rather narrow range of classroom activities—listening to the teacher, writing answers to questions, and taking tests and quizzes.
- Large percentages of the students surveyed appeared to be passively content with classroom life.
- Even in the early elementary years there was strong evidence of students not having time to finish their lessons or not understanding what the teacher wanted them to do.
- The teacher has little influence or involvement in schoolwide and other extra-classroom matters. (1984, pp. 123–124, 186)

Goodlad proceeds to analyze the conditions under which teachers work. The theme of autonomous isolation stands out. Although teachers functioned independently, "their autonomy seemed to be exercised in a context more of isolation than of rich professional dialogue" (p. 186). Inside schools, "teacher-to-teacher links for mutual assistance or collaborative school improvement were weak or nonexistent" (p. 186). A large majority said that they never observed another teacher teaching, although 75% at all levels of schooling stated that they would like to observe other teachers at work (we shall return to the potential of this latter finding later in this chapter). Teachers also reported that they were not involved in addressing schoolwide problems. Outside the school, aside from casual contacts at in-service workshops and meetings, Goodlad found that "there was little . . . to suggest active, ongoing exchanges of ideas and practices across schools, between groups of teachers, or between individuals even in the same schools" (p. 187).

A few years later, Rosenholtz's study of 78 schools in Tennessee (1989) corroborated many of Goodlad's observations. The majority of schools (65 of the 78) were classified by Rosenholtz as relatively "stuck" or "learning impoverished" for both teachers and students. She described these schools as showing little or no attention to schoolwide goals. These schools were also characterized by isolation among teachers, limited teacher learning on the job, teacher uncertainty about what and how to teach, and low commitment to the job and the school. This constellation of factors functioned in these schools as a vicious negative cycle to suppress teacher and student desire and achievement. Rosenholtz says "stuck schools" are characterized by

> [l]ittle attachment to anything or anybody. Teachers seemed more concerned with their own identity than a sense of shared community. Teachers learned about the nature of their work randomly, not deliberately, tending to follow their individual instincts. Without shared governance, particularly in managing student conduct, the absolute number of students who claimed teachers' attention seemed greater. . . . teachers talked of frustration, failure, tedium and managed to transfer those attributes to the students about whom they complained. (p. 208)

Rosenholtz explains that isolation and uncertainty are associated with settings where teachers are able to learn little from their colleagues, and therefore are not in a strong position to experiment and improve.

Fast forward another decade from Goodlad and we find Hargreaves (1994) talking about "the intensification of teachers' work," in which demands have increased relentlessly:

- Intensification leads to reduced time for relaxation during the working day . . .
- Intensification leads to lack of time to retool one's skills and keep up with one's field
- Intensification creates chronic and persistent overload . . .
- Intensification leads to reductions in the *quality* of service, as corners are cut to save on time. (Hargreaves, 1994, pp. 118–119, emphasis in original)

More recently, in a study of teachers in four countries (Australia, New Zealand, United Kingdom, and the United States), Scott, Stone, and Dinham (2000) found that teachers still point to the psychic rewards of "seeing children progress" and "making a difference in young people's lives," but they also found a prominent negative theme across the four countries, which the authors labeled "the erosion of the profession." This domain included decrease in status and recognition of the profession; outside interference in and deprofessionalization of teaching, pace, and nature of educational change; and increased workload (Scott et al., 2000, p. 4).

In teachers' words:

> Teaching isn't like it used to be and the money isn't worth the abuse we cop day in and day out (Australia).
>
> Classroom teachers are bombarded with paperwork. We spent so much time on useless paperwork that planning, evaluating, and teaching time are seriously impacted (U.S.).
>
> Teachers feel like puppets—other people pull our strings. There is little vision left in the teaching profession—it's been weeded out over the last 10 years (U.K.).

ENTER CHANGE

Of course, change has already entered, and the question is, How can we deal with it and turn it to our and others' advantage? Aside from being inevitable, change is needed. It is necessary because high proportions of students are alienated, performing poorly or dropping out. Their life in school is far less than it should be (see Chapter 9).

But here we are talking about teachers. In a direct sense, change is needed because many teachers are frustrated, bored, and burned out. Even Lortie's teachers were not exactly thriving on psychic rewards, primarily because they did not have access to new ideas and had few opportunities for growth. As Sarason (1971, pp. 166–167) observes, "If teaching becomes neither terribly interesting nor exciting to many teachers, can one expect them to make learning exciting to students?"

In an indirect sense, teachers need to increase their capacity for dealing with change because if they don't they are going to continue to be victimized by the relentless intrusion of external change forces.

Teacher isolation and its opposite—collegiality—provide the best starting point for considering what works for the teacher. It may be recalled from Chapter 5 that at the teacher level the degree of change was strongly related to the extent to which teachers *interact* with each other and others providing technical help. Within the school, collegiality among teachers, as measured by the frequency of communication, mutual support, help, and so forth, was a strong indicator of implementation success. Virtually every research study on the topic has found this to be the case. And it does make eminent sense in terms of the theory of change espoused in this book. Significant educational change consists of changes in beliefs, teaching style, and materials, which can come about *only* through a process of personal development in a social context. As Werner (1980) observes in explaining the failure of social studies curriculum in Alberta,

> Ideally, implementation as a minimum includes shared understanding among participants concerning the implied presuppositions, values and assumptions which underlie a program, for if participants understand these, then they have a basis for rejecting, accepting or modifying a program in terms of their own school, community and class situations. To state the aim another way, implementation is an ongoing construction of a shared reality among group members through their interaction with one another within the program. (pp. 62–63)

There is no getting around the *primacy of personal contact*. Teachers need to participate in skill-training workshops, but they also need to have one-to-one and group opportunities to receive and give help and more simply to *converse* about the meaning of change. Under these conditions teachers learn how to use an innovation as well as to judge its desirability on more information-based grounds; they are in a better position to know whether they should accept, modify, or reject the change. This is the case with regard to both externally developed ideas and innovations decided upon or developed by other teachers. Purposeful interaction is essential for continuous improvement.

Fortunately, over the past decade, research has provided a much more specific picture of how purposeful interaction operates within successful schools. The key term is "professional learning community" (or what we refer to as "collaborative work cultures") (Fullan & Hargreaves, 1992).

We can start with Rosenholtz's (1989) description of the collaborative work culture of the 13 "moving" or "learning-enriched"
work environments in her study. Figure 7.1 contains an adapted
summary of the main school-based elements associated with the
successful schools in Rosenholtz's research. There are other factors
influencing the six themes and the interactions among the themes
are multifaceted, but the composite picture of how successful collaborative schools work is clear and convincing.

As Rosenholtz observes, teacher uncertainty (or low sense of
efficacy) and threats to self-esteem are recurring themes in teaching
(Ashton & Webb, 1986). In comparing learning-enriched schools
with learning-impoverished schools, Rosenholtz found that teachers and principals collaborated in goal-setting activities (or vision-
building) that "accentuated those instructional objectives toward
which teachers should aim their improvement efforts" (p. 6), and
that shared goals served to focus efforts and mobilize resources
in agreed-upon directions. Principals and teacher leaders actively
fostered collegial involvement: "Collective commitment to student
learning in collaborative settings directs the definition of leadership
toward those colleagues who instruct as well as inspire awakening
all sorts of teaching possibilities in others" (p. 68). In effective
schools, collaboration is linked with norms and opportunities for

Figure 7.1. Learning-enriched schools.

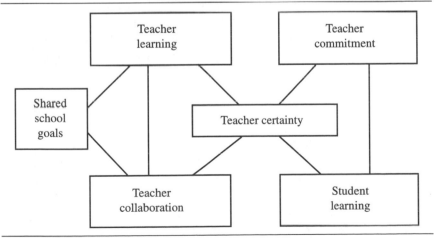

continuous improvement and career-long learning: "It is assumed that improvement in teaching is a collective rather than individual enterprise, and that analysis, evaluation, and experimentation in concert with colleagues are conditions under which teachers improve" (p. 73). As a result, teachers are more likely to trust, value, and legitimize sharing expertise, seeking advice, and giving help both inside and outside of the school. They are more likely to become better and better teachers on the job: "All of this means that it is far easier to learn to teach, and to learn to teach better, in some schools than in others" (p. 104).

Becoming better teachers means greater confidence and certainty in deciding on instructional issues and in handling problems. Rosenholtz (1989) found that:

> Where teachers request from and offer technical assistance to each other, and where school staff enforces consistent standards for student behavior, teachers tend to complain less about students and parents. Further, where teachers collaborate, where they keep parents involved and informed about their children's progress, where teachers and principals work together to consistently enforce standards for student behavior, and where teachers celebrate their achievements through positive feedback from students, parents, principals, colleagues, and their own sense, they collectively tend to believe in a technical culture and their instructional practice. (p. 137)

Teacher certainty and teacher commitment feed on each other, as Rosenholtz found, increasing teachers' motivation to do even better. All of these factors served to channel energy toward student achievement. Teachers in the learning-enriched schools were less likely to conform to new state or district policies that they judged ill-conceived or as directing energies from classroom priorities, and more likely to assess innovations in terms of their actual impact on students.

Newmann and his colleagues (Louis & Kruse, 1995; Newmann & Wehlage, 1995) have gone ever further in tracing the link between professional learning community, teacher learning, and student performance. In essence, their argument about the internal workings of successful schools is that professional communities make the difference because, in their words:

- Teachers pursue a clear purpose for all students' learning.
- Teachers engage in collaborative activity to achieve the purpose.
- Teachers take collaborative responsibility for student learning . . . [And]
- Schoolwide teacher professional community affected the level of classroom authentic pedagogy, which in turn affected student performance.
- Schoolwide teacher professional community affected the level of social support for student learning, which in turn affected student performance. (Newmann & Wehlage, 1995, pp. 30, 32)

What happens in these schools is that teachers as a group and as subgroups examine together how well students are doing, relate this to how they are teaching, and then make improvements (see Figure 7.2). We have called this the need for teachers to become "assessment literate" (Hargreaves & Fullan, 1998). Assessment literacy involves:

1. The capacity to examine student performance data and results, and to make critical sense of it.
2. The capacity to act on this understanding by developing classroom and school improvement plans in order to make the kinds of changes needed to increase performance.
3. The capacity of teachers to be effective players in the accountability arena by being proactive and open about school

Figure 7.2. The nature of professional learning communities. (Adapted from Louis & Kruse, 1995; Newmann & Wehlage, 1995).

performance data, and by being able to hold their own in the contentious debate about the uses and misuses of achievement data in an era of high-stakes testing.

Let us consider three more examples in order to be crystal clear about the power of collaborative work cultures. Bryk and colleagues (1998) have been tracing the evolution of reform in the Chicago school system. After 10 years of monitoring the results and beginning to see success in more and more elementary schools, Bryk and colleagues draw the following conclusion:

> In schools making systemic changes, structures are established which create opportunities for such interactions to occur. As teachers develop a broader say in school decision making, they may also begin to experiment with new roles, including working collaboratively. This restructuring of teachers' work signifies a broadening professional community where teachers feel more comfortable exchanging ideas, and where a collective sense of responsibility for student development is likely to emerge. These characteristics of systemic restructuring contrast with conventional school practice where teachers work more autonomously, and there may be little meaningful professional exchange among co-workers. (Bryk et al., 1998, p. 128)

Goldenberg's study of Freeman (pseudonym) Elementary School outside Los Angeles is also instructive because he worked with the school from its initial state of isolation and poor performance to a fully developed collaborative school in which the literacy achievement of students continued to climb (Gallimore & Goldenberg, 2001; Goldenberg, in press).

Goldenberg (in press) quotes a teacher in Freeman referring to the past:

> We never had grade level meetings where we had to talk to each other and see what was going on and where everyone was . . . and I had no idea if I was on track or off track or things like that. (p. 17)

The goal of the project was to develop norms of collaboration and interaction in order to produce improvements in student learning. Literacy did improve substantially over a 3-year period both relative to baseline measures, and compared to the performance of other schools in the district. There was no doubt in the minds of teachers that the gains were caused by the concerted efforts of the principal and teachers:

> Now ... with [the] principal's leadership, it's kind of a given that there's more communication within the staff, especially within the grade levels, as it pertains to the goals and just communication in general. It's really good. (Goldenberg, in press, p. 22)

Other teachers reported much the same:

> All teachers are working together at this point, in grade levels and in teacher work groups. And they're focused on, in all of the groups, to work towards the goals and objectives that were written for all grade levels. All teachers had input on that.... It's allowed them to be unified. It's allowed them to feel good about what they are doing. (p. 23)

One teacher commented that her teaching had improved "100% to 200%" because they meet to plan, learn together, and review progress on an ongoing basis. She observed: "It's like one big classroom instead of one big school" (p. 26).

Freeman is an elementary school (albeit a fairly large one with 800 students), but what about high schools? I must say, as others have, that they need major surgery, if not burial. Put positively, we need whatever it will take to create purposeful learning communities and this certainly will require smaller schools (e.g., 600 students rather than 3,000). We do get confirmation of the problem and specific glimpses of the desired direction in some very recent research, especially that of McLaughlin and Talbert (2001) (see also Murphy, Beck, Crawford, & Hodges, et al., 2001).

McLaughlin and Talbert conducted a study of the role of professional learning communities in 16 high schools in California and Michigan. What they found was confirmatory and revealing as they got inside complex high schools more specifically than other researchers have. They suggest that there are three patterns of teaching practice:

1. Enacting traditions of practice (in which traditional subject-based teaching occurs, and only traditional students succeed).
2. Lowering expectations and standards (in which teachers water-down subjects in the face of low-motivated students, which has limited success).
3. Innovating to engage learners (in which subjects and teaching are considered dynamic in order to involve all students, which leads to greater learning by all).

In lowering expectations, for example, teachers tend to locate the problem in the student, as in the following comment from a math teacher:

> Oh man, you just sit here and you think how can anybody be that stupid . . . how can they be this damn stupid. The kid is where the problem is today. There is nothing wrong with the curriculum. If I could just get people that wanted to learn, then I could teach and everything would be wonderful. (McLaughlin & Talbert, 2001, p. 13)

By contrast, innovating to engage students involves

> teachers [who] move beyond or outside established frames for instruction to find or develop content and classroom strategies that will enable students to master core subject concepts. . . .
> An English teacher uses writing groups; a math teacher creates groups of three ["no more than that," he advises], a science teacher has all but abandoned texts to connect students through lab-based group projects. (pp. 17, 20)

Dovetailing with the theme of this chapter, McLaughlin and Talbert (2001) found that "a collaborative community of practice in which teachers share instructional resources and reflections in practice appears essential to their persistence and success in innovating classroom practice" (p. 22). In other words, teachers who were successful with all students, especially those traditionally turned off by school, were constantly figuring out and sharing what works (much like Stigler and Hiebert's [1999] Japanese teachers). More to the point here, these teachers "taught in schools and departments with a strong *professional community* engaged in making innovations that support student and teacher learning and success" (p. 34, emphasis in original).

Overall, McLaughlin and Talbert found that most high school departments lacked a culture of sharing and jointly developing practice. But they found some exceptions, such as differences between departments *within* the same school, whole high schools that were more collaborative. In one school, for example:

Oak Valley's English department has the strongest technical culture of any department in our sample while the same school's social studies department ranks among the weakest. (McLaughlin & Talbert, 2001, p. 47)

A veteran English teacher at Oak Valley comments:

It's everyday practice that teachers are handing [out] sample lessons they've done, or an assignment that they've tried, and [discussed] when it worked [or] how they would do it differently. Or a new teacher joins the staff and instantly they are paired up with a couple of buddies . . . and file drawers and computer disks and everything are just made readily available. (p. 50)

In contrast, teachers in the social studies department speak of "my materials" but never mention their colleagues as resources.

Most revealing is that teachers talk about students with radically different assumptions about learning. English teachers' comments are uniformly positive: "We have excellent students, cooperative, and there's good rapport with the teachers." A Social Studies teacher in turn says, "The kids—there's no quest for knowledge. Not all, but that's in general . . . it's not important to them. They just don't want to learn." Note that these teachers are talking about the *same* students!

McLaughlin and Talbert sum up Oak Valley's two departments:

In the social studies department, autonomy means isolation and reinforces the norms of individualism and conservatism. In the English department, professional autonomy and strong community are mutually reinforcing, rather than oppositional. Here collegial support and interaction enable individual teachers to

reconsider and revise their classroom practice confidently because department norms are mutually negotiated and understood. (p. 55)

McLaughlin and Talbert show what a dramatic difference these
experiences have for the motivation and career commitments of
teachers:

When teachers from the Oak Valley English and Social Studies
departments told us how they feel about their job, it was hard
to believe that they teach in the same school. Oak Valley English
teachers of all pedagogical persuasions express pride in their
department and pleasure in their workplace: "Not a day goes
by that someone doesn't say how wonderful it is to work here,"
said one. In contrast, social studies teachers, weary of grappling
alone with classroom tensions, verbalize bitterness and professional disinvestment. Several plan to leave the school or the
profession. (pp. 83–84)

McLaughlin and Talbert proceed with similar analyses that we
need not report in detail here. For example, comparing two math
departments in different schools, one has a well-developed professional community, the other is steeped in isolationism. Across all
16 schools, they found only three schoolwide learning communities.

In short, weak departments contain teachers who disengage
from their jobs, while strong departments evidence teachers who
see themselves as lifelong learners.

We will return to McLaughlin and Talbert's study in later
chapters (Chapter 8 on the role of leadership, Chapter 9 on the
student, and Chapter 15 on professional development), but here's
one more critical observation. It is not just any kind of professional
learning community that counts. Collaboration is powerful, which
means it can be powerfully bad as well as powerfully good.

Little (1990a) warned us about this problem a decade ago:

The content of teachers' values and beliefs cannot be taken
for granted in the study or pursuit of teachers' collegial norms
of interaction and interpretation. Under some circumstances,
greater contact among teachers can be expected to advance the
prospects for students' success; in others, to promote increased

teacher-to-teacher contact may be to intensify norms unfavorable to children. (1990a, p. 524)

And:

Bluntly put, do we have in teachers' collaborative work the creative development of well-informed choices, or the mutual reinforcement of poorly informed habit? Does teachers' time together advance the understanding and imagination they bring to their work, or do teachers merely confirm one another in present practice? What subject philosophy and subject pedagogy do teachers reflect as they work together, how explicit and accessible is their knowledge to one another? Are there collaborations that in fact erode teachers' moral commitments and intellectual merit? (p. 525)

In a wonderfully insightful summary diagram, McLaughlin and Talbert make the same point (Figure 7.3). Weak professional communities are bad, no matter how you cut it. Strong teacher communities can be effective or not depending on whether they collaborate to make breakthroughs in learning or whether they reinforce methods which do not get results. In other words, when teachers collaborate to reinforce each others' bad or ineffective practices, they end up making matters worse.

One final clarification. We cannot assume that autonomy is bad and collaboration is good. One person's isolation is another person's solitude; one person's collaboration is another person's groupthink (Fullan & Hargreaves, 1992). Let's not forget that we are talking about purposeful, critical improvements in learning for all students—and it should be clear, learning for all teachers.

PROFESSIONALISM AT THE CROSSROADS

Teaching needs to become a highly intellectual as well as a highly caring profession. Because it takes place under intense social and political circumstances it is also a profession that demands great emotional intelligence. The question is, can the profession become that good? This will entail (1) understanding what an effective teacher and teaching profession is; and (2) working at creating it at all levels in the system.

Figure 7.3. Communities of practice and the work of high school teachers. (From McLaughlin & Talbert, 2001).

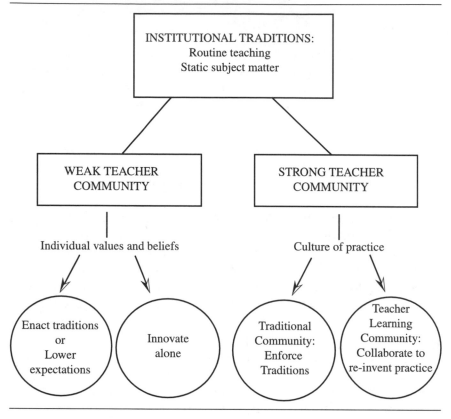

The management consultant firm of Hay/McBer recently carried out a study in England in order "to provide a framework describing effective teaching" (Hay/McBer, 2000) (see also the National Board for Professional Teaching Standards, 1993; Darling-Hammond, in press). Observing teaching in the context of start-of-year and end-of-year student attainment, Hay/McBer found that effective teachers displayed three sets of characteristics, which in turn accounted for over 30% of the variance in pupil progress. The three domains pertained to teaching skills, classroom climate, and professional characteristics.

Teaching skills included a variety of teaching methods, planning, high expectations, monitoring assessment, and the like. Climate involved how students felt in the classroom with respect to clarity, fairness, participation, care, interest, safety, and so on. Professional characteristics consisted of 16 dimensions in five clusters. The clusters with illustrative dimensions were:

- Professionalism (challenge, respect)
- Thinking (analytic and conceptual)
- Planning and setting expectations (drive for improvement, information-seeking)
- Leading (passion for learning, holding people accountable)
- Relating to others (teamwork, empathy)

Their conclusion:

> The integrating analyses found that pupil progress is most significantly influenced by a teacher who displays both high levels of professional characteristics and good teaching skills which lead to the creation of a good classroom climate. . . . [This analysis] is based on clear evidence of pupil progress . . . Above all, it re-emphasizes how important and influential the teacher is in raising standards in schools whatever the existing situation. (Hay/McBer, 2000, p. 29)

Add to this reference to the work in Tennessee referred to by the Education Commission of the States (ECS) (2000), which found that

> students who had good teachers three years in a row showed a significant increase in their percentile rankings on state examination—regardless of socioeconomic factors. (ECS, 2000, p. 5)

In short, we are talking about something truly powerful, and frightening.

As this whole book claims, this is not just an individual problem, it is a system problem. Thus, it must be attacked at all levels. It should be abundantly clear as well, from this chapter, that this is not a matter of establishing a bunch of policies and requirements.

We are talking about *reculturing* the teaching profession—the process of creating and fostering purposeful learning communities.

It is also the case that teachers and unions must take a lead role in asking what kind of culture do we have, what do we want, and how do we get there (Hargreaves & Fullan, 1998). Teachers and principals must reculture their schools, but so must administrators work on reculturing their districts; universities, their teaching preparation programs; and states, their policies of accountability and development. All of these topics are addressed in subsequent chapters.

It is possible to obtain short-term gains in student achievement scores without reculturing, but these less powerful strategies produce superficial gains. They do not get at the heart of learning, which is what students need. They have no depth and they have no staying power. The development of professional learning communities does have depth, and the beauty is that these communities integrate development and accountability seemlessly in new cultures of improvement. Teachers in the learning communities I have described in this chapter are challenged day in and day out. They are supported, but they also must deliver because it is so noticeable when they don't.

The trouble, as I said at the outset, is that we have too few of these learning communities; they are very hard to get, and even harder to sustain. Teachers, individually and collectively, need to work on this agenda. It is in their interest and in the interests of their students. But if there is any changing to be done, *everyone is implicated*. The infrastructure surrounding teachers is critical and at this point not all that helpful in fostering powerful learning communities. Let us turn to the most immediate source of help or hindrance—the school principal.

CHAPTER 8

The Principal

Effective principals attack incoherence.
                                    —Bryk et al. (1998)

Forget about the principal as head of the school for a moment and think of her or him as someone just as buffeted as the teacher is by wanted or unwanted and often incomprehensible changes—and, what is more, *expected to lead these very changes.* Change is only one of the forces competing for the principal's attention, and usually not the most compelling one. Yet some principals are actively engaged as initiators or facilitators of continuous improvements in their schools. The principal is in the middle of the relationship between teachers and external ideas and people. As in most human triangles there are constant conflicts and dilemmas. How the principal approaches (or avoids) these issues determines to a large extent whether these relationships constitute a Bermuda triangle of innovations.

An understanding of what reality is *from the point of view of people within the role* is an essential starting point for constructing a practical theory of the meaning and results of change attempts. This phenomenology is social science's contribution to addressing the frequent lament, "No one understands me." In the field of educational change, everyone feels misunderstood. One of the most revealing and frustrating indicators of the difficulties in educational change is the participants' frequent experience of having their intentions not only misunderstood but interpreted exactly opposite of what they meant. Principals should have no problem claiming their fair share of frustration, since the role of the principal has in fact become dramatically more complex, overloaded, and unclear over the past decade. On the optimistic side, very recent research has identified some specific change-related behaviors of principals who deal effectively with educational change. It is time to go beyond the empty phrase, The principal is the gatekeeper of change.

While research on school improvement is now into its third decade, systematic research on what the principal actually does and its relationship to stability and change is quite recent. Some of the earlier implementation research identified the role of the principal as central to promoting or inhibiting change, but it did not examine the principal's role in any depth or perspective. During the 1980s research and practice focusing on the role of the principal-ship, assistant principalship, and other school leaders mounted, resulting in greater clarity, but also greater appreciation of the complexities and different paths to success.

I start with a description of where principals are. I then turn to the part of their role that interests us the most—what principals do and don't do in relation to change. In the last section of the chapter, I talk about the complexity of leadership, and offer some guidelines for how principals might lead change more effectively. I should also acknowledge at the outset that effective principals share—in fact, develop—leadership among teachers. So we are really talking about assistant principals, department heads, grade-level coordinators, and teacher leaders of all types in the school.

WHERE PRINCIPALS ARE

"Pressure drives heads to drink" blares a recent headline in the *London Times Education Supplement* in England (Times Educational Supplement [TES], 2000, p. 5). The article reports that among the principals and deputy principals in the district of Warwickshire (a district with 250 schools), 40% had visited the doctor with stress-related problems in the past year, and 30% were taking medication. Warwickshire was selected, says the article, because it was considered to be a well-run district—a good employer!

With the move toward the self-management of schools, the principal appears to have the worst of both worlds. The old world is still around with expectations to run a smooth school, and to be responsive to all; simultaneously the new world rains down on schools with disconnected demands, expecting that at the end of the day the school should be constantly showing better test results, and ideally becoming a learning organization.

In *What's Worth Fighting for in the Principalship* (Fullan, 1997), I reported on a study of 137 principals and vice principals in Toronto (Edu-Con, 1984). The growing overload experienced by principals was evident over 15 years ago: 90% reported an increase over the previous 5 years in the demands made on their time, including new program demands, the number of board priorities and directives, and the number of directives from the Ministry of Education. Time demands were listed as having increased in dealing with parent and community groups (92% said there was an increase), trustee requests (91% reported an increase), administration activities (88%), staff involvement and student services (81%), social services (81%), and board initiatives (69%).

Principals and vice principals were also asked about their perceptions of effectiveness: 61% reported a *decrease in principal effectiveness*, with only 13% saying it was about the same, and 26% reporting an increase. The same percentage, 61%, reported decreases in "the effectiveness of assistance . . . from immediate superiors and from administration." Further, 84% reported a decrease in the authority of the principal, 72% a decrease in trust in leadership of the principal, and 76% a decrease in principal involvement in decision making at the system level; 91% responded "no" to the question, "Do you think the principal can effectively fulfill all the responsibilities assigned to him/her?"

The discouragement felt by principals in attempting to cover all the bases is aptly described in the following three responses from interviews conducted by Duke (1988) with principals who were considering quitting:

> The conflict for me comes from going home every night acutely aware of what didn't get done and feeling after six years that I ought to have a better batting average than I have.
>
> If you leave the principalship, think of all the "heart-work" you're going to miss. I fear I'm addicted to it and to the pace of the principalship—those 2,000 interactions a day. I get fidgety in meetings because they're too slow, and I'm not out there interacting with people.

The principalship is the kind of job where you're expected
to be all things to all people. Early on, if you're successful, you
have gotten feedback that you are able to be all things to all
people. And then you feel an obligation to continue to do that
which in your own mind you're not capable of doing. And that
causes some guilt. (p. 309)

Duke was intrigued by the "dropout rate" of principals after
encountering an article stating that 22% of Vermont administrators
employed in the fall of 1984 had left the state's school systems by the
fall of 1985. In interviewing principals about why they considered
quitting, he found that sources of dissatisfaction included policy
and administration, lack of achievement, sacrifices in personal life,
lack of growth opportunities, lack of recognition and too little
responsibility, relations with subordinates, and lack of support
from superiors. They expressed a number of concerns about the
job itself: the challenge of doing all the things that principals are
expected to do, the mundane or boring nature of much of the work,
the debilitating array of personal interactions, the politics of dealing
with various constituencies, and the tendency for managerial concerns to supersede leadership functions (Duke, 1988, p. 310).

Duke suggested that the reasons principals were considering
quitting were related to fatigue, awareness of personal limitations,
and awareness of the limitation of career choices. All four principals
experienced reality shock, "the shock-like reactions of new workers
when they find themselves in a work situation for which they have
spent several years preparing and for which they thought they
were going to be prepared, and then suddenly find that they are
not." Duke (1988) concludes:

A number of frustrations expressed by these principals derived
from the contexts in which they worked. Their comments send
a clear message to those who supervised them: principals need
autonomy *and* support. The need for autonomy may require
supervisors to treat each principal differently; the need for support may require supervisors to be sensitive to each principal's
view of what he or she finds meaningful or trivial about the
work. (p. 312)

There is no question that the demands on the principalship
have become even more intensified over the past 10 years, 5 years,
1 year. . . . More and more principals in almost every Western country are retiring early; more and more potential teacher leaders are
concluding that it is simply not worth it to take on the leadership
of schools:

> Wanted: A miracle worker who can do more with less, pacify
> rival groups, endure chronic second-guessing, tolerate low levels
> of support, process large volumes of paper and work double
> shifts (75 nights a year). He or she will have carte blanche to
> innovate, but cannot spend much money, replace any personnel,
> or upset any constituency. (Evans, 1995)

Is this an impossible job? A job that is simply not worth the
aggravation and toll it takes? Even students notice, such as this
secondary student:

> I don't think being a head is a good job. You have to work too
> hard. Some days [the head] looks knackered—sorry, very tired.
> (Day, Harris, Hadfield, Toley, & Bereford, 2000, p. 126)

At the present time the principalship is not worth it, and therein
lies the solution. If effective principals energize teachers in complex
times, what is going to energize principals? We are now beginning
to see more clearly examples of school principals who are successful. These insights can help existing principals become more effective; even more, they provide a basis for establishing a system
of recruiting, nurturing, and supporting and holding accountable
school leaders (see Chapter 15).

THE PRINCIPAL AND CHANGE

I know of no improving school that doesn't have a principal who
is good at leading improvement. "Almost every single study of
school effectiveness has shown both primary and secondary leadership to be a key factor" says Sammons (1999) in her major review.
Building on the previous chapter, let us see more precisely what
this means. Especially, what does it mean in the year 2000 and

beyond, because these are very different times for school leadership.

Fortunately, there are several recently released studies of school leadership across different countries that provide consistent and clear, not to say easy, messages (Brighouse & Woods, 1999; Bryk et al., 1998; Day et al., 2000; Donaldson, 2001; Elmore, 2000; Leithwood, 2000; Leithwood, Jantzi, & Steinback, 1999; McLaughlin & Talbert, 2001; Newmann, King, & Youngs, 2000).

Bryk and his colleagues have been tracing the evolution of reform in Chicago schools since 1988. In schools that evidenced improvement over time (about one third of 473 elementary schools):

> [P]rincipals worked together with a supportive base of parents, teachers, and community members to mobilize initiative. Their efforts broadly focused along two major dimensions: first, reaching out to parents and community to strengthen the ties between local school professionals and the clientele they are to serve; and second, working to expand the professional capacities of individual teachers, to promote the formation of a coherent professional community, and to direct resources toward enhancing the quality of instruction. (Bryk et al., 1998, p. 270)

These successful principals had (1) "inclusive, facilitative orientation"; (2) an "institutional focus on student learning"; (3) "efficient management"; and (4) "combined pressure and support." They had a strategic orientation, using school improvement plans and instructional focus to "attack incoherence":

> In schools that are improving, teachers are more likely to say that, once a program has begun, there is follow-up to make sure it is working and there is real continuity from one program to another. . . . In our earlier research, we dubbed schools with high levels of incoherence "Christmas tree schools." Such schools were well-known showcases because of the variety of programs they boasted. Frequently, however, these programs were uncoordinated and perhaps even philosophically inconsistent. (Bender Sebring & Bryk, 2000, pp. 441–442)

Other studies of schools improving are variations on themes. In Chapter 7, we saw the effects of strong and weak professional communities in the high schools studied by McLaughlin and Talbert. Leadership (or lack of it) at the department and/or school level accounted for a large part of these differences:

> These very different worlds reveal how much department leadership and expectations shape teacher community. The English department chair actively maintained open department boundaries so that teachers would bring back knowledge resources from districts and out of district professional activities to the community. English faculty attended state and national meetings, published regularly in professional journals, and used professional development days to visit classrooms in other schools. The chair gave priority for time to share each others' writing, discuss new projects, and just talk. . . . English department leadership extended and reinforced expectations and opportunities for teacher learning provided by the district and by the school, developing a rich repertoire of resources for the community to learn.
>
> None of this applied down the hall in the social studies department, where leadership enforced the norms of privatism and conservatism that Dan Lortie found central to school teaching. For example, the social studies chair saw department meetings as an irritating ritual rather than an opportunity: "I don't hold meetings once a week; I don't even necessarily have them once a month." Supports or incentives for learning were few in the social studies department . . . This department chair marginalized the weakest teachers in the department, rather than enabling or encouraging their professional growth. (McLaughlin & Talbert, 2001, pp. 107–108)

Recall from Chapter 7 that only 3 of 16 high schools demonstrated schoolwide professional communities. In these comparisons McLaughlin and Talbert talk about "the pivotal role of principal leadership":

> The utter absence of principal leadership within Valley High School . . . is a strong frame for the weak teacher community we found across departments in the school; conversely, strong leadership in Greenfield, Prospect and Ibsen has been central to engendering and sustaining these school-wide teacher learning communities. . . .

> Principals with low scores [on leadership, as perceived by teachers] generally are seen as managers who provide little support or direction for teaching and learning in the school. Principals receiving high ratings are actively involved in the sorts of activities that nurture and sustain strong teacher community. (McLaughlin & Talbert, 2001, p. 110)

Day and his colleagues (2000) in England wrote a book on the leadership roles in 12 schools, all of which "had consistently raised student achievement levels—in this sense they were 'improving schools'—and all the headteachers were recognized as being instrumental in this and in the overall success of the schools." (p. 1) We observe a now familiar refrain:

> The vision and practices of these heads were organized around a number of core personal values concerning the modeling and promotion of respect (for individuals), fairness and equality, caring for the well-being and whole development of students and staff, integrity and honesty. (Day et al., 2000, p. 39)

These school leaders were "relationship centered," focused on "professional standards," "outwards looking in" (seeking ideas and connections across the country), and "monitoring school performance."

In summarizing, Day and associates conclude:

> Within the study, there was also ample evidence that people were trusted to work as powerful professionals, within clear collegial value frameworks which were common to all. There was a strong emphasis upon teamwork and participation in decision-making (though heads reserved the right to be autocratic). Goals were clear and agreed, communications were good and everyone had high expectations of themselves and others. Those collegial cultures were maintained, however, within contexts of organization and individual accountability set by external policy demands and internal aspirations. These created ongoing tensions and dilemmas which had to be managed and mediated as part of the establishment and maintenance of effective leadership cultures. (p. 162)

These findings are reinforced in Donaldson's (2001) new book, in which he claims that effective school leadership "mobilizes for moral purpose" by fostering "open, trusting, affirmative relationships," "a commitment to mutual purposes and moral benefit," and a "shared belief in action-in-common."

Similarly, Leithwood and his colleagues provide numerous case studies, and cross case synthesis to show that school leaders at both the elementary and secondary levels concentrate on fostering the conditions for school growth by helping to obtain and target resources, developing collaborative cultures across subgroups of teachers, supporting and pushing teacher development, creating facilitative structures, and monitoring teacher commitment as an indicator of organizational capacity (Leithwood, 2000; Leithwood et al., 1999).

Probably the clearest integration of the ideas in Chapters 7 and 8 is contained in the new work by Newmann and his colleagues (King & Newmann, 2000; Newmann et al., 2000). Recall that Newmann & Wehlage (1995) provided us with great new insights about the inner workings of professional learning communities. In their most recent case studies, Newmann and his colleagues use the more comprehensive concept of "school capacity," which in turn affects instructional quality and student assessment in the school as a whole.

The five components of capacity and their cumulative relationships are most revealing. Newmann et al., (2000) define school capacity as consisting of:

- Teachers' knowledge, skills, and dispositions
- Professional community
- Program coherence
- Technical resources
- Principal leadership

Basically, they claim, with backing from case studies, that professional development often focuses on the knowledge, skills, and dispositions of teachers as *individual* staff members. Obviously this is important and can make a difference in individual classrooms.

They also observe that individual development is not sufficient. In addition, they say (and certainly backed up strongly in previous citations in this chapter) there must be *organization* development because social or relationship resources are key to school improvement. Thus, schools must combine individual development with the development of *schoolwide professional communities*.

However, individual development combined with professional communities is still not sufficient, unless it is channeled in a way that combats the fragmentation of multiple innovations by working on *program coherence*, "the extent to which the school's programs for student and staff learning are coordinated, focused on clear learning goals, and sustained over a period of time" (Newmann et al., 2000, p. 5). Program coherence is organizational integration.

Fourth, instructional improvement requires additional *resources* (materials, equipment, space, time, and access to expertise).

Fifth, school capacity is seriously undermined if it does not have quality leadership. Put differently, *the role of the principal is to cause the previous four factors to get better and better*. Elmore (2000) agrees:

> [T]he job of administrative leaders is primarily about enhancing the skills and knowledge of people in the organization, creating a common culture of expectations around the use of those skills and knowledge, holding the various pieces of the organization together in a productive relationship with each other, and holding individuals accountable for their contributions to the collective result. (p. 15)

Elmore also notes that only a minority of current leaders are like this, and that it is a "systems" problem; that is, we will continue to reproduce only small numbers of heroic leaders (heroic because they are going against the grain) until we change how we recruit, support, and develop leadership on the job. In this sense schools get the leaders they deserve. I consider in later chapters how other levels of the system can make it more or less likely that school capacity will grow or deteriorate. In the meantime, it should be absolutely clear that school improvement is an organizational phenomenon and therefore the principal, as leader, is the key for better or for worse.

THE COMPLEXITY OF LEADERSHIP

There are at least four ways in which school leadership is complex: (1) the changes we are seeking are deeper than we first thought; (2) as such, there are a number of dilemmas in deciding what to do; (3) one needs to act differently in different situations or phases of the change process; and (4) advice comes in the form of guidelines for action, not steps to be followed.

First, then, is the realization that what is at stake is "reculturing" schools, a deep and more lasting change once it is attained. Any other changes are superficial and nonlasting. For example, one can increase scores on standardized achievement tests in the short run with tightly led and monitored changes. However, as Bryk and associates warn:

There is a growing body of case evidence documenting that it is possible to raise standardized test scores quickly under high stakes accountability systems based on standardized tests. . . . However, there is also some evidence that these effects may not generalize beyond the specific accountability instruments and may not persist over time . . . [test scores improve] without undertaking the fundamental change necessary to achieve effects that are more likely to persist over time. (Bryk et al., 1998, p. 354)

Win the battle and lose the war, because the results are neither deep (what is learned is not transferable) nor lasting. These types of superficial learnings are not what Gardner (1999), Bransford, Brown, & Cocking (1999), and other cognitive scientists are talking about when students really come to understand and apply what they learn; they aren't the kinds of changes that will help disadvantaged students move forward, as Oakes and associates (1999) confirm. For this level of reform we need new learning cultures where many teachers are working in a concerted way both inside and outside of the school—something that requires sophisticated school leadership.

Second, developing learning communities is not a dilemma-free process, and once established, they are intrinsically problematic. This is what makes them valuable as adaptive learning environments. Day and associates talk about several enduring tensions and dilemmas faced by the teachers' effective school heads in their study, including balancing and integrating "internal versus external change demands," deciding on the boundaries and occasions of "autocracy versus democracy," finding "personal time versus professional tasks" with the latter becoming more and more consuming, and "development versus dismissal" in working with staff who are not progressing.

Also difficult is deliberately valuing differences of opinion and even dissent. It is a mistake for principals to go only with like-minded innovators. As Elmore (1995) puts it: "[S]mall groups of self-selected reformers apparently seldom influence their peers" (p. 20). This strategy just creates an even greater gap between the innovators and others, which essentially becomes impossible to bridge. It is counterintuitive, but effective, "to respect those you wish to silence" (Heifetz, 1994). Incorporating naysayers in complex times is necessary because they often have some valuable ideas and criticisms, and you need them for implementation, but how do you know when you are going too far in this direction?

Third, we are beginning to find out that effective leaders combine different leadership characteristics depending on the phase of the change process or on circumstances over time. To turn "failing schools" around you need assertive leadership; schools on the move need facilitation, coaching, and assistance; more fully developed professional communities need a greater scope for participative problem solving (see Boyle, 2000).

These variations in effective leadership are confirmed in a revealing way by Goleman's (2000) analysis of Hay/McBer's database in a random sample of 3,871 executives. Goleman examined the relationship between leadership style, organization climate (or culture), and performance. He identified six leadership styles, four of which positively affected climate, and two that had negative influences. The six styles were:

- Coercive (demands compliance, or "do what I tell you")
- Authoritative (mobilizes people toward a vision, or "come with me")
- Affiliative (creates harmony and builds emotional bonds, or "people come first")

- Democratic (forges consensus through participation, or "what do you think?")
- Pacesetting (sets high standards for performance, or "do as I do, now")
- Coaching (develops people for the future, or "try this"). (Goleman, 2000, pp. 82–83)

The two styles that negatively affected climate, and in turn performance, were coercive (people resent and resist) and pacesetting (people get overwhelmed and burnt out). All four of the other styles positively affected climate. Goleman concludes that "leaders need many styles":

> [T]he more styles a leader exhibits, the better. Leaders who have mastered four or more—especially the authoritative, democratic, affiliative, and coaching styles—have the very best climate and business performance. And most effective leaders switch flexibly among the leadership styles as needed. . . . Such teachers don't mechanically match their style to fit a checklist of situations— they are far more fluid. They are exquisitely sensitive to the impact they are having on others and seamlessly adjust their styles to get the best results. (Goleman, 2000, p. 87)

No matter how you cut it, effective leaders are energy creators (Brighouse & Woods, 1999, p. 84).

Incidentally, although these results come from business executives, they apply to leadership in all complex organizations. Certainly they pertain to the superintendent (Chapter 10). Increasingly they apply to the principal because the principal in a professional learning community is a CEO. The long-term trend, if we are to be successful, will see school principals with more leeway at the school level operating within a broad framework of standards and expectations—not only for charter schools, but for all schools.

The fourth way in which leadership is complex pertains to the realization that it cannot be captured in a checklist. We can provide guidelines for action but no definitive list of steps. It is always the thinking leader who blends knowledge of local context and personalities with new ideas from the outside who is going to do best. Our own recent set of six guidelines for principals is a case in point:

1. Steer clear of false certainty (there is no ready-made answer out there to the "how" question).
2. Base risk on security (promote risk-taking but provide safety nets of supportive relationships).
3. Respect those you want to silence (incorporate and learn from dissenters).
4. Move toward the danger in forming new alliances ("out there" may be dangerous, but you need external partners).
5. Manage emotionally as well as rationally (work on your emotional intelligence, don't take dissent personally).
6. Fight for lost causes (be hopeful against the odds).

In short, the principal's role has become decidedly more daunting, more complex, and more meaningful for those who learn to lead change, and are supported in that role.

Chapters 7 and 8, in combination, present a powerful message for school reform. Remember the Tennessee study that found that students who got three good teachers in 3 successive years did better? Well, students in schools led by principals who foster strong professional communities are much more likely to encounter three good teachers in a row, whether it be on the same day or over the years.

CHAPTER 9

The Student

Why in a democratic society, should an individual's first real contact with a formal institution be so profoundly antidemocratic?
—Bowles and Gintis (1976, pp. 250–251)

In the field of educational innovation it is surprising how many times a teacher will finally shout out of desperation, "But what about the students?" Innovations and their inherent conflicts often become ends in themselves, and students get thoroughly lost in the shuffle. When adults do think of students, they think of them as the potential beneficiaries of change. They think of achievement results, skills, attitudes, and jobs. *They rarely think of students as participants in a process of change and organizational life.* While research of the 1980s began to look at students as active participants in their own education, and it has become clearer what should be done, too little has actually happened to enhance the role of students as members of the school as an organization.

In this chapter, I continue to pursue the main theme of the book. Educational change, above all, is a people-related phenomenon for each and every individual. Students, even little ones, are people, too. Unless they have some meaningful (to them) role in the enterprise, most educational change, indeed most education, will fail. I ask the reader not to think of students as running the school, but to entertain the following question: What would happen if we treated the student as someone whose opinion mattered in the introduction and implementation of reform in schools?

Little progress has been made since the first edition of this book in 1982 in treating the student as a serious member of the school. It looks like we may be at the early stages of a breakthrough

151

because of the serendipitous linkage between two strange bedfellows: cognitive scientists and sociologists. To be clear about the argument at the outset, cognitive scientists claim that, traditionally, teaching has "focused too narrowly on the memorization of information, giving short shrift to critical thinking, conceptual understanding, and in-depth knowledge of subject matter" (National Research Council [NRC], 1999, p. 25). Teaching and learning for deep understanding (which means learners can critically apply what they know to comprehending and addressing new problems and situations) has now become the goal of this new and radical pedagogy (Bransford et al., 1999; Gardner, 1999).

At the same time, but operating entirely independently, sociologists have long argued that schools reproduce a hierarchical status quo in a way that actually increases the gap between those who are well off in the first place and those who are disadvantaged. This inequitable circumstance, they say, is deeply embedded in the structures and cultures of society, manifested in turn in school systems (Oakes et al., 1999).

The new common ground for both cognitive scientists and sociologists concerns *motivation and relationships*, that is, it is only when schooling operates in a way that connects students relationally in a relevant, engaging, and worthwhile experience that substantial learning will occur. That only a small proportion of any students are so engaged is a measure of the seriousness of the problem.

To state the matter differently, the more that accountability systems become focused only on cognitive achievement, the greater the gap will become between those students who are doing well and those who are not. This is so because the main problem with disengaged students is that they lack a meaningful personal connection with teachers and others in the school; in other words, they lack the motivational capacity to become engaged in learning. Incidentally, this is why emotional development for children must go hand-in-hand with cognitive development. Emotionally developed students have the individual and social skills that enable them to become motivationally engaged with other learners, which in turn is a route to greater cognitive achievement. Of course, emotional intelligence is a desired goal in its own right because it produces better citizens who can function well in a complex, stressful world (Goleman, 1995, 1998).

In short, we must combine the ideas of cognitive scientists, who are working on the problem of how to engage all learners, with the insights of sociologists, who show how power relations in the school must be altered if we are to make substantial progress on this agenda. When these two forces become integrated into the culture of professional learning communities, in effect that educators in these types of schools function as "moral change agents," or in Oakes's (1999) phrase, educators with "a passion for the public good." But where are students now in this equation?

WHERE STUDENTS ARE

Tremendous numbers and diversity of students, combined with minimal research from the students' point of view, make it impossible to do justice to the question of where students are. Instead I will present a summary of some of the main issues that seem to concern students.

In 1970–1977, I was involved in a research project focusing on the role of students in Ontario schools (see Fullan & Eastabrook, 1973; Fullan, Eastabrook, & Biss, 1977). My colleagues and I started with a survey of students in 46 Ontario schools representing a range of large-city, medium-sized-city, suburban, and rural settings. Information was gathered from a random sample of students in grades 5 through 13 (Ontario high schools went up to grade 13 at the time). The information was collected directly by us in classrooms using a questionnaire. The original sample was 3,972, from which we obtained 3,593 returns, or a 90% response rate. Questions included both fixed choice formats and open-ended questions that asked for comments. We categorized the responses according to three levels: elementary school (grades 5–6, or 5–8 in some schools), junior high (grades 7–9), and high school (grades 9–13, or 10–13 in some schools). The following summarizes our main findings:

1. A minority of students think that teachers understand their point of view, and the proportion decreases with educational level—41%, 33%, and 25% from elementary, junior high, and high school, respectively.

2. Less than one fifth of the students reported that teachers asked for their opinions and ideas in deciding what or how to teach (19%, 16%, 13%), a finding that we consistently replicated in subsequent work in a large number of classrooms in other schools.
3. Principals and vice principals were not seen as listening to or being influenced by students.
4. Substantial percentages of students, including one out of every two high school students, reported that "most of my classes or lessons are boring" (29%, 26%, 50%).

Written comments on open-ended questions elaborate the meaning of the fixed-format responses. About 1,000 students (of the total of almost 3,600) wrote comments about the school. Of these, about 30% reflected such positive attitudes as:

- Teachers are friendly. (elementary)
- This school is great. (junior high)
- I think the school I go to is good the way it is now. It doesn't need any changes. (junior high)
- I like my school because it has modern techniques, teaching methods, and facilities. It is a clean and up-to-date school. I think they should keep the school just the way it is. (high school)

The other 70% of the comments are indicative of what we labeled generally "the alienation theme":

- I think schools should make students feel comfortable, and not tense. (high school)
- I feel that teachers don't really care about what happens to students as long as they get paid. (elementary)
- I know that school is important to me and that I need it to get anywhere in life. But I'm beginning to realize that this reason is not good enough. I don't enjoy school at this point. It is the last place I want to be. If I wasn't so shy I imagine I could express these feelings to a teacher, but I've never spoken to one, not even about extra help. (high school)

- I'm only in school so I can go to university so as to make more money than if I quit school now. I do not particularly like school, in fact sometimes I hate it, but I don't particularly want to be poor. (high school)

Our questions on principals and vice principals stimulated many comments from junior high and senior high students along the following lines:

- I have never spoken to the principal, and I don't even know who the vice principal is.
- It's hard to say anything about the principal. He's always hiding.
- We never see him and I think the only kids he knows is the head boy and the head girl. He seems like a nice man, but who really knows, when he is always in his office.

Finally, we asked students an open-ended question about what they thought of the questionnaire and the project. This opened a floodgate. Over one third of the students wrote responses, nearly all of which indicated that students were interested in the topics and had something to say. Typical of these 1,200 responses were the following:

- I think this project is very interesting in many ways. It asks many questions that I have never been asked before. (elementary)
- I think it's great the grown-ups want our opinion. I feel that they treat us like babies. (elementary)
- It brought me to thinking about things I had never thought much about, and is giving you at the institution, knowledge of what we students think about the school. (junior high)
- No comment. Only that this may help the teachers or planning board realize what lousy classes and subjects we are taking. (high school)
- I think this is an excellent project. It gives the man at the bottom of the ladder a chance to unleash his feelings and say something about this damn school. (high school)

Over the years, not much has changed for most students, other than the fact that life has become more complicated. Based on his nationwide study, Goodlad (1984) states that "learning appears to be enhanced when students understand what is expected of them, get recognition for their work, learn quickly about their errors, and receive guidance in improving their performance" (p. 111). Yet, he found that "over half of the upper elementary students reported that many students did not know what they were supposed to do in class" (p. 112). At least 20% of high school students did not understand teachers' directions and comments.

Striking at the core of the theme in this book, Goodlad observes:

> Somewhere, I suspect, down in the elementary school, probably in the fifth and sixth grades, a subtle shift occurs. The curriculum—subjects, topics, textbooks, workbooks, and the rest—comes between the teacher and student. Young humans come to be viewed only as students, valued primarily for their academic aptitude and industry rather than as individual persons preoccupied with the physical, social, and personal needs unique to their circumstances and stage in life. (p. 80)

As students moved through the grades, Goodlad (1984) and his colleagues found that "there was increasingly less use of teacher praise and support for learning, less corrective guidance, a narrowing range and variety of pedagogical techniques, and declining participation by students in determining the daily conduct of their education" (p. 125). We see, says Goodlad, "a decline from lower to upper grades in teachers' support of students as persons and learners" (p. 126).

Sarason (1982) similarly claims that students at the elementary level are not party to how classroom patterns are established. He conducted an informal observational study to see how the rules of the classroom were formed (what he calls the "constitution of the classroom"), and what assumptions about students were implicit in the process. In Sarason's words, "the results were quite clear": The rules were invariably determined by the teacher, and teachers never solicited the opinions and feelings of students in developing rules. Sarason suggests several assumptions underlying the observed behavior.

1. Teacher knows best;
2. Children cannot participate constructively in the development of rules;
3. Children are not interested in such a discussion;
4. Rules are for children, and not for the teacher (rules state what children can and cannot do, but not what a teacher could or could not do), and so on. (pp. 175–176)

Sarason observed that teachers rarely, if ever, discussed their own thinking about planning and learning. Issues never came up pertaining to teachers' assumptions and theories of learning and thinking, whether children were interested in these matters, and whether they were able to talk about them. Rather, the task of the student was to get the right answer and know the facts. Sarason comments that teachers "unwittingly [created] those conditions that they would personally find boring" (p. 182).

The central issue, however, is contained in the following passage:

> The point I wish to emphasize is that it appears that children know relatively little about how a teacher thinks about the classroom, that is, what he takes into account, the alternatives he thinks about, the things that puzzle him about children and about learning, what he does when he is not sure of what he should do, how he feels when he does something wrong. (Sarason, 1971, p. 185)

I referred earlier to students' lives becoming more complex. Dryden (1995) spent a year observing in classrooms in a high school in Ontario, and concluded that "so much is going on in each kid's life, every story is so complicated" (p. 84). Students are often disengaged from their own learning, and it is enormously difficult for teachers to enter their world. Many teachers, reports Dryden, end up, metaphorically speaking, teaching "to the front row," reaching 10 or fewer students in a class of 30. Noddings (1992) captures this frustration in the student-teacher relationship:

> [T]he single greatest complaint of students in school is, "They don't care" . . . They feel alienated from their school work, sepa-

rated from adults who try to teach them, and adrift in a world perceived as baffling and hostile. At the same time, most teachers work very hard and express deep concern for their students. In an important sense, teachers do care, but they are unable to make the connections that would complete caring relationships with their students. (p. 2)

A starting point, then, is to understand the fundamental reasons and consequences of student disengagement in learning. In one of the very few studies that asked students what they thought, Rudduck, Chaplain, & Wallace (1996) provide a comprehensive summary of the consequences of disengagement as perceived by students:

1. *Perceptions of themselves*—disengaged pupils:
   - have lower self-concepts and self-esteem than engaged peers;
   - have characteristics that tend to make it difficult to achieve academically, these include: "giving up easily at school work" . . . ;
   - are more likely to be fed up with school on a regular basis.

2. *Perception of school work*—disengaged pupils:
   - find homework difficult, given they are often struggling in class;
   - dislike subjects with a high proportion of writing (e.g., English);
   - dislike subjects where they do not understand (esp. modern languages);
   - have increased anxiety about their ability, as they near exams. . . .

3. *Relationship with peers*—disengaged pupils:
   - are more likely to have been involved in bullying incidents;
   - feel under pressure from their immediate friends if they exhibit achievement behavior;
   - are perceived by many of their engaged peers as a hindrance and annoyance to their own classroom work.

4. *Relationship with teachers*—disengaged pupils:
   - perceive teachers as generally unfair to pupils, but particularly unfair to them;
   - believe teachers express negative behaviors toward them both verbally and non-verbally;
   - would like a teacher they could trust to talk things through with;
   - consider teachers to be largely responsible for their failure at school.

5. *Perceptions of the future*—disengaged pupils:
  - show high levels of anxiety about their future chances in the working world;
  - despite negative messages from the school want to persist and have some examination success;
  - see a direct relationship between examination success and getting a job;
  - are more likely to plan to get a job at 15. (Rudduck et al., 1996, p. 111)

Sadly, high percentages of students are disengaged, and the proportion increases as the student gets older. (For further confirmation, see Coleman's (1998) chapter on the students' perspective with respect to "the good teacher").

THE STUDENT AND CHANGE

I have already foreshadowed in the previous two chapters how professional learning communities work on the problems of relevance (teaching for understanding) and relationships (treating students differently). To use the Hay/McBer (2000) framework, these teachers work on continually expanding and refining their teaching repertoire designed to reach all students; they work on classroom climate in a way that students find fair and demanding, and they develop their professionalism individually and in relation to others (see Bennett & Rolheisher (2001) for a powerful coverage of "the artful science of instructional integration").

And students notice! Especially affected are what McLaughlin and Talbert (2001) call "nontraditional students" (meaning those who do not come from advantaged backgrounds—these days, the majority of students). Even traditional students don't reach deep understanding if we use more advanced indicators of learning (e.g., applying knowledge to solve problems in novel situations), but they do get good grades and like the clarity of knowing what is expected.

However, McLaughlin and Talbert note that nontraditional students struggle in these "teacher-directed, sometimes impersonal classrooms":

For example, a high-achieving Latina at Valley described her experience with the math teacher who feels all of his students are "the problem."

Ooh . . . I dread that class . . . I didn't do well. At the end I got a B, but it wasn't what I was hoping for . . . it was a hard class, because he didn't really explain the material. It was like he taught college also at the same time that he teaches high school. So it's sort of like, he brought those techniques to high school. And he'd move around really quick, and you couldn't follow him. And it was just really difficult. (McLaughlin & Talbert, 2001, p. 27)

By changing this situation, teachers make a difference:

Teachers who understand their non-traditional students are of a voice in saying that changes in classroom practices are essential not only to meet the needs of contemporary students, but also to support teachers' sense of efficacy.

Said one teacher:

Teachers have been used to lecturing and teaching the lesson . . . and they aren't getting satisfaction from kids' achievement now, because they aren't achieving. We need to grow and change and evolve too. (McLaughlin & Talbert, 2001, pp. 28–29)

Teachers who were successful with all students, need we remind ourselves, "taught in schools and departments with a strong professional community engaged in making innovations that support student and teacher learning and success" (p. 34).

So far I have been talking about teachers, figuring out what they have to do differently in order to reach more students. But what if we invited students into this arena? What if student voice mattered? Rudduck, Chaplain, and Wallace (1996) make this very suggestion:

[T]hose bent on improvement in schools might usefully start by inviting pupils to talk about what makes learning difficult for them, about what diminishes their motivation and engagement, and what makes some give up and others settle for a "minimum risk, minimum effort" position—even though they know that doing well matters. (p. 31)

Rudduck and associates also makes the point that "behind the mask of nonchalance that some pupils wear to hide their anxiety about the future is a concern to succeed and some realization of the consequences of not making the grade" (p. 3). Further:

> The pupils interviewed had quite a sophisticated understanding of those aspects of the school system which obstructed their learning and those aspects that were supportive . . . [they] all had their own concerns about school, even those who were achieving well across the curriculum. Their comments showed that they had ideas about how schools should be, that they were prepared to explain their views, and that teachers could learn from consultation with them. (1996, p. 85)

Another program that has been treating students seriously is the Manitoba School Improvement Program (Earl & Lee, 2000). For 8 years this program has been supporting grassroots teachers to change how they work with students and fellow teachers. Students who once seemed sullen and unreachable often became the most ardent advocates for positive change once the right connection had been made. One student spoke about how "what seemed to be an impossible path to walk in life, has been altered" thanks to teachers who had worked with her. "But what I am most thankful for is that all of you have exposed me to an atmosphere of hope and strength." The MSIP has just entered a second phase that is primarily based on developing its strategies and mechanisms for high school students to participate in helping to shape new directions for student engagement and learning.

Elementary school students also have insights and ideas as we reported in our survey cited earlier in this chapter; primary students even have clear views about their principals, especially if these principals are visible leaders, as Day and associates (2000) found:

> There was a recognition that all students, in exchange for a safe and caring environment, were expected to work hard, and that hard work would be rewarded. (p. 123)

Children, in other words, are vastly underutilized resources. A dramatic example is contained in Senge and associates' (2000) field book on education in an article entitled "Children as Leaders," which describes the efforts of the Children's Peace Movement in Columbia, organized by young people age 6 through 18. Against horrendous odds, they are trying to raise questions about improving what is a daily lethal environment:

> More than 850,000 Columbia children have been forced out of their homes by violence during the past dozen years. Sixty percent of those displaced children dropped out of a school. At least 2000 children under the age of 15 are enlisted or in paramilitary groups, some as young as eight years old. More than 4000 children were murdered in 1996 alone, with the number continuing to rise each year; and impunity is widespread. (Senge et al., 2000, p. 546)

The Children's Peace Movement responds, perhaps initially raising more questions than providing answers:

> The level on which most children "understood" this complex situation is different from that of adults. They think less about political and economic concerns and more about justice and fairness. Perhaps as a result, their definition of peacemaking is very broad—it includes any activity that improves the quality of life in a community affected by violence. (Senge et al., 2000, p. 549)

This is obviously an extreme situation, but it illustrates a point. Society is complex. Children's characteristics and needs are diverse. Not only must they be part of the solution, but in many cases, they may even have better ideas for solutions.

Integral to the argument in this chapter is that treating students as *people* comes very close to "living" the academic, personal, and social educational goals that are stated in most official policy documents. But more than that, involving students in constructing their own meaning and learning is fundamentally pedagogically essential—they learn more, and are motivated to go even further.

In the same way that professional learning communities establish powerful pressure and support learning conditions for motivating disengaged teachers (seamless capacity-building and lateral accountability, if you will), working through the difficulties of connecting with disaffected students is the route to both cognitive and affective attainment with students.

The irony is that the majority of teachers want to do well by their students; and the majority of students know that success in school is beneficial. Meaning must be accomplished at every level of the system, but if it is not done at the level of the student—the vast majority of students—all is lost.

Chapter 10

The District Administrator

To get the whole world out of bed, and washed, and dressed, and warmed, and fed, Believe me, Saul, costs worlds of pain . . .
—John Masefield, "The Everlasting Mercy" (1911)

It is possible for an individual school to become highly collaborative despite the district it is in, but it is not likely that it will *stay* collaborative. If the district does not foster professional learning communities by design, it undermines them by default. We now know that schools will not develop if left to their own devices.

Not all systems have school districts, and a local authority in the United States is not the same as one in Canada, or England or Sweden. Nonetheless, it is abundantly clear that if a district is part of the system, it can play a vital role, again, for better or for worse. Just as Chapter 8, on the principal, is a short-hand reference to school leadership, this chapter on the district administrator is meant to encompass district leadership more generally.

I comment first on where district administrators are, and then take up the question of what we are learning about the role of districts—moving from the negative to the positive.

WHERE DISTRICT ADMINISTRATORS ARE

District administrators in North America work in school systems ranging in size from fewer than 100 to more than 300,000 students. Districts in provinces in Canada, compared to most states in the United States, tend to be much larger. Ontario, for example, has some 72 districts, while Illinois and Ohio have more than 600 each. Thus, the conditions and tasks can vary tremendously.

165

In smaller districts, the administrators frequently carry out several functions with few resources, and in larger districts they are constantly dealing with conflicts and crises and large financial and personnel issues through an elaborate bureaucracy of specialists. The vast majority of superintendents are appointed (and fired) by locally elected school boards. Although there is a fair amount of evidence about the role of the administrator and change (which is the subject of the next section), there is little representative information on what administrators do and think in their total roles. Goldhammer (1977) reviewed the changing role of the American school superintendent from 1954 to 1974 and suggests that the major change over the 20-year period has been away from the role of educational spokesperson and executive manager of a relatively homogeneous system, toward one where negotiation and conflict management of diverse interests and groups predominate. School boards have become more politically active, as have teacher unions and community and other special-interest groups. Communities have become more heterogeneous. Federal and state government agencies and courts in the United States have become major participants in educational programming through financial and legislative means. The superintendent, notes Goldhammer (1977, p. 162), has become more of a negotiator than a goal-setter, a reactor and coordinator of diverse interests, and a person who must learn to lead and involve teams of specialists.

Blumberg (1985) studied 25 school superintendents, interviewing them about their roles, responsibilities, and perceptions of impact. Overwhelmingly, his respondents described their role as one of "conflict" and ambiguity mediated by everyday tasks. Blumberg (1985) observes that superintendents face

> the necessity of having to live daily with conflictual or potentially conflictual situations in which the superintendent plays a focal role as decision maker, mediator, or simply as a human lightning rod who attracts controversy. Some of the conflicts take on major, systemic proportions, affecting the entire school district. Some are major but affect only individuals. Some are minor. Some relate to the superintendent as a person, some to his job and career, and some to his family. Regardless of the focus or substance, a seemingly absolute condition of the superintendency

is that there are only rarely days when the superintendent is not
called upon to make a decision that will create some conflict, or
is not involved somehow in conflicts of his own making. All of
this seems to occur irrespective of the person involved: "it comes
with the territory." (p. 1)

In Blumberg's perception, the role of the superintendent is
different from that of other chief executive officers, due to

the public perception of the superintendent as guardian of a
sacred public enterprise, the education of the community's children; the politicalness of the relationship between the superintendent and the school board; and the fact that superintendents
once held the same job—that of a teacher—as the people over
whom they are now expected to exercise authority; the huge
number of community and governmental groups with one or
another stake in the school; the superintendent's visibility and
accessibility as public property. (p. 188)

As one superintendent described it,

It's always a balancing act because there are so many pressure
groups. More so than ever before, and the funny thing is that
we have made it happen that way. We have really pushed the
idea that everyone should be involved in schools. So now I have
so many different constituencies out there with so many different
interests that my problem is to try and keep them all appeased.
(p. 67)

What is most revealing about Blumberg's extensive exploration
of the working lives of chief superintendents is the infrequency
with which curriculum and instruction matters "naturally" arise in
the interviews. Superintendents talk about politics, school boards,
teacher unions, stress, public exposure, conflict, and so on. Curriculum, instruction, and professional development rarely arise in a
prominent way and do not appear at all in the index of Blumberg's
book. This is not to say that these 25 superintendents had no impact
on curriculum and student achievement in their districts, only that
keeping conflict at bay preoccupies superintendents unless they
take extraordinary steps to go beyond it.

Several years ago we conducted an extensive study of "supervisory officers" in Ontario (those above the role of principal in line positions up to and including the director or chief superintendent). Over 200 supervisory officers were interviewed in 26 school districts (one quarter of the total) in the province. Three summative-style dimensions were developed: system-driven versus school-driven, reflective versus fire-fighting, and generalist versus specialist (Fullan et al., 1987). As might be expected, directors, compared with other central office superintendents, scored consistently higher on the system, reflective, and generalist dimensions.

In further analysis of our data focusing on the 22 directors of education in the study, Allison (1988) identified three distinct sectors of work: board (trustees), system, and community. In comparing the situation of chief executive officers in the United States with those in Ontario, Allison suggests that the Ontario directorship evolved from a more stable tradition. By contrast, Allison states that the emergence of the superintendent's role in the United States is characterized by a culture of "conflict, insecurity and uncertainty" (p. 5).

Some specific features provide support for Allison's observation. Compared with their American counterparts, Ontario and, more broadly, Canadian superintendents are more likely to head larger, more stable school systems, are less laterally mobile, are more likely to be appointed from within their own systems, and have longer tenure as chief executive officers (Allison, 1988; Fullan et al., 1987). Superintendents in Ontario in our study had an average tenure of 7 years. In the United States it is commonly thought that the average superintendency is about 3 years, but Hodgkinson and Montenegro (1999) report that 5 years is more accurate. Still, turnover in many districts in the United States is very high, presenting enormous problems for schools; in particular, instability, episodic changes in direction, and lack of follow-through all exacerbate the problem of finding meaning and coherence.

In a more recent study of the superintendency, Johnson (1996) followed the work of 12 newly appointed superintendents during the first 2 years of their appointments. She talks about the turmoil and complexity of current school district leadership. Based on past experiences, teachers and principals were skeptical about the promises, intentions and skills of their new superintendent. They withheld their support until they were convinced that these new administrators deserved it; in the end, they judged some to be worthy, others not. (p. 23)

Johnson found that three types of leadership were evident in the work of all the influential superintendents: educational leadership (focus on pedagogy and learning), political leadership (securing resources, building coalitions), and managerial leadership (using structures for participation, supervision, support, and planning). Johnson summarizes:

When educational leadership was weak, teachers and principals often discredited the superintendent as being misguided and preoccupied with the wrong things. When political leadership was weak, the schools suffered undue financial cuts, became the captives of special interests on the school board, or became the battleground for citizens with competing priorities. When managerial leadership was weak, people became preoccupied with bureaucratic errors, communication among educators faltered, and potential school leaders could not act constructively. (p. 24)

Of the 12 districts, two sought leaders who could bring about major change, four looked for leaders who could provide continuity, and six districts had experienced disruption of such magnitude that their search committees primarily sought candidates "who could stabilize the system" (Johnson, 1996, p. 41). This range is likely not atypical of the larger numbers of districts. Almost all of these situations involve change under complex circumstances. Even districts seeking stability after disruption still must go through a sophisticated change process, and inevitably they find themselves grappling with student improvement, which is all the more difficult because they often don't have the basic capacity to move ahead.

Johnson concludes that superintendents must be "teachers" in all three domains—educational, political, and managerial—modeling, coaching, and building the capacity of principals, teacher leaders, school board members, and so on. Once again, change with any depth must be cultivated by building relationships while pushing forward. In districts that were on the move, "superintendents . . .

were active participants in the change process—raising concerns, voicing expectations, asking questions, offering encouragement, making suggestions, and insisting that change occur" (Johnson, 1996, p. 280).

Finally, I referred in Chapter 8 to the problem of attracting candidates to the principalship. The problem is worsening for superintendents as well. There are fewer and fewer candidates for positions and conflict on the job has intensified. The representation of women and minorities in the role has increased over the years, but it is still small.

The irony in all of this is that with the return to large-scale reform, the role of the district has taken on an increased prominence (Fullan, 2000a). As we shall see shortly, most districts are not prepared for this new role, but there are now enough examples of success to provide conceptual and strategic lessons for future development.

THE DISTRICT ADMINISTRATORS AND CHANGE

If we take a quantitative approach, the majority of districts are not effective. To be fair, stimulating, coordinating, and sustaining "coherent" development across many schools is exceedingly difficult because it requires balancing top-down and bottom-up forces.

In any case, districts do make a difference. I referred in Chapter 7 to Rosenholtz's (1989) study of 78 elementary schools, which she classified as "stuck," "moving," and "in-between" schools. Rosenholtz also found that a disproportionate number of stuck schools came from certain districts; likewise, moving schools were clustered in certain other districts. This prompted her to write a chapter on stuck and moving districts (two of the eight districts were in the latter category).

Rosenholtz comments:

> The contrast between stuck and moving districts, nowhere more apparent than here, underscores how principals become helpful instructional advisors or maladroit managers of their schools. It is also clear that stuck superintendents attribute poor performance to principals themselves, rather than accepting any re-

sponsibility to help them learn and improve. This again may indicate their lack of technical knowledge and subsequent threats to their self-esteem. If districts take no responsibility for the inservice needs of principals, of course, principals become less able colleagues, less effective problem-solvers, more reluctant to refer school problems to the central office for outside assistance, more threatened by their lack of technical knowledge, and, most essential, of substantially less help to teachers. Of equal importance, with little helpful assistance, stuck superintendents symbolically communicate the norm of self-reliance and subsequently professional isolation—that improvement may not be possible, or worthy of their time and effort, or that principals should solve their school problems by themselves—lugubrious lessons principals may unwittingly hand down to poorly performing teachers, and thus teachers to students. (Rosenholtz, 1989, p. 189)

Similar findings are contained in LaRocque and Coleman's (1989) analysis of "district ethos" and quality in school districts in British Columbia. The authors compiled performance data by aggregating school results on provincewide achievement tests. They rated the districts according to high, medium, and low performance. They selected ten districts for more detailed analysis, taking into account size and type of school community. LaRocque and Coleman (1989, p. 169) hypothesized that positive district ethos would be characterized by a high degree of interest and concern relative to six sets of activity and attitude "focuses":

1. Taking care of business (a learning focus);
2. Monitoring performance (an accountability focus);
3. Changing policies/practices (a change focus);
4. Consideration and caring for stakeholders (a caring focus);
5. Creating shared values (a commitment focus); and
6. Creating community support (a community focus).

Three of the ten districts were classified as having a strong district presence in the schools, which is described in the following terms:

The district administrators provided the principals with a variety of school-specific performance data; they discussed these data with the principals and set expectations for their use; and they monitored through recognized procedures, how and with what success the schools used the performance data. . . .

The district administrators used their time in the schools purposefully to engage the principals in discussion on specific topics: school performance data, improvement plans, and the implementation of these plans. . . .

In spite of the emphasis on school test results, the nature of the discussions was collaborative rather than prescriptive. The district administrators acknowledged good performance. They helped the principals interpret the data and identify strengths and weaknesses, and they offered advice and support when necessary. Ultimately, however, plans for improvement were left up to the principal and staff of each school—this point was stressed by the principals—although their progress in developing and implementing the plans was monitored. The features of collaboration and relative school autonomy probably reinforced the perception of respect for the role of the principal and recognition of the importance of treating each school as a unique entity. (LaRocque & Coleman, 1989, p. 181)

All three of these districts had high performance ratings on the achievement tests.

At the other end of the continuum, three districts were characterized by an absence of press for accountability: Little or no data were provided to the schools, and no structures or processes were established to monitor or discuss progress. All three of these districts were found to be low on achievement results.

More often than not, the district is perceived by schools as less than helpful. Little and Dorph's (1998) summary evaluation of School Bill (SB) 1274 in California is instructive. As stated in the request for proposals:

The demonstration of restructuring is intended to be a five-year effort aimed at improving student learning. . . . All students, regardless of race, ethnic, linguistic or socioeconomic background need to think critically, solve problems individually or as part of a team, analyze and interpret new information, develop convincing arguments, and apply their knowledge to new situations. SB 1274 invites educators to consider radical changes in the way schools and districts operate in order to create a better environment for engaging all students in powerful learning experiences. . . . (Little & Dorph, 1998, p. 1, emphasis added)

SB 1274 was, to be sure, a school-focused initiative, but the role of the district was recognized, at least on paper. What happened was that not many schools were able to accomplish and sustain improvement, due largely, say the evaluators, to "shortcomings [arising] from failing to appreciate the magnitude of the change in district-school relations anticipated by comprehensive school restructuring" (Little & Dorph, 1998, p. 51). The problem, now familiar to us, was that districts treated SB 1274 as one of many school improvement projects:

> Absent was the collaborative crafting of a restructured school, and the corresponding shift in district policy and practice. Rather, the district component and collaborative agreement were typically viewed as a conventional form of "district sign-off," and the restructuring demonstration was one among many special projects supported by state, federal, or private funding. (p. 51)

As with most examples of "projectitis," district support diminished over time "after the first flush of excitement when grants were awarded."

It won't take too many false starts for motivated teachers and principals before they come to take future initiatives less seriously. Spillane's (1999) examination of the district's role in a context of state policy found this to be the case. Teachers and principals were "reluctant to engage in learning about instructional change because they were skeptical that the latest reform initiative wouldn't last very long" (Spillane, 1999, p. 38). Teachers barely have a chance to learn one new idea when there is a change to something else. The result is a "this too shall pass," and "I can wait this out" mindset. Spillane (1999) concluded:

> Reform fads sapped teachers' desire to change. It had bred cynicism about instructional change among teachers that did not lend itself to in-depth engagement with learning. (p. 39)

In a related study of the implementation of mathematics reform in nine districts, Spillane (2000) found that even when districts endorsed the reform, and focused on all its components, they often lacked a deeper understanding. Thus, implementation was weak and piecemeal:

> [D]istrict leaders' understandings tended to lack "a big picture" or "holistic" frame that might integrate the various reform ideas. Thirty-nine of the 65 district leaders . . . understood the reforms as an assemblage of instructional, motivational, and classroom management tools rather than a coherent pedagogy or instructional philosophy designed to support more integrated changes in mathematics education. (p. 162)

Once again, underlying meaning and coherence are key to manageable, powerful reform, but remain elusive in most cases.

In McLaughlin and Talbert's (2001) study of high schools, teachers describe their district professional context in terms that range from "demeaning and demoralizing" to "supportive and respectful" (p. 119). They compare Mostaza with Oak Valley (pseudonyms):

> Mostaza teachers' extraordinarily negative feelings of their district are no surprise given their comments that the district is "the worst in the state" as a professional setting . . . Teachers complain about the "insulting and demeaning relations with 'downtown'" . . . "We received absolutely no preparation or help from the district. . . . " (p. 120)

A principal complains that district policy is neither very clear nor consistent with the schools' realities, yet it permeates the school (p. 119). Mostaza administrators complain about "inadequate structures or strategies for sharing information, confusion about responsibilities, and a general lack of trust block communication up and down the district" (p. 122).

Oak Valley is another story:

> Teachers and administrators in Oak Valley, in stark contrast to their colleagues in Mostaza, praise their district as an exciting professional setting, one that expects much and provides much to support professional excellence . . . The union representative praised the district's commitment to high levels of professionalism. (p. 124)

WHAT SCHOOL SUCCESS LOOKS LIKE

The enemy of improvement is inertia, and it is clear that districts must do more than just stay out of the way. Until recently, very few reform efforts and consequently very few research studies focused on entire school districts; that is, reforms in which *all* schools in the district were implicated. Two of the most insightful case studies deal with District 2, New York City, and the Chicago school system. Similar ideas are evident in the Memphis district in Tennessee, and in Durham, Ontario.

Nothing presents a clearer example of district "reculturing" with a focus on instruction, meaning, capacity, and coherence than Elmore and Burney's (1999) study of District 2. In 1987 the district ranked tenth in reading and fourth in mathematics out of 32 subdistricts. By 1996, it ranked second in both reading and math. Elmore and Burney describe the superintendent's (Alvarado) approach:

> Over the eight years of Alvarado's tenure in District 2, the district has evolved a strategy for the use of professional development to improve teaching and learning in schools. This strategy consists of a set of organizing principles about the process of systemic change and the role of professional development in that process; and a set of specific activities, or models of staff development, that focus on system-wide improvement of instruction. (p. 266)

Within this framework, there are seven "organizing principles" of the reform strategy:

1. It's about instruction and only instruction;
2. Instructional improvement is a long, multistage process involving awareness, planning, implementation and reflection;
3. Shared expertise is the driver of instructional change;
4. The focus is on system-wide improvement;
5. Good ideas come from talented people working together;
6. Set clear expectations, then decentralize;
7. Collegiality, caring and respect.

Further, in District 2, professional development is a management strategy rather than a specialized administrative function. Professional development is what administrative leaders do when they are doing their jobs, not a specialized function that some people in the organization do and others do not. Instructional improvement is the main purpose of district administration, and professional development is the chief means of achieving that purpose. Anyone with line administrative responsibility in the organization has responsibility for professional development as a central part of his or her job description. Anyone with staff responsibility has the responsibility to support those who are engaged in staff development. It is impossible to disentangle professional development from general management in District 2 because the two are synonymous for all practical purposes. (p. 272)

More particularly, the district uses a combination of "instructional consulting services," "inter-visitation and peer networks," "off-site training," and "oversight and principal site visits"—all of which provide mechanisms for developing the capacity to recognize and solve problems. District 2 does not represent all the answers, but it is a very clear example of focus, capacity-building, coherence in the service of instructional improvement, and enhanced student learning.

A second case example, and messier to be sure, involves the 550 schools in the Chicago school system. Prior to 1988, when decentralization was legislated, Chicago was the embodiment of excessive bureaucracy that literally had ground the system to a halt. Too much structure took the form of an "uncoordinated congery of bureaucracies [which] produced a maze of extra-school layers" (Bryk et al., 1998, p. 277). Overnight, in 1988 the system was decentralized with individual school authority handed over to 550 local school councils. From 1988 to 1994 the system operated in the decentralized fashion with little functional contact between schools and the district. In other words, too little structure characterized the operation. The result in the first instance (1988–1994) was what Bryk and associates (1998, p. 261) called the story of "three-thirds." One third of the schools engaged in "self-initiated active restructuring," one third "struggled with improvement," and one third of the schools were "left behind." Even the self-initiating schools did not go very deep in instructional improvement. The district office, while much less influential, was still a negative factor: "Four years into reform the basic orientation of the central office remained focused on program compliance and emphasized control of local school practice" (Bryk et al., 1998, p. 278).

Since 1994, the central district has been reorganized and restructured as a key player. It is still too early to assess its impact, but the gist of the change was to retain decentralized development within a context of capacity-building and external accountability. Two of the external researchers who have been tracking the reform (Bryk and Easton) had the opportunity to work full time in the district office during this reorganization. Their projective account of "a new vision of central action" is thus particularly instructive, albeit partly speculative.

Bryk and associates (1998, p. 279) argue that decentralization "entails a renorming toward becoming advocates for local schools rather than acting as their superpatrons"; they refer to the need for new capacity-building external to the school, namely the establishment of "the *extra-school infrastructure* needed to promote improvement" (p. 279, italics in original).

Essentially, Bryk and colleagues advocate that four critical extraschool functions must be developed:

1. Policy Making to Support Decentralization;
2. A Focus on Local Capacity-building;
3. A Commitment to Rigorous Accountability;
4. Stimulation of Innovation. (Bryk et al., 1998, pp. 279–281)

First, policies and goals and procedures need to be developed to support school development in the context of system expectations (much as we have just seen in District 2).

Second, there is a "need for significant advances in the knowledge, skill, and dispositions of local school professionals, in their ability to work cooperatively together toward a more coherent school practice, and their ability to effectively engage parents and the local community" (p. 280).

Third, a system of rigorous external accountability must be established "that tracks the progress of schools' improvement efforts and that can intervene in failing situations" (p. 270). Further, "[I]t is central . . . that this accountability operate in ways that advance, rather than undermine, local capacity-building." Thus:

> Decentralization is based on the premise that the best account-
> ability is not regulatory. While it may be necessary from time
> to time to use bureaucratic intervention in very troubled schools,
> the ultimate aim is a stronger base of professional norms of
> practice for educating all children well, coupled with supportive
> parent and community involvement toward the same ends. (Bryk
> et al., 1998, p. 280)

Fourth, even though a decentralized system of schools no longer mandates programs for every school to implement, it still maintains a strong interest in spawning innovations and diffusing effective improvement efforts (p. 281).

I will not go into detail with other examples, but the evidence is mounting. The early evaluation of the Annenberg Challenge initiative in several U.S. cities and rural areas is a case in point (see Cervone & McDonald, 1999; Fullan, 2000a). So is the story of the Durham School District in Ontario, in which the system's 114 schools progressed from being a "stuck" school district in 1988 to being awarded the Bertelsmann prize in 1996 for being an outstand-ing, innovative school system (Bertelsmann Foundation, 1996).

Similar lessons can be learned from Memphis, where the whole district of 117,000 students has moved forward by implementing schoolwide reform models (see the evaluation by Ross et al., 1999). It is interesting to note the seven lessons as reported by the superin-tendent in a recent article (House, 2000). In recreating a school system, argues House, we have learned that:

1. Professional development is critical;
2. The model and the school culture must be a good match;
3. Benchmarks are important;
4. Strong partnership with the teachers' union is necessary;
5. Schools need both autonomy and support;
6. Technology is a critical component;
7. Parent and community support are key.

Note the similarity between an effective school (the same seven criteria could be applied to a school) and an effective district. It is a difference in level of complexity rather than a difference in kind.

So, if we can now visualize success, what's the problem? In a word, plenty.

CAUTIONS AND IMPLICATIONS

The first problem is that all districts should be improving, but only a very small percentage are as good as the ones we just reviewed.

Second, the "successful" case examples took about 6 to 8 years, but we have no reason to believe that they can be sustained. In each case—District 2, Durham, and Memphis—superintendents who have led the reform have recently left. This is not just a matter of the school board maintaining continuity. The larger policy context can also take its toll on district energy and morale.

Third, as impressive as the accomplishments have been, the achievement results are on the surface. Basic literacy and numeracy have advanced in many, but not all, schools, which is no small feat; but teaching for deep understanding and addressing equity concerns have not gone far. In the bigger scheme of things, only baby steps have been taken.

Fourth, as I have implied, there are all kinds of other agencies to contend and work with in the larger infrastructure. There are more resources and more pressures, but also more complexity (see Hill, Campbell, & Harvey, 2000; Newmann & Sconzert, 2000 for excellent analysis of this bigger picture of complexity).

Fifth, it is not at all clear that the strategies used by effective districts in the 1990s will be the ones most appropriate for the 2000s decade. The former strategies were best for moving systems ahead on some of the basics; different, more sophisticated strategies may be necessary to lead learning organization in the complex cultures of change of the future (Fullan, 2001).

The above notwithstanding, the agenda for school superintendents is becoming clearer.

The first task for superintendents is to recognize and unleash the power they have to do good. Block (1987) states it best in *The Empowered Manager*:

> The core of the bureaucratic mind-set is not to take responsibility for what is happening. Other people are the problem. . . . Re-

awakening the original spirit means we have to confront the
issue of our own autonomy. To pursue autonomy in the midst
of a dependency-creating culture is an entrepreneurial act. (pp.
1, 6)

Block suggests that maintenance means being preoccupied with
playing it safe. He acknowledges that maintenance and caution
are often necessary (and the superintendent, more than most, is
frequently in such a situation). However, Block argues that to break
the mold we must practice "enlightened self-interest" by engaging
in activities that have as their basis *meaning* (activities that are
genuinely needed); *contribution and service* (the decision to do things
that seriously contribute to the organization and its purpose); *integrity* (putting into words what we really see is happening, making
only those promises we can deliver on, feeling that the authentic
act is always the best for business); *positive impact on others' lives*
(in the long run it is in our self-interest to treat other people well);
and *mastery* (simply learning as much as we can about the activity
in which we are engaged).

Second, the main message is reculturing toward interactive,
accountable, inclusive professional learning communities. Some
related guidelines:

1. *Choose a district in which change has a chance of occurring or do not
   expect much change.* Some communities are dominated by a power
   structure that is more interested in the status quo; other communities are so fractious that the superintendent is the inevitable
   victim; others expect administrators to lead change. Although
   the classification is greatly oversimplified, the main message is
   sound—the interest in change, or leverage for change, in a district must be minimally present. Without that, the chief executive
   officer is as powerless as anyone else, and in fact will likely
   become the convenient scapegoat. Other district administrators
   (below the level of the chief executive officer) will have to make
   similar choices, and will also have to determine whether the
   superintendent with whom they will be or are working is knowledgeable and actively supportive of change—ideally, someone
   who can teach them something about how to implement change
   effectively.

2. *Once in a district, develop the management capabilities of administra-tors—other district administrators and principals—to lead change.* Using a combination of promotion criteria, in-service training emphasizing development and growth, and replacement of ad-ministrators through attrition or forced resignation (in extreme cases), the goal is to develop incrementally the district's adminis-trative capability to lead and facilitate improvement. Among other things, the administrator must require and help principals to work with teachers, which means that he or she, as district administrator, must have the ability and willingness to work closely with principals.

3. *Invest in teacher development* from prerecruitment to professional development throughout the career (see Chapters 14–15).

4. *Focus on instruction, teaching, and learning, and changes in the culture of schools.* Both short-term and long-term strategies should be used consistently and persistently to establish norms and the capacity for collaboration and continuous improvement in the learning environments of students and educators.

5. *Monitor the improvement process.* The need for monitoring is never ending. The information-gathering system to assess and address problems of implementation must be institutionalized. The more horizontal and vertical two-way communication that exists, the more knowledge there will be about the status of change. Bench-marks, transparent information, and intervention in persistently failing schools are all part of the monitoring process.

6. *Foster an identity with the district.* Principals who are interested in only whether their own school does well and are not interested in other schools in the district will not find themselves in sup-portive districts in the long run. Superintendents can change that by developing districtwide identity in the service of individual school development for all schools.

7. *Move toward the danger in selectively forming external partnerships* with the community, city, and other agencies in order to further the work of the schools in the district.

8. Above all, work on continually *conceptualizing* the purpose, de-sign, and process of continuous district reform. The best leaders evolve, articulate, and reflect on their theories of change. For example, most districts need to be reorganized in order to func-tion in the new way but a superintendent would be at sea without

a conception of what design principles should drive the new organization.

If you want to consider a "pathways" problem, take a look again at the seven lessons from Superintendent House cited above: professional development is critical, strong partnership with the union is needed, parent and community support is key, and so on. The pathways problem is how does one get these factors in place if one doesn't have them. This is why I contend that 25% of the solution is knowing what to work on, and 75% is figuring out how to get there given local context, culture, personalities, and prehistory.

The superintendent also needs to model learning. Negroni talks about the shift he made from "lone ranger" to lead learner. During the first 3 years of his superintendency in Springfield, Massachusetts, his overriding goal was "to change this inbred system":

> Intent on the ends, I operated as Lone Ranger. I didn't try to build relationships with the teachers' union or with the board. Instead, I worked around them. Most of the time, I felt that I was way out in front of them. I would change things on my own. (quoted in Senge et al., 2000, p. 426)

For all the changes he pushed through, Negroni says, "these were three brutal years for all of us"; "I was running so fast and making so many changes that I was getting tired. People around me were even more sick and tired" (pp. 426–427).

Eventually, through reflective practice and feedback, Negroni moved to transforming the district into a learning institution. He explains:

> Our most critical role at the central office is to support learning about learning, especially among principals—who will then do the same among teachers in their schools. At the beginning of the year, three or four central office administrators and I conducted forty-six school visits in forty-six days, with the principals of each school alongside us. Then the administrators and all forty-six principals met together to summarize what we had seen. This is one of a series of walk-throughs that principals do during the course of a school year—with me, with other central

office administrators, and with each other. The sequence includes a monthly "grand round," when every principal in the district goes with me and the eight academic directors to spend the day in one school. We break up into subgroups for hour-and-a-half visits, then come back and (still in subgroups) discuss what we saw. Then a representative from each sub-group makes a presentation to all of the principals. (Senge et al., 2000, p. 431)

Recall Goleman's (2000) six leadership styles of chief executives: coercive, authoritative, affiliative, democratic, pace-setting, and coaching. Negroni moved from coercive and pace-setting (the two negative styles, in terms of impact on climate and performance) to a combination of the remaining four (which positively impact the organization).

I want to emphasize how very fundamental the change we are talking about is to the current cultures of schools and districts. Most school systems are still "loosely coupled," despite top-down efforts to the contrary. What is necessary, as Elmore (2000) also argues, is a change in the organization itself—in its very culture:

Improvement at scale is largely a *property of organizations*, not of the pre-existing traits of the individuals who work in them. Organizations that improve do so because they create and nurture agreement on what is worth achieving, and they set in motion the internal processes by which people progressively learn how to do what they need to do in order to achieve what is worthwhile. (p. 25, emphasis in original)

And:

It seems clear that administrators in the districts that are improving avoid pointless and distracting arguments about centralization and decentralization. Instead, they spend a lot of time building a sense of urgency and support in specific schools and communities around issues of standards and performance. It also seems clear that if they communicate that urgency to principals and teachers, as well as to schools collectively, they will have to accept a high degree of responsibility for the detailed decisions. (Elmore, 2000, p. 33)

In the same way that effective principals "cause" teachers' work to improve, effective superintendents impact the work of school leaders through very specific mechanisms, as we have seen.

Leading like this is hard to do when the board and the state are breathing down your neck to get better results on standardized tests. I can't help but think, however, that superintendents who lead, like Alvarado, House, and Negroni, get better results on most measures, and have more political allies when they need them. You can get some short-term results through heavy-handed leadership, but they are surface gains, and they are extracted at a high price. Besides, "why get better at a bad game" (Block, 1987); instead, why not change the game? The superintendent is in a position to help do just that.

CHAPTER 11

The Consultant

. . . the omnibus portfolio . . .

How are these for two recent titles: *Flawless Consulting* (Block, 1999), and *Flawed Advice and the Management Trap* (Argyris, 2000)? They both have the same message. Consultancy is about building capacity, motivation, and commitment to engage in improvements. They also both claim that it hardly ever happens that way, because of the complexity of doing it and the many obstacles that stand in the way.

We do a lot of consultancy for schools and school districts. Every time a school district has been working diligently on a problem and they ask us to help them go further, it almost always helps. Every time a district is experiencing a problem and they want us to provide the solution, it never works. The irony is that we need external help, but it is so easy to treat it as cosmetic or to become dependent on it.

I pursue some of the complexities of consultancy from these vantage points: the ins and outs of the current situation, the point of view of the external consultant, and the perspective of the client or user of consultants.

THE PROBLEM AND PROMISE OF CONSULTANCY

In any society with complex problems and constantly shifting environments, the demand for solutions is ever present. In this same society, new ideas are being generated and tried out all over the place. We are reminded day in and day out that things must improve, and that being open to change is a prime requirement.

Then things go awry. First is the problem of taking on the latest innovation without a careful assessment of its strengths and weaknesses, its fit to local context, or how it can be integrated with what is already going on. Baker, Curtis, and Benenson (1991) provide an illustration:

> A superintendent attends a national meeting where Madeline Hunter gives a speech. He comes back convinced that she can solve the district's instructional problems and promptly arranges for everyone to be trained in the Hunter method of teaching. When teachers learn more about Hunter's "scientific" methods and want to dispute her philosophic or pedagogical assumption, the innovators and administrators in charge of improvement dismiss these concerns as "unscientific." The thoughtful teachers who raised questions are labeled as "resisters" and their attitude as "uncooperative." Instead of a dialogue in the school on the prospects of improved teaching, the Hunter plan for improvement becomes the occasion to fragment teachers into at least three groups: the believers, the resisters, and those who are still unsure. The superintendent does not seem to worry about minor problems of faculty fragmentation. He is pleased by his efforts to provide a concrete plan that the school board can understand. (p. 12)

Baker and associates conclude:

> Planned change for these teachers is not the cumulative development of a comprehensive strategy. Rather, it is "one damned thing after another." Planned change becomes the preoccupation of the administrators who continue to try to fix the system. For teachers, change becomes a matter of coping with management's penchant for educational fads. (p. 13)

Second, even when an innovation represents a potentially valuable fit, it is often one of many initiatives underway in the same district. We have already seen in Chapter 2 what happens "when multiple improvement initiatives collide" (Hatch, 2000). They create an additional overload, fragmentation, and dissipation of energy.

Third, solid innovations seem to work in some situations, but not in others. For example, those who have developed schoolwide models of reform have been nonplussed to find that the same model works wonders in one district and fails miserably in another. To put this down to the motivation and commitment of administrators and teachers is to egregiously beg the question of change. Even in situations where teachers have "voted" to adopt a particular innovation, it does not necessarily represent a considered decision.

Yet to ignore the outside is hardly an acceptable response for a would-be learning organization. We do consistently find that improving schools and districts reaches outside. Baker and associates' (1991) study of 48 school districts in Illinois confirms that internal development and external involvement must go together. Thirteen of the 48 districts were classified as engaged in "systematic improvement" on a sustained basis. It is no accident that all 13 successful districts were found to be users of external support from regional educational service centers and several other sources. By contrast, in all eight cases that had no external support, there was no evidence of school improvement. Time and again we find that seeking external support and training is a sign of vitality. It is the organizations that act self-sufficient that are going nowhere. And, as we have seen in Chapter 8, it is the schools that have their internal acts together that both seek outside support and know good ideas when they see them.

It is clear that consultants providing service and those using it have a lot to learn. In general terms, what is needed is that external initiatives and those relating to them must base their work on both a high quality *theory of learning* and a high quality *theory of action* (or, if you like, a theory of pedagogy and a theory of change, which constantly feed on each other). A theory of pedagogy focuses on assumptions about learning, instruction, and performance; a theory of action tends to local context such as the conditions under which the model will work.

Stokes, Sato, McLaughlin, and Talbert (1997) analyzed several intervention models with these criteria in mind, and found that those models that got high marks for focusing on both pedagogy and local context got better results in terms of student learning. The Child Development Project (CDP) is a good case in point. CDP is an intervention that consists of three components: a classroom program (instructionally focused with student involvement); a schoolwide program (fostering student participation and development of values such as helpfulness, responsibility, understanding of others); and a family involvement program (making school welcoming to families and promoting home activities). The approach to change is to provide materials, assistance, and support for developing local capacity to implement the three program components. An evaluation study of 12 schools in six districts found that (1) despite strong external support, only about half the schools showed widespread implementation, thereby confirming the difficulty of schoolwide reform, and (2) those schools that did accomplish implementation "significantly increased in a number of resilience-related outcomes and academic attitudes, including attachment to school, intrinsic academic motivation, preference for challenging tasks, frequency of reading outside school, democratic values, intrinsic prosocial motivation, and conflict resolution skills" compared to matched nonprogram schools (Lewis et al., 1998, p. 1). In other words, innovations are more successful if they have a strong instructional focus *combined with* strategies to obtain support at the school, community, and district levels.

McLaughlin and Mitra (2000), working on the same framework and set of models, pursue the same theme in more depth. They argue that models of reform will only go deeper if they develop a "theory-based change." They identify five key components of this theory: resources, knowledge of first principles, a supportive community of practice, a supportive principal, and a compatible school district. Essentially, the theory of pedagogy concerns the first two: most well-developed models do pay more attention to resources (time, materials, professional development) and to first principles (the learning theory underlying, for example, cooperative learning, Success for All, etc.). These same models pay less attention to the theory of action (how do you get a supportive community of practice, a committed principal, and a compatible district?).

Focusing on the theory of action, McLaughlin and Mitra (2000) note that:

> Sustaining practice . . . requires a community of practice to provide support, deflect challenges from the broader environment, and furnish feedback and encouragement essential to going deeper. (p. 10)

They found, for example, that CDP, after initial frustration in working with schools and districts, "now incorporates the role of teacher community as the primary vehicle of learning and a major goal of reform itself" (p. 10).

Similarly, most reformers have now learned that it is a mistake to bypass the principal. Principals need to understand the model, value it, and work on the interaction that is at the core of successful teacher (and consequently) student learning. In McLaughlin and Mitra's terms:

> The social relationships and caring that were supported in strong communities were an important ingredient in teachers' trust for one another, willingness to put in the extra effort reform change requires, as well as the sense of professional satisfaction they were denied from their work. In a number of our sites, teachers attributed the presence of these strong social ties to the principal's investment in social interaction. (p. 14)

Compatible district context was also seen as crucial: "[E]ven the most dedicated teachers and principals will have a hard time sustaining reform practices and philosophy if their district context is hostile or pushing in an incompatible direction" (p. 15). And, we would add from Chapter 10, that the district must establish a number of focused, proactive procedures and habits if it's to develop strong communities of practice.

In this talk about communities of practice, supportive principals, and compatible districts, the reader will notice that there is a fair amount of "question-begging" going on. The issue, of course, is how you get these conditions if they are not present. There are more sophisticated answers elsewhere in this book, but the short one here is that external reformers should use two means: one concerns "readiness criteria" (don't work with districts that are not ready and willing to support the reform at several levels); the second is, build into the reform model strategies for working on the missing ingredients (such as communities of practice, principal and district support). It is not so much that external models can solve these problems, but that they at least must work on them if they are to have a chance.

This line of thinking is similar to that of Hill and his colleagues, in which they observe that the models of change they reviewed all contained "zones of wishful thinking," or things that must happen if the reform is to be successful but over which the model has no control. Again, the first step is to identify these factors, and start taking them into account. Such a working list has been formulated by Datnow and Stringfield (2000) in their review of adoption, implementation, and sustainability. Their lessons are:

1. There is no substitute for a finite set of widely shared goals.
2. The goals must be tied to a long-term, whole-team focus on key measures of school improvement.
3. Districts need a coordinated and broad-based plan for disseminating information about reform options.
4. Schools must engage in a thoughtful, critical process of inquiry about what needs to change at their school and why before they select reforms. Good decisions about reform take time.
5. Reform designs (and reform designers) must (a) view local context and the diversity of the language, race, class, and gender of those involved as strengths to build on; (b) see teachers as an asset and as collaborators, not simply implementers of reform; (c) affect the whole school, not just be a "pocket program"; (d) address technical, normative, and political dimensions of change; and (e) include equity as an explicit goal.
6. Multidimensional, ongoing support and leadership are required from design teams, district personnel, and school site educators.
7. Policy systems need to be aligned in order to support reform.
8. Successful implementation requires sensitivity and adaptability (without academic compromise) on the part of the design developers, local policymakers, and educators in schools. States, districts and design teams must be willing to change along with schools. Such active, shared growth is at the heart of both co-construction and high reliability. (pp. 199–200)

It is a formidable list, but ignoring these factors altogether when they are so critical is the worst one can do.

A more fundamental conclusion is that it is not so much the *product* of reforms that worked elsewhere that needs to be replicated, but the conditions under which the reforms worked. Analogous to my earlier point that implementation is 25% having good ideas and 75% figuring out how to put them in place, effective consultancy is 25% having good products and 75% helping to develop local conditions. Healey and De Stefano (1997) draw the same conclusion:

> Success stories are success stories because: (1) the reform addressed a well-understood local need, (2) there is a significant local demand for the reform, (3) the reform itself is locally derived, (4) it is championed by one or more "messiahs," (5) it is adequately financed, and (6) there is widespread ownership of the reform. Attempting to replicate the reform itself (i.e., take it to scale) *inevitably* violates some of the very conditions that render certain innovations successful in the first place. The fact is that people's educational aspirations, needs and contexts differ from place to place. Accordingly, what works in one location won't necessarily work in another. And even in those instances where an "outside" innovation addresses some of the specific needs and aspirations of a particular location, its fate is still precarious, for unless there is widespread ownership of the innovation (a factor largely engendered through the development of local solutions), chances are that it will not become a permanent part of that location's educational landscape. Instead of replication of the reform itself, we contend that it is the *conditions which give rise to the reform in the first place* that should be replicated. (Healey & De Stefano, 1997, pp. 10–11, italics in original)

All of these issues of consultancy have increased dramatically in prominence over the past decade with the return of large-scale reform and the presence of more and more external agencies in the infrastructure. It is not just state departments, intermediate agencies, universities, and the like, but also the new presence of profit and not-for-profit groups. Foundations, for example, have become more prevalent, pouring huge sums of resources into school reforms. They have also changed their modus operandi from doling out money, and from specifying criteria and conditions, toward becoming part of the action themselves through their professional staff.

The Annenberg Challenge, for instance, has established a number of new "secretariats" who are now part of the new landscape of providing training, support, and—let's face it—"pressure" for engaging in reform. Just in Chicago alone, Annenberg has been responsible for generating nine new partners—five are university-based, two community-based, two community advocacy, and one a cultural institution (Newmann & Sconzert, 2000). These partners are involved in dozens of activities that Newmann and Sconzert classify under "four promising strategies":

- Offering professional development;
- Creating new roles to assist instruction;
- Providing materials to assist instruction;
- Establishing new school organization structures.

These are promising indeed, but not until we tackle the problem of coherence:

> help from different sources tended to exacerbate overall program fragmentation and incoherence. Program incoherence limited school development, because in most situations it prevented staff from investing the degree of focused, sustained energy and attention that any given high-quality intervention requires ... The lack of program coherence is due in part to "principals" difficulty in channeling available help from many sources into a focused, sustained program ... we found no powerful incentives or accountability structures that led universities, foundations, and other improvement organizations to coordinate their efforts in each school toward a comprehensive design. (Newmann & Sconzert, 2000, pp. 59–60)

In sum, external involvement is essential for success. There are a growing number of possibilities available, but figuring out how to dance with many partners is problematic for schools and districts. In the rest of this chapter I consider some of these issues first from the perspective of the consultant, and in turn from those who must figure out how to use consultants.

EXTERNAL CONSULTANTS: OUTSIDE-IN

Block (1999) provides the best comprehensive advice for external consultants. He identifies three sets of skills that all consultants will need: technical (expertise about the content of the problem), interpersonal (expertise to listen, give support, disagree reasonably, and to build and maintain relationships), and consulting skills (entry, contracting, problem identification, feedback, engagement and implementation, extension and termination). Block repeatedly warns us that "techniques are not enough" (p. 13). He emphasizes that being authentic is key:

> In thirty years of consulting, all my failures (which I remember with distressing clarity) occurred either because I was so carried away by how *I* was going to solve the client's problem that I didn't pay attention to client motivation or because I wanted to contract so badly that I didn't care what the contract looked like. (Block, 1999, p. 50)

Block, as I have, places special emphasis on implementation when he observes that consultants have traditionally given too much attention to analysis and recommendations and too little attention to the complexity of translating those answers into action. (p. 247)

Block notes that the goal of implementation is to create the conditions for engagement or emotional commitment to taking action:

> The greatest service of the consultant may be to raise the consciousness of the client about the value of engagement in the implementation process. (p. 265)

"Start measuring your work," advises Block, "by the optimism and self-sufficiency you leave behind. Consulting is fundamentally an educational and capacity-building function" (p. 324).

Argyris (2000) draws a similar conclusion in talking about managers:

> When managers ask for commitment, they usually want employees to:
>
> • Implement the strategy process, and job requirements as faithfully, reliably, and effectively as they can;
> • Monitor such implementation to assess effectiveness;
> • Be vigilant about recognizing actual or potential gaps, errors, and inconsistencies, as well as new and unrecognizable challenges.
>
> The first two points can be implemented by the use of either external or internal commitment. The third requires internal committment because it asks employees to go beyond what is defined by vision, strategy, and management process—indeed, to question policies and practices, especially for difficulties that were not recognized at the outset. (pp. 40–41)

External commitment, notes Argyris, "is triggered by management policies and practices that enable employees to accomplish their work" (p. 40). Conversely, "internal commitment draws from energies internal to human beings that are activated because getting the job done is intrinsically rewarding" (p. 40). In this sense, the goal of external consultants is to help organizations develop greater internal commitment (while in practice, external interventions often end up preserving the status quo because they result in surface changes at best, thereby giving change a bad name). Argyris's (2000) basic solution is that we should move to what he calls Model II:

> Every significant Model II action is evaluated in terms of the degree to which it helps the individuals generate valid and useful information (including relevant feelings), share a problem in ways that lead to productive inquiry, solve the problem such that it remains solved, and do so without reducing the present level of problem-solving effectiveness. (p. 76)

The advice from Block and Argyris dovetails with the themes in this book. Let me summarize the advice for external consultants in my own terms. First, whatever your model, build up the theory of change that needs to go along with it—a theory that generates strategies to obtain local support from parents, teachers, principals, and others. Be wary of superficial acceptance or adoption decisions. Argyris (2000) refers to this as "choices appear to get made, but fall apart" (p. 202):

> False consensus occurs when one or more members of the management team [or the organization members more generally] do not agree with the choice that emerges but do not reveal their concerns or discomfort to the group . . . If the concerns of these silent members are not voiced, the concerns cannot be resolved in the process and commitment cannot be built . . . The result: the silent but doubting members of the team drag their feet in implementation or work actively to subvert implementation. (pp. 202–203)

Thus, the first order of business is to combine good ideas with the more difficult process of building commitment over time.

Second, don't focus only on your model, but on how it relates or not to the multiple initiatives that might be underway in the district or school. Program coherence, connectedness, and alignment are crucial, otherwise your model will be "one more damn thing to do." In short, if impact is your concern, being a consultant requires having good ideas (theories of learning) and being very sophisticated about the complexities of relationships and motivations (theories of change).

USING CONSULTANTS: INSIDE-OUT

The advice to those within organizations is pretty much the flip side of the previous section. First and probably foremost is the realization that *all* successful schools and districts are proactively plugged into an external network of resources, professional development, and other forms of assistance. So, it is not whether you should be in the game that is at issue, but how you should play it.

Second, in considering external ideas, assess how "actionable the advice is" (Argyris, 2000). Does the external idea have a theory of action to address key aspects to support the process of implementation?

Third, worry a great deal about the problem of multiple innovations colliding (Hatch, 2000). If an idea is not "integratable," if it takes its place alongside a set of other ideas that are coming and going, it probably should not be taken on, even if it has some appeal.

Fourth, focus on capacity-building; that is, how the external idea can increase the motivation and know-how of leaders within the organization to help lead others in generating commitment.

The final dilemma is a troublesome one. Hatch (2000) reminds us that "it takes capacity to build capacity." What if a school or district is persistently failing and dysfunctional—organizations that are good at continually making the wrong decisions. In a direct sense, this is not the external consultant's problem. It is a problem for leadership at the school, district, community, or state levels. In failing situations, as I discussed earlier, it will require more assertive front-end steps, but initial compliance will not be sufficient. If it is to go anywhere, the school/district must go beyond these first steps toward greater capacity to engage in actions that generate internal commitment for continuous improvement. Ironically, as this kind of self-sufficiency increases, schools become greater natural users of outside resources, including the very valuable quality of knowing when to say no.

CHAPTER 12

The Parent and the Community

Whose school is it, anyway?

—Gold and Miles (1981)

In *What's Worth Fighting for Out There*, Hargreaves and I (1998) argued that the "out there" is now "in here." We observed that the boundaries of the school are now more permeable and more transparent, and that this development was both *inevitable and desirable*. It is inevitable because there is a relentless press for accountability from our public institutions and many more means these days of acting on this interest, including the growing accessibility to information in a technology-based society. It is desirable because in postmodern society you can no longer get the job of education done unless you combine forces. It has become too complex for any one group (like teachers) to do alone. These new ways of partnering are threatening and complex. But we concluded that if the "out there" is going to get you anyway on its terms, why not move toward the danger, and have a chance of getting some of it on your terms. This chapter is about parents and communities, on the one hand, and administrators and teachers, on the other hand, moving toward each other—a process that is a far more dangerous journey at the outset (when you are working from a base of mutual ignorance) than it is once you are underway.

If teachers and administrators who spend 40 to 60 hours a week immersed in the educational world have trouble comprehending the meaning of educational change, imagine what it is like for the parent. Highly educated parents are bewildered; what of the less educated ones who have always felt uncomfortable in dealing with the school?

The question of parent and community involvement in schools has been the subject of hundreds of books and articles over the past 30 years. At first glance this literature appears to be a mass of contradictions, confusion, and hopelessness for understanding— let alone coping with—the relationship between communities and schools. Yet emerging from this research is a message that is remarkable in its consistency: *The closer the parent is to the education of the child, the greater the impact on child development and educational achievement.* Of course, it is not quite that simple, because such a statement encompasses a multitude of variables that make it more or less probable that closeness will occur. And we can certainly imagine situations in which closeness per se could be harmful to the growth of the child. Moreover, decisions about the precise nature of parent involvement must take into account cultural, ethnic, and class differences as well as variations related to the age and gender of students.

In determining under what conditions parent and community involvement is most beneficial, we have to understand the different forms of parent participation and their consequences for the student and other school personnel. Stated another way, why do certain forms of involvement produce positive results while others seem wasteful or counterproductive?

I start with the role of parents because this is where the most powerful instrument for improvement resides. I also consider the role of school boards and communities. The final section identifies guidelines and resources for how schools and communities might better cope with educational change together.

PARENT INVOLVEMENT IN SCHOOLS

Nowhere is the two-way street of learning more in disrepair and in need of social reconstruction than with concerning the relationship among parents, communities, and their schools. Teachers and principals need to reach out to parents and communities, especially when the initial conditions do not support such efforts. Henry's (1996) study of parent-school collaboration in poor neighborhoods concluded:

Educators have to go out into their communities with empathy, and interact meaningfully with their constituents. Being professional can no longer mean remaining isolated in the school (p. 132).

This will involve shifts in power and influence. But it is not power in and of itself that counts. It is what new power arrangements can accomplish that matters:

To seek power is to raise and begin to answer the question: to seek power to change what? Changing the forces of power in no way guarantees that anything else will change ... To seek power without asking the "what" question is not only to beg the question but to avoid, and therefore to collude in cosmetic changes. (Sarason, 1995, p. 53)

The "what" question is: "What will it take to mobilize more people and resources in the service of educating all students?" The research is abundantly clear about the answer: Teachers cannot do it alone. Parents and other community members are crucial and largely untapped resources who have (or can be helped to have) assets and expertise that are essential to the partnership. However well or badly they do it, parents are their children's very first educators. They have knowledge of their children that is not available to anyone else. They have a vested and committed interest in their children's success, and they also have valuable knowledge and skills to contribute that spring from their interests, hobbies, occupations, and place in the community.

The research is very clear about the benefits, indeed the necessity, of parent engagement. In Coleman's (1998) study of schools in two districts, he calls this the "power of three" (parent, student, and teacher collaboration). Based on his interviews and surveys of parents, students, and teachers, Coleman argues that:

Student commitment to schooling (or engagement in learning) is primarily shaped by parents through the "curriculum of the home"; but this parent involvement is an alterable variable which can be influenced by school and teacher practices. (p. 11)

Coleman expounds on this:

When the development of student responsibility occurs it is a function of the attitudes and practices of all three triad members. The vital elements are: (a) for teachers, beliefs about parental involvement, student capabilities, and the importance of deliberate teaching of responsibility in classrooms; (b) for students, communication with parents about school, confidence in the ability to do the work, valuing school for its importance to the future, and collaboration with teachers; (c) for parents, valuing school, an "invitational" teacher attitude, and communication with students about school. (p. 14)

Coleman (1998) concludes that "student commitment can indeed be sustained and strengthened by collaborative teacher attitudes, expressed in and through their practices; strong connections with the home are essential to the task" (p. 139). Coleman (1998, p. 150, emphasis in original) argues that "teachers [can] facilitate and encourage parent collaboration through some simple practices, all well-known *but not implemented consistently* in any of our schools (or we believe in many schools anywhere). Most parents," he adds, "are conscious that much more could be done to help their students learn, in classrooms and in the home" (p. 150). The irony, as I shall discuss below, is that most teachers want more parent involvement as well.

In the meantime the research over the years has been consistent (and fortunately more precise) about the role of parents. Mortimore and colleagues' (1988) large study of school effectiveness found that parental involvement practices represented one of 12 key factors that differentiated effective from less effective schools.

Our findings show parent involvement in the life of the school to be a positive influence upon pupils' progress and development. This included help in classrooms and on educational visits, and attendance at meetings to discuss children's progress. The headteacher's accessibility to parents was also important; schools operating an informal, open-door policy being more effective. Parent involvement in pupils' educational development within the home was also clearly beneficial. Parents who read to their children, heard them read, and provided them with access to books at home, had a positive effect upon their children's learning. (p. 255)

Rosenholtz's (1989) research, with which we are familiar, found important differences in how teachers in "moving" versus "stuck" schools related to parents. Teachers from stuck schools "held no goals for parent participation" (p. 152), while teachers from moving schools "focused their efforts on involving parents with academic content, thereby bridging the learning chasm between home and school" (p. 152). Teachers in stuck schools were far more likely to assume that nothing could be done with parents, while teachers in moving schools saw parents as part of the solution.

In the Chicago evaluation conducted by Bryk and associates (1998), those schools that were more successful were found to be committed to developing "the engagement of parents and community resources." In their words:

> Schools pursuing a systemic agenda have a "client orientation." They maintain a sustained focus on strengthening the involvement of parents with the school and their children's schooling. They also actively seek to strengthen the ties with the local community and especially those resources that bear on the caring of children. As these personal interactions expand and become institutionalized in the life of the school, the quality of the relationships between local professionals and their community changes. Greater trust and mutual engagement begins to characterize these encounters. In contrast, schools with unfocused initiatives may set more distinct boundaries between themselves and their neighborhood. Extant problems in these relationships may not be directly addressed. The broader community resources that could assist improvement efforts in the school are not tapped. These schools remain more isolated from their students' parents and their communities. (Bryk et al., 1998, p. 127–128)

The flip side of teachers needing help is that parents and communities need it, too. As Steinberg (1996) observes:

> The first, and most significant, problem is the high prevalence of disengaged parents in contemporary America. By our estimate,

nearly one in three parents in America is seriously disengaged from his or her adolescent's life, and especially from the adolescent's education. (1996, p. 187)

The most systematic research and development in this whole domain has been conducted by Epstein and her colleagues over the past decade and a half. In 1988, she had already concluded that:

There is consistent evidence that parents' encouragement, activities, interest at home and their participation at school affect their children's achievement, even after the students' ability and family socioeconomic status is taken into account. Students gain in personal and academic development if their families emphasize schooling, let their children know they do, and do so continually over the years. (Epstein, 1988, Chap. 1)

Epstein has identified six types of school and parent/community involvement which in combination improve student learning and adult engagement with their children's education:

Type 1—Parent skills
Type 2—Communication
Type 3—Volunteering
Type 4—Learning at home
Type 5—School decision-making
Type 6—Collaboration with communities agencies (Epstein,
    1995; Epstein et al., 1997)

Note that school governance (Type 5) represents only one of six forms, and is not the most important. Most parents do not want to run the school; they want their child to do better. Put another way, it is only when the majority of teachers are collaborating with the majority of parents that any sizeable impact on student learning will occur. And this, of course, makes perfect sense even if it is not practiced much.

Over the years Epstein has found that parent involvement is critical to success, but there is no evidence that schools and parents have become substantially closer (except for the minority that have deliberately set out to do this with external training and support). In a statewide survey, Epstein found that 58% of the parents reported rarely or never having received requests from the teacher to become involved in learning activities at home, while over 80% said they could spend more time helping children at home if they were shown how to do specific learning activities (Epstein, 1986, p. 280).

There were significant differences between the teacher-leaders in parent involvement and the comparison teachers, even though the two groups were matched on characteristics and type of community. For example, teacher-leaders involved parents from differing educational backgrounds compared with the control groups, which reported that parents with little education "could not or would not help at home." Parents of children in the classes of teacher-leaders reported significantly more frequent use of 9 of the 12 parent involvement practices. The effect on parents was positive and multifaceted. Parents increased their understanding about school most when the teacher frequently used parent involvement practices. Epstein (1986) states:

> What is important in our findings is that teachers' frequent use of parent involvement practices improved parents' knowledge about their child's instructional program, after the grade level, racial composition, and parent education composition of the classroom were taken into account. (pp. 288–289)

Epstein concludes:

> Parents were aware of and responded positively to teachers' efforts to involve them in learning activities at home. Parents with children in the classrooms of teachers who built parent involvement into their regular teaching practice were more aware of teachers' efforts, received more ideas from teachers, knew more about their child's instructional program, and rated the teachers higher in interpersonal skills and overall teaching quality. Teachers' practices had consistently strong and positive effects on parent reactions to the school program and on parent evaluations of teachers' merits for parents at all educational levels. . . . Teacher practices of parent involvement had more dramatic positive links to parents' reactions than general school-to-home communication or parent assistance at the school. (p. 291)

In related work, Epstein and Dauber concentrated, respectively, on *teacher attitudes and practices of parent involvement* (Epstein & Dauber, 1988) and *parents' attitudes and practices* (Dauber & Epstein, 1989) in eight inner-city schools in Baltimore (five elementary and three middle schools). In examining teacher attitudes and practices of the 171 teachers, Epstein and Dauber (1988) found:

- Almost all teachers express strong, positive attitudes about parent involvement in general. But the strength of school programs and teachers' actual practice vary considerably, with elementary school programs stronger, more positive, and more comprehensive than those in middle grades.
- The individual practices of each teacher at particular grade levels and in particular subject areas are the keystone for strong programs of parent involvement.
- The individual teacher is not, however, the only factor in building stronger programs. Analyses of "discrepancy scores" showed that differences between self and principal, self and teacher colleagues, and self and parents were significantly associated with the strength of schools' parent involvement programs. Programs and practices were stronger in schools where teachers saw that they, their colleagues, and the parents all felt strongly about the importance of parent involvement.
- Without the schools' assistance, parents' knowledge and actions to help their children are heavily dependent on the parents' social class or education. But schools—even inner city schools—can develop strong programs of parent involvement to help more families become knowledgeable partners in their children's education. (pp. 11–12)

Epstein and Dauber also report that teachers with more positive attitudes toward parent involvement report more success in involving "hard-to-reach parents including working parents, less educated parents, single parents, parents of older students, young parents, parents new to the school, and other adults with whom children live" (p. 5).

The work of Epstein and her colleagues in establishing the National Network of Partnership Schools (NNPS) has done a great deal to further both the research knowledge base and the corresponding developmental strategies required to strengthen the family and school connection. Established in 1996, NNPS now includes 1,050 schools from 1,125 districts in 11 states in the United States (Epstein & Sanders, 2000; Sanders & Epstein, 2000). Members of the network are provided with tools and strategies to implement their school improvement efforts, the six types of involvement (see Epstein et al., 1997, handbook).

These strategies have proven successful in elementary schools, but what about the dreaded high school, the focus of their recent research? I quote at some length because of the powerful message:

> Analyses of data from 243 parents of high school students revealed a number of important findings. Over 90% of the parents surveyed agreed that parent involvement was needed at the high school level. More than 80% indicated that they wanted to be more involved in their teens' learning and that they needed more information in order to effectively help their teens at home. Few were involved in school activities such as volunteering, fundraising, or committee participation. Most (75%) reported that their high schools had never contacted them about such activities. About 72% of the parents surveyed believed that high schools should start new programs or improve their present partnership programs to help families understand more about adolescent development and other topics related to their teens' growth and learning.
>
> Further analyses revealed that when families perceived that their high schools implemented activities for specific types of involvement, parents had more positive attitudes about the schools, and responded by conducting practices for those types of involvement. For example, when schools implemented more practices of Type 1 Involvement (Parenting) and Type 4 Involvement (Learning at Home), parents reported that they were more involved with their teens' learning at home. Similarly, when schools conducted more practices for Type 3 Involvement (Volunteering) and Type 5 Involvement (School Decision Making), parents reported more involvement at their teens' schools. The study also indicated that school practices for Type 2 (Communicating) were essential for improving the other types of involve-

ment. These findings were strong and significant even after controlling for parents' educational backgrounds. Thus, regardless of years of formal schooling, more parents became involved in their adolescents' education if high schools implemented specific practices to guide their involvement at school or at home.

Data from about 1,300 ninth graders indicated that students' attitudes about involvement were influenced by their high schools' practices to involve families. For example, students whose families were already involved in their education in the ninth grade were more willing to interact with their families about schoolwork in a number of ways. Importantly, after statistically accounting for their families' social and economic background and present level of involvement, students who said that their high schools and teachers had stronger programs of partnership were more willing than were other students to conduct more interactions about school with family members. . . . (Sanders & Epstein, 2000, p. 67)

And further,

High school teachers were more willing to work to improve their schools' partnership programs if they had experience on teams with other teachers, and if they perceived high collegial support in the school and district for family and community involvement. (p. 68)

A familiar story to the reader of this book. Every time a school collaborates to do something to improve learning, positive things happen. Epstein and colleagues have been providing training and support for Action Team Partnerships (ATP)—parents, teachers, principal, other school staff, students—at the school level. They find that:

Schools report higher quality programs if they have effective ATPs; widespread support from school personnel, community members, and district leaders; and adequate funding to implement partnership activities. Analyses also showed that high schools are less likely than middle and elementary schools to find widespread support for school, family and community partnerships. High schools, then, need additional assistance from organizations like the National Network, and from their district and state leaders to help them garner the general support that contributes to the quality and success of partnership programs. (Sanders & Epstein, 2000, p. 72)

It is, to be sure, a chicken-and-egg problem. When you have collaborative relationships they produce results. But if you don't have these qualities, how do you get them? The obvious but still useful answer is to work on these capacities by joining NNPS or other similar development efforts. The deeper answer concerns the "pathways problem" that I keep raising, which means entering the complexities of relationship building. Dolan (1994) puts it best:

> In a school, where mistrust between the community and the administration is the major issue, you might begin to deal with it by making sure that parents were present at every major event, every meeting, every challenge. Within the discomfort of that presence, the learning and the healing could begin. (Dolan, 1994, p. 60)

The good news is that all three partners—parents, teachers, and yes, even students—potentially want more interaction. But they don't trust it to be helpful, don't see the possibilities, are not confident about initiating it, and so on. These issues are compounded when there are ethnic, age, and class differences, but all researchers still find parent involvement as a crucial and *alterable* variable regardless of parents' education and ethnic background. Goldenberg (in press, Chap. 7), for example, describes how he and other teachers were reluctant to contact parents (in this case, mostly of Latino students) and made certain assumptions about parents' lack of interest. He also shows that deliberate training of teachers and parents to enhance home-school connections produces greater academic engagement of parents and students and greater achievement in the vast majority of cases. Reticent teachers and parents became more mutually supportive as a result of these new experiences, even though they were skeptical to begin with. Dodd and Konzal (1999) make the same case for high schools, and provide a set of strategies for developing rapport and involvement:

> The tendency to assume that parents don't care may be greater in schools with poor and minority students. In a study that

compared two urban schools—one affluent and one working
class—researchers found that cultural and social differences, not
lack of parent interest accounted for less parental involvement
in the working-class school. (p. 238)

Up to this point, however, not enough schools have tried to
find the particular pathways of involvement appropriate for their
setting. Thus, the power of three, at the very time it is most needed,
remains an unleashed force as far as the majority of schools and
communities are concerned.

SCHOOL BOARDS AND COMMUNITIES

The role of school boards (in the United States, usually made up
of circa seven locally elected trustees who are responsible for over-
seeing the work of schools within the district) is difficult to discern.
Danzberger and colleagues (1987) call boards "the forgotten players
on the education team." They undertook a national study of local
school boards in the United States, in which they surveyed 450
board chairpersons of city districts and 50 in rural districts, and
interviewed a variety of local leaders. Danzberger and her colleagues found that state governments were becoming more and
more directive, that the role of local boards was unclear, that board
members received little preparation and training for their roles,
and that only one third of the boards surveyed had any process
for evaluating or monitoring the board's role. They observed that
boards could be crucial agents for school improvement, and recommended that state reforms should be concerned with strengthening
the capacity of local boards to bring about and monitor change,
and that boards themselves should be engaged in self-improvement
through in-service and by establishing systems to assess their own
effectiveness.

School boards, depending on their activities, can make a difference. LaRocque and Coleman (1989) investigated the role of school
boards in relatively successful compared with less successful districts (as measured by student achievement) in ten districts in British
Columbia. On the surface, many of the policies and initiatives were
similar across all boards. Through interviews and the examination

of specific activities, LaRocque and Coleman found that school trustees in the more successful boards

(a) Were considerably more knowledgeable about district programs and practices;
(b) Had a clearer sense of what they wanted to accomplish, based on a set of firmly held values and beliefs; and
(c) Engaged in activities which provided them with opportunities to articulate these values and beliefs. (p. 15)

Successful boards also worked more actively and interactively with superintendents and the district administration.

Greely, quoted in Senge and associates (2000, p. 432), also talks about "a school board that learns." She notes that there are built-in obstacles to learning:

- External funding from federal and state sources fragments programs and promotes a "command-and-control" mindset;
- Individual board members, elected by constituencies, often do not vet in the interest of the whole community;
- There is large turnover, with new majorities often being established every 2 to 4 years;
- It is hard for school board members to learn as a team because they are frequently in public, political settings.

Greely draws a number of lessons for countering these forces:

- Create a public record of private connections;
- Resist the temptation to involve business examples;
- Keep returning to the observable data;
- Set up alternative meeting formats;
- Practice talking about values;
- Have your behavior model the behavior you want from the schools. (cited in Senge et al., 2000, pp. 436–438)

Despite the obvious conclusion that school superintendents and trustees should engage in mutual training and learning, and that it can be done—at least for short periods of time—in a minority of cases, it may be an impossible task if we expect large-scale reform. I am not saying that boards and superintendents should give up trying. Indeed, they should diligently apply the learning principles in this book in their own development. What I am saying is that they may need more help and involvement of the larger infrastructure if we are to see deeper and more widespread reform.

Hess's (1999) study of school district policymaking indicates that the prevailing system is not likely to improve. As quoted in Hill and associates (2000) school boards are often caught in a "policy churn". Hess states:

> District policymakers constantly embrace politically attractive changes, producing prodigious amounts of reform at a pace inimical to effective implementation. . . .
>
> [Districts] recycle initiatives, constantly modify previous initiatives, and adopt innovative reform A to replace practice B even as another district is adopting B as an innovative reform to replace practice A. . . .
>
> Urban districts appear to do a number of things in a stop-and-start, chaotic fashion that is not part of any clear strategy to improve specific elements of school performance. (Hess, 1999, p. 5)

Elmore (2000) summarizes Hess:

> [R]elatively unstable political factors advance new "reforms" as ways of satisfying their electoral constituencies, pausing only long enough to take credit for having acted, and quickly moving on to new reforms, with no attention to the institutionalization or implementation of previous reforms. The political rewards in the pluralistic structure, Hess argues, are in the symbolisms of initiations and enactment of reform, not in its implementation. Among the pathologies the incentive structure creates is high turnover of leadership, both political and administrative. . . . Factions are fickle, political opportunities about board majorities hold onto school superintendents just long enough for them to advance their reform proposals, . . . and at the first sign of opposition, move onto the next superintendent. (Elmore, 2000, p. 19)

Yes, training for trustees is desirable, but it is not likely to be a sufficient solution. Instead we must move to local communities and to the larger infrastructure in municipalities. Starting with parents, we have to ask along with Steinberg (1996), "If so many parents really want their child to do well in school, why do only a minority of parents do what they ought to be doing?" (p. 103). One answer is that it is exceedingly difficult to create a home atmosphere conducive to positive child development. It involves combining approaches that don't easily go together: acceptance (versus rejection), firmness (versus leniency), and autonomy (versus control). The integration of acceptance, firmness, and autonomy in parents is complex and demanding work. Steinberg (1996) describes parents who practice this combination well as "authoritative." The ability to work with these paradoxes of parenting distinguishes "good parents from bad ones" (p. 106).

Steinberg also notes that despite good intentions, nearly one in three parents end up being disengaged from their children:

> Disengaged parents have for one reason or another, "checked out" of childrearing. They have disengaged from responsibilities of parental discipline—they do not know how their child is doing in school, have no idea who their child's friends are, and are not aware of how their child spends his or her free time—but they have also disengaged from being accepting and supportive as well. They rarely spend time in activities with their child, and seldom just talk with their adolescent about the day's events (p. 188).

Parent-school connections can counter the problem to some extent. Neighborhoods and communities can also make a difference:

> Adolescents who live in neighbourhoods in which a large proportion of families are authoritative [combine acceptance, firmness, autonomy] perform better in school and are less likely to get into trouble than adolescents who come from identical home environments—and who go to the same school—but who live in neighborhoods in which the population of authoritative families is much lower. (p. 153)

Thus, training and development in local communities and neighborhoods in which communities and schools form partnerships, to work on implementing the Epstein and associates (1997) framework, for example, are essential. Schools can take the first step as some are now doing, or it can be community initiated; in either case it must be jointly designed once started. Note, for the moment we are talking about individual schools and communities, not districts. With the trend toward school-based development (recall that this does not eliminate the district role, but changes it, as we saw in Chapter 10), the most powerful training and development for parents and school people will be *school by school*.

Beyond the individual school, Mathews (1996) and Hill and associates (2000) conclude that community and municipal involvement will be required. They say that a strong public school system is necessary for a strong democracy, that the public system is weakening rather than getting stronger and that it is a *system* problem, that is, a societal problem. Mathews (1996) asks, "Is there a public for public schools?" and suggests:

> [S]chool reform may need to be recast as community building
> . . . certain things may have to happen in our communities before
> we can see the improvements we want in our schools (p. 3)

Stated in our terms, simultaneous development of schools and communities will be required. This is not the place to formulate a detailed plan. Hill and associates (2000) provide one version, which involves mayors, business leaders, and community and school people and requires the establishment of new entities, including: "a civic reform oversight group," an "independent educational analysis agency," "a schools inspectorate," "a schools incubator," and "a real estate trust to manage and lease school buildings" (pp. 108–109). Elmore (2000) formulates a compatible set of requirements in revamping what leaders at all levels of the school system will need to do.

Whatever the case, the "loosely coupled" school system of the past is now existing on borrowed time. To accomplish the reforms we are talking about in this book, it will take a city, a community, and a professional learning community. It is, in a word, a systems-change proposition.

IMPLICATIONS

There are, of course, great implications for policymakers and other leaders who have the opportunity to alter the larger infrastructure (see, for example, Chapters 13–15). Individuals (and combinations of individuals) can also work in their own ways with a system perspective, that is, they can in their own way move toward the danger in working out new ways of working between communities and schools. We have seen the research, and it is convincing. We have seen that the pathways and obstacles in getting there involve working through the discomfort of each other's presence until new patterns of relationships are established. There is a growing set of guidelines and resources for acting on these matters. Epstein and associates' (1997) handbook contains action steps and checklists with respect to implementing the framework of six forms of parent/community/school involvement.

Dodd and Konzal (1999) contain many suggestions for what principals, teachers, and parents can do. Coleman (1998) and Goldenberg (in press) provide both the research and strategies for school people to take the initiative with parents. Coleman (1998) summarizes it this way:

> Teachers must (1) realize that parent efficacy with respect to instructional involvement (collaboration) is dependent upon teacher invitation; (2) legitimize collaboration through an assertion to parents of their rights and responsibilities with respect to collaboration; (3) facilitate collaboration by arranging for parent-teacher conversations of various kinds, and by providing parents with the knowledge of curriculum and methodology they need; (4) encourage collaboration by providing activities that parents and their children can do together; that is, accepting the role of instructional mediator between parents and their children; and (5) acknowledge the results of collaboration by providing adequate and timely information about student performance. (Coleman, 1998, p. 61)

As for parents, I have said that schools do not capitalize enough on the interest in and knowledge of their own children's learning that many parents have. It is also true that many parents are insufficiently involved in the education of their children. While schools have often not made parental involvement easy or have otherwise resisted it, many parents may need to act differently as well. Hargreaves and I suggested the following four guidelines for parents:

1. *Press Governments to Create the Kind of Teachers You Want*
   Help make education a sophisticated election issue that goes beyond hackneyed slogans to address how we can make teaching better so that learning will get better too. Demand answers regarding the kinds of resources that will be dedicated to that end. How will we get and keep quality teachers? How will teachers be helped and encouraged to maintain and improve that quality over time? Better learning needs better teaching—how, precisely, will governments bring that about? Push them for answers.

2. *Leave Nostalgia Behind You*
   Make more efforts to understand what schools are striving to achieve in today's world. Try and get firsthand knowledge and experience of what your children's school is doing now. Consider the knowledge and skills your children will need as they become citizens and workers in the future, and what kinds of teaching and learning are necessary to create these. Don't long for your children to have exactly the kind of education you think you remember having yourself, just because that is what's familiar to you. The science of learning is profoundly different today. Find out more about these new developments. What worked in 1965 is unlikely suitable for 1995 or 2005 (Stoll & Fink, 1996). Remember the words of Christopher Lasch (1991)—"nostalgia is the abdication of memory."

3. *Ask What You Can Do for Your School As Well As What Your School Can Do for You*
   What can you offer and contribute to support your school? The best place to start is at home. If you expect the school to develop a work ethic in your child, do you also insist on this at home by making sure he or she really does mow the lawn, shovel the snow, complete his or her homework, etc. The more you give to your school and its teachers, the more responsiveness you are likely to get when you want something in return. Once more, relationships are the key.

4. *Put Praise Before Blame*

If you have criticisms to make of your children's education, remember that the teachers will be as anxious about meeting you as you are about meeting them. Try to put teachers at their ease. Put compliments before criticism. Wherever you can, see what the school is doing firsthand so you know your complaints aren't groundless. Contact teachers and thank them spontaneously when things are going well (which will make the more difficult encounters easier and put them into perspective). Take responsibility to build relationships with your children's teachers *before* problems arise. (Hargreaves & Fullan, 1998, pp. 124–125)

In the meantime, the simple and powerful conclusion of this chapter is threefold. First, the vast majority of parents find meaning in activities related to their own children rather than in school- or systemwide endeavors. Second, educational reform requires the conjoint efforts of families and schools. Parents and teachers should recognize the critical complementary importance of each other in the life of the student. Otherwise, we are placing limitations on the prospects for improvement that may be impossible to overcome. Third, it is also time for systems change. The larger infrastructure does make a difference, usually for the worse. The big system must get its house in order, too. Hence, Part III.

PART III

EDUCATIONAL CHANGE AT THE REGIONAL AND NATIONAL LEVELS

CHAPTER 13

Governments

The state is an incredibly blunt instrument; it gets hold of one overarching idea and imposes it without any sensitivity to local context . . . [And there] is the desperate craving of politicians for a magical solution.
—Micklethwait & Wooldridge (1996)

Hargreaves and I wrote the *What's Worth Fighting For* trilogy on the assumption that on any given day, the "system" might not know what it is doing. Thus, we tried to equip teachers and principals with insights and action guidelines so that they could make headway despite the system. This is still valuable advice.

But later we realized that only small-scale, nonlasting improvement can occur if the system is not helping. I then wrote the *Change Forces* trilogy with the system as the focus—the chaotic, complex, nonlinear forces that could be better understood and acted upon, especially if people at all levels worked on building learning organizations. Now in 2001, more than ever before, we find people grappling with not only the issue of how to go to scale, but also the issue of how to go deeper at the same time. In other words, we have come to the conclusion that the larger infrastructure matters.

Governments face a dilemma, as Micklethwait and Wooldridge pointed out above. Their world is one of wanting quick solutions for urgent problems. Yet bringing about change on a large scale is enormously complex. If it is difficult to manage change in one classroom, one school, one school district, imagine the scale of the problems faced by one state or province or country in which numerous agencies and levels and tens or hundreds of thousands of people are involved. It is infinitely more difficult for that government if its personnel do not venture out to attempt to understand the culture and the problems of local school people.

If we are to achieve large-scale reform, governments are essential. They have the potential to be a major force for transformation. The historical evidence to date, however, suggests that few governments have gotten this right.

In this chapter I take up the role of governments in three ways. First, I address what we know about their effect on local implementation. Second, I use the National Literacy and Numeracy Strategy in England as a case example to illustrate many of the issues that will require attention. Third, I draw out the implications for what governments need to do if they are interested in greater improvement across all or most schools. The issues at stake are what governments are doing and what they can do to make a difference.

THE ROLE OF GOVERNMENTS

By "governments" I mean federal and state departments in the United States, provinces in Canada (because there is virtually no federal policy presence in education), and national governments in countries that are governed as one system.

I want to provide an advance organizer. Governments can push *accountability, provide incentives* (pressure and supports), and/or foster *capacity-building*. We will see that if they do only the first and second they can get results that, I will argue, are real but not particularly deep or lasting. If they do all three they have a chance of going the distance. Many governments have put all their eggs in the accountability basket; a few have been good at combining pressure and support; and none have seriously affected capacity, although several are now working on it.

In the United States, starting with the publication of *A Nation at Risk* in 1983, attention shifted to what governments should do to accomplish badly needed large-scale reform. By and large the efforts of the decade following 1983 concentrated on beefing up accountability expectations and requirements. These early policy initiatives, focusing only on accountability, did more damage than good. They put tremendous pressure on local systems, provided little help, and actually increased the overload and fragmentation of effort.

Firestone, Rosenblum, and Bader (1992) studied the evolution of reform in six states—Arizona, California, Florida, Georgia, Minnesota, and Pennsylvania—over a 7-year period between 1983 and 1990. They make a similar observation:

> Government fragmentation . . . runs from central agencies to peripheral ones—that is, from federal and state governments to districts, schools, and ultimately classrooms. The study of policy implementation since the 1960s has been a history of efforts to identify ways for agencies at one level to influence those at the next level down; authoritative directions and responsive compliance turn out to be the exception. The best that can usually be expected of efforts to get districts to implement state and federal policy is mutual adaptation through which central expectations adapt to local preferences at least as much as the opposite occurs. High-quality implementation is the exception. (Firestone et al., 1992, p. 256)

In addition to the fragmentation in the above vertical relationships, there are also enormous horizontal disconnections. Countless agencies, many of them government entities or government-sponsored groups, fail to coordinate their work, so that multiple initiatives do collide in a haphazard fashion.

Let us not forget that governments also live in a world of "adoption," not implementation—the timeline for implementation is always longer than the next election. Related to this is that it is easier to adopt *structural* changes rather than it is to engage in the hard work of *cultural* changes in relationships, capacity, and motivation. Most policies (e.g., vouchers, charters, and site-based management), argues Elmore (2000, p. 10), "are quintessential structural changes in that they imply absolutely nothing about either the content or quality of instruction."

Lusi's (1997) detailed case studies of the role of State Departments of Education (SDE) in Kentucky and Vermont confirms that accountability-driven strategies by themselves can never work because you cannot "change the practice of a large number of prac-

titioners over whom [you] have little control and no proximity"
(p. 11). I will return later to the new work that states have begun
to do to enhance the likelihood of widespread reform at the local
level.

In any case, in complex systems heavy-handed accountability
schemes can never work because they cannot cause the beliefs and
behaviors necessary for success. The next logical step, then, is to
add incentives (an amalgamation of pressure and support). The
history of policymaking over the past decade concerning teacher
quality is very instructive. A good summary is provided by Darling-
Hammond from the work of the National Commission on Teaching
and America's Future:

> Of the 50 states, North Carolina and Connecticut undertook the
> most substantial and systematic investments in teaching during
> the mid-1980's. Both of these states, which share relatively large
> high poverty student populations, coupled major statewide in-
> creases in teacher salaries and improvements in teacher salary
> equity with intensive recruitment efforts and initiatives to im-
> prove preservice teacher education, licensing, beginning teacher
> mentoring, and ongoing professional development. Since then,
> North Carolina has posted the largest student achievement gains
> in mathematics and reading of any state in the nation, now
> scoring well above the national average in 4th grade reading
> and mathematics, although it entered the 1990s near the bottom
> of state rankings. Connecticut has also posted significant gains,
> becoming one of the top scoring states in the nation in mathemat-
> ics and reading (ranked first at the 4th grade level in mathematics
> and reading, and in the top five at the 8th grade level), despite
> an increase in the proportion of low-income and limited English
> proficiency students during the time. (Darling-Hammond, 2000a,
> p. 13)

Even more revealing is Darling-Hammond's comparison of
states that employed accountability-only strategies versus those
that combined accountability with incentives (skill training, rewards, etc.):

> State reform strategies during the 1980s that did not include
> substantial efforts to improve the nature and quality of classroom

work have shown little success in raising achievement, especially
if the reforms relied primarily on student testing rather than
investments in teaching. For example, the two states to reorga-
nize their reforms around new student testing systems were
Georgia . . . and South Carolina . . . These states developed extensive testing systems coupled with rewards and sanctions
for students, teachers, and schools. Although both states man-
dated tests for teachers, they did not link these assessments to
emerging knowledge about teaching or to new learning standards, nor did they invest in improving schools of education or
ongoing professional development. (Darling-Hammond, 2000b,
pp. 14–15)

In comparing student achievement in geographically proxi-
mate states that used different strategies (Connecticut versus New
Jersey; North Carolina versus Georgia; and West Virginia versus
Virginia), Darling-Hammond concluded:

Although the states that have aggressively pursued investments
in teacher knowledge and skills have equal or higher levels of
student poverty than nearby states that pursued other distinc-
tively different strategies, their students now achieve at higher
levels. (Darling-Hammond, 2000b, p. 15)

It appears that the more successful states have indeed invested
in *capacity-building*, but I am going to conclude later that these are
really baby steps, more in line with what incentives will produce—
some degree of commitment and achievement, but not very deep.
Nonetheless, it is a start. A principal from Kentucky in Goertz's
(2000) study of local accountability in nine states puts it this way:

[The state assessment program] has probably been driving everything we've done. You can say you're doing it to raise students'
achievement. To be honest you're doing it because of accountability and assessment. I don't know if the whole accountability
piece with rewards and sanction is still the deal. It was at the
beginning. Now it's a matter of pride. Before, we didn't want
the scores to slip; now it's self-examination. Without the state
assessment, I don't think that would have come into play. We
may have been able to make some changes, maybe start some

good things. But the degree and speed we have changed never would have happened. (p. 12)

We can debate whether the side effects have been worse than the cure, or whether strong interventions were absolutely essential to get anywhere. McNeil (2000) takes the former position with respect to the standards involvement in Texas in talking about devastating "collateral damage" on the quality of teaching. Grissmer and Flanagan (1998), as summarized in Elmore (2000), take a different view about the events in that same state:

> [Grissmer and Flanagan] demonstrate that the achievement gains are, in fact, larger than one would predict based on performance of similar students in other states, and that the achievement gains seem to be occurring disproportionately among traditionally low-performing students. They offer as explanations for these gains a number of factors, including clearly stated content and performance standards, an incentive structure that focuses on the performance of all students, not just on average school performance, consistency and continuity of focus among political leaders, clear accountability processes, and a willingness to give flexibility to administrators and teachers in crafting responses to the accountability system. (Elmore, 2000, pp. 27–28)

In high-stakes states, however, most local leaders do not perceive much flexibility. Put another way, it takes an extraordinarily courageous principal to act flexibly under these conditions, and by definition this means only a small percentage will, even if invited on paper to do so.

In any case, I am willing to conclude that the combination of accountability and incentives produces results. The question is: At what price? And are they substantial, lasting results? I return to these questions in the concluding section.

Let us now turn the question on its head. What is the importance of external assistance and policy for school capacity? Recall the latest work of Newmann and colleagues, discussed in Chapter 8. They found that some schools had high capacity for reform, defined as individual skill and knowledge of teachers, professional learning communities, program coherence, availability of resources, and a school principal who helped develop the previous four factors. Of interest here, they also asked whether external assistance and external policy coordination at the district and state levels had contributed to the high-capacity schools. Essentially they found a weak relationship using *the standard of high capacity*; that is, external assistance and policy sometimes made partial contributions (and sometimes made matters worse) but were not formulated in a way that could help with comprehensive, schoolwide reform. Policy support thus remains at best potentially helpful.

We can also state this in another fashion. Schools and districts that have high capacity to begin with do take advantage of external policy and assistance (the rich get richer). High capacity schools and districts are less likely to toe the line with rigid impositions, more likely to take a risk when flexible options are available, and more likely to be resource-hungry when it comes to exploiting the larger infrastructure. High-capacity systems tend to take new policies seriously if the policies represent a wake-up call with respect to unmet goals or if they represent new resources to go further on goals already being pursued. Two conclusions stand out, however. First, only a minority of schools and districts have the confidence and competence—the capacity, if you like—to hold their own and then some in this kind of environment. Second, those that have low capacity are by definition vulnerable. Because they do not have the confidence, because they literally don't know what to do, they at best comply superficially to external demands.

The dilemma for well-intentioned governments is considerable. If they trust local entities to take policies seriously, to take advantage of resources, only a few will systematically do so. If they force the issue by increasing accountability, they foster cultures of superficial dependence.

These issues can be most fruitfully pursued by considering the case of the National Literacy and Numeracy Strategy (NLNS) in England.

THE CASE OF THE NATIONAL LITERACY AND NUMERACY STRATEGY

Here is the proposition: A new government comes into power in 1997 and the prime minister declares that his three priorities are "education, education, education." We have heard that before, but this government goes further. It says that the initial core goal is to raise the literacy and numeracy achievement up to age 11. The government sets specific targets. The base line they observe is that the percentage of 11-year-olds scoring 4 or 5 on the test of literacy was 57% in 1996 (level 4 being the level at which proficient standards are met); for numeracy the base line was 54%. The minister announces that the targets for 2002 are 80% for literacy (from 57) and 75% for numeracy (from 54). He makes a commitment that he will resign as Secretary of State if those targets are not met—a commitment that implicates 20,000 primary schools and 7 million students.

Further, the leaders of the initiative in the Department for Education and Employment set out to "use the change knowledge base" to design a pressure and support set of strategies to accomplish this remarkable feat. Finally, they know they are going to be watched carefully as this highly political and highly explicit initiative unfolds, and they add an external evaluation component. A team of us at University of Toronto are monitoring and assessing the entire NLNS strategy as it unfolds into the 1998–2002 period.

This is not the place to tell the full story (see Barber, 2000; Earl, Fullan, Leithwood, & Watson, et al., 2000), but the essence of it can be told in three brief parts: (1) the strategy, (2) its impact, and (3) lessons and question marks.

The Strategy

The main elements of the implementation strategy are summarized by Michael Barber, the head of the government initiative:

- A nationally prepared project plan for both literacy and numeracy, setting out actions, responsibilities, and deadlines through to 2002;
- A substantial investment sustained over at least 6 years and skewed toward those schools that need most help;
- A project infrastructure involving national direction from the Standards and Effectiveness Unit, 15 regional directions, and over 300 expert consultants at the local level for each of the two strategies;
- An expectation that every class will have a daily math lesson and daily literacy hour;

- A detailed teaching programme covering every school year for children from ages 5 to 11;
- An emphasis on early intervention and catch up for pupils who fall behind;
- A professional development programme designed to enable every primary school teacher to learn to understand and use the proven best practice in both curriculum areas;
- The appointment of over 2,000 leading math teachers and hundreds of expert literacy teachers, who have the time and skill to model best practice for their peers;
- The provision of "intensive support" to circa half of all schools where the most progress is required;
- A major investment in books for schools (over 23 million new books in the system since May 1997);
- The removal of barriers to implementation (especially a huge reduction in prescribed curriculum content outside the core subjects);
- Regular monitoring and extensive evaluation by our national inspection agency, OFSTED;
- A national curriculum for initial teacher training requiring all providers to prepare new primary school teachers to teach the daily math lesson and the literacy hour;
- A problem-solving philosophy involving early identification of difficulties as they emerge and the provision of rapid solutions or intervention where necessary;
- The provision of extra after-school, weekend, and holiday booster classes for those who need extra help to reach the standard. (Barber, 2000, pp. 8–9)

The Impact

The impact of the strategies on achievement, as a percentage of pupils reaching levels 4 or 5 is, in many ways, astounding (recall that 20,000 schools are involved). The whole country has progressively moved from 57% proficient achievement in literacy in 1996 to 75% in 2000; and from 54% to 72% in numeracy (see Table 13.1).

We have no doubt that the targets of 80% and 75% will be achieved by 2002.

TABLE 13.1 Percentage of 11-Year-Olds Achieving Level 4 or 5 on the National Tests for Literacy and Numeracy

	*Literacy	Numeracy
1996	57	54
1997	63	62
1998	65	59**
1999	70	69
2000	75	72

*   Reading increased substantially, while writing improved marginally
** A new mental arithmetic component was added

The evaluation framework we have developed to interpret these results is contained in Figure 13.1.

Lessons/Question Marks

We have already seen the many "policy levers" as summarized above by Barber. I particularly want to focus on what we call local challenges—motivation, capacity, situation. Motivation is the willingness to put effort into implementing the reform; capacity involves preexisting or newly developed skills and conceptions; situation is local context. In our interpretation, almost all of the gains can be attributed to an increase in *motivation*. In other words, the pressure and support strategies, the quality of materials, and so on influenced initially skeptical teachers to put effort into literacy and numeracy practices and the monitoring of results. The strategy has not been powerful enough to substantially affect "capacity." What the set of strategies did in effect was to mobilize *existing unfocused capacity* into an increased effort on literacy and numeracy; hence the results.

There are a number of direct question marks, and more substantial points to raise about the meaning of the NLNS strategy up to this point.

First, are the results real or are they a false representation of how well pupils can read, write, and enumerate? We believe, and heads of schools and teachers confirm, that these gains are valid.

FIGURE 13.1. The framework guiding the external evaluation. (From Earl, Fullan, Leithwood, & Watson, 2000, p. 4)

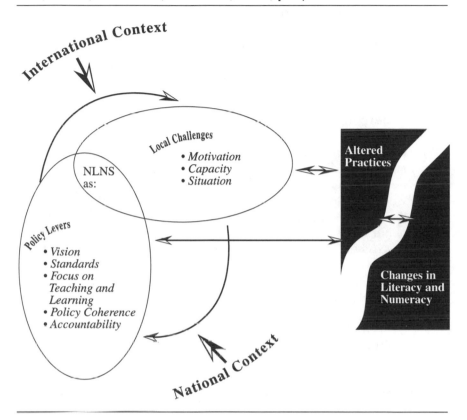

By and large, schools have adopted the strategy, have attended the training, have found the training to be very good, have welcomed the materials, and have begun to enjoy and value the methodology, not the least of which because it works.

Second, is there collateral damage—for example, other subjects being downplayed, burnout of teachers, neglect of special education students? The answer is, to some extent—although there is no direct evidence that NLNS is the culprit.

Third, is the larger infrastructure being aligned and mobilized to help? There are actually two aspects to this question: aspects of the infrastructure that are directly helpful or harmful; and aspects that are indirectly, yet powerfully connected. Barber (not using these terms) talks about both.

As to the direct supporting infrastructure, he says:

> While the overall strategy impacts directly on teaching, learning and student achievement, a series of other measures are designed to provide the necessary underpinning:
>
> - pre-school education has been introduced for all four year olds whose parents want it and for around 60 per cent of three year olds;
> - class sizes for 5, 6 and 7 year olds are being reduced to a maximum of 30 across the system;
> - learning mentors (school-based counsellors) are being provided to help remove barriers to learning outside school from thousands of primary age pupils in the disadvantaged parts of our large cities;
> - after-school and/or summer learning opportunities are being offered in over 25 per cent of primary schools;
> - campaigns, including government-funded television advertisements, have been run to promote parental support for reading and mathematics;
> - the National Year of Reading (in 1998–9) and Maths Year 2000 have opened up opportunities for businesses, community groups, library, churches and others to join the national crusade;
> - family literacy schemes are supporting parents whose own levels of literacy prevent them from assisting their children as much as they would like;
> - growing investment, year-on-year, is being made to provide extra assistance in literacy and maths for children whose first language is not English. (Barber, 2000, p. 11)

Barber then proceeds to talk about the chief components of the wider infrastructure, including:

- Transformation of Secondary Education (so that the growing success of the primary sector is built-on rather than dissipated);
- Excellence in Cities (so that community development occurs along with school development);

- Modernization of the Teaching Profession (so that quality people are attracted to and find rewarding the teaching profession);
- The Strengthening of Leadership (so that school leaders are nurtured, supported and otherwise developed) (Barber, 2000, p. 15).

We are still on the third point—the role of the larger infrastructure. The question is whether the infrastructure will get its act together so that it does no further harm, and indeed turns out to be helpful by coordinating policies, providing resources, and holding people accountable in a fair and reasonable way.

Fourth, is the pace of change—not only NLNS, but the other components just described—too overwhelming? Most principals and teachers think so. This is not an easy matter to get right. Problems are urgent, elections are on the horizon, the pace must be brisk. But is it at the expense of exhausting the system?

Fifth, are the changes deep and lasting? We don't think so. Don't get me wrong. The gains are real and they represent not a bad day's work—to get millions of pupils reading and engaged in numeracy. But they do not represent the kinds of transformation in teaching and learning that are being identified by cognitive scientists, or the closing of achievement gaps by disadvantaged groups (see Chapter 3). The gains are neither deep nor lasting because we don't have any evidence that the learning cultures in schools have been transformed. We don't, in other words, have any reason to believe that the professional learning communities we described in Chapters 7 and 8 are part and parcel of the strategy. Without the latter we will not see the problem-solving and internal commitment needed for substantial and continuous reform.

To summarize using the advance organizers I started with in this chapter, the government in England has moved beyond the accountability role to incorporate incentives. They have blended accountability and incentives effectively to produce gains in literacy and numeracy. They have not yet seriously acted on capacity-building, and they cannot do so effectively with the present strategies. Rather, the next stage of advance is the creation and fostering of learning communities where local schools evolve to leading their own destiny within a framework of accountability and support. I will discuss this further in a moment.

IMPLICATIONS

It is exceedingly difficult to combine accountability, incentives, and capacity-building, as evidenced by the fact that no government has ever done it effectively. It is complex and there are in-built tensions. It is easy to err in providing too much or too little control.

The main outlines at the general level are clear enough. Massell (1998) claims that the eight states in her sample shared four common capacity-building strategies: "building external infrastructure to provide professional development and technical assistance; professional development and training standards; providing curriculum materials, and organizing and allocating resources" (p. 3).

Recall from Chapter 5 the five lessons from the Education Commission of the States (ECS) (2000). Lesson three was "state education development support is key to long-term success," in which the authors report:

> In the last two years, an increasing number of state education agencies are doing the following:
> - Using comprehensive school reform to further their states' goals on accountability, standards, and assessments;
> - Developing long-term strategies to help schools implement comprehensive reform;
> - Helping districts and schools identify federal, state and district funding to support comprehensive reform;
> - Assisting schools in choosing comprehensive reform models that match their needs. (ECS, 2000, p. 12)

In *What's Worth Fighting for Out There*, Hargreaves and I offered five guidelines for governments:

> 1. *Invest in the Long Term*
>   In her impressive review of large scale social programmes, Schorr (1997) found that "successful programs have a long-term, preventive orientation, a clear mission, and continue to evolve over time." As hard as it is for politicians to do, if they are serious about reform, they must base their strategies on approaches that have

the best record of success educationally, not what is easy or popular politically. This means investing in the right long-term solutions that will make a difference, but that may not come to fruition before the next election. We have shown that early childhood education is one of the best investments there is, but its benefits are seen long after governments who introduce it have gone out of office. Most change strategies that make a difference in the classroom take five years or more to yield results—again, out of phase with most political election cycles. Governments must put educational investment beyond their own needs for political survival. By showing such integrity they may paradoxically gain greater political support.

2. *Go Beyond Left and Right*

Neither idealize conventional state bureaucracies of the past, nor overzealously embrace the idea of more market-like systems of school choice (with all their divisive consequences). Beyond the ideologies of left and right, the real issues are how can local level bureaucracies be agencies of support rather than interference and control for schools and parents? How can parents be offered choice within parameters that protect equity and diversity? How can school systems and collective agreements be made more flexible so schools can open up to and get more help from their communities without exploiting teachers or creating excessive insecurity for them? These are the real rather than rhetorical challenges of school system reorganization.

3. *Use Data for Improvement, not Embarrassment*

Ensure that assessment and accountability measures aren't used gratuitously or exploitatively to shame public education and create government pretexts for reorganizing it. How can data be contextualized fairly to present schools' performance in relation to the communities they serve? How can we hold schools accountable for how they improve over time (i.e., value-added measures of achievement) more than how they compare with schools in other very different communities? How can data be used as a spur to greater success rather than as a way to justify government's obsession with educational failure (which they then have an excuse to fix)?

4. *Put Capacity-Building Before Compliance*

Don't humiliate teachers for their alleged failures, or bluntly demand they do better—but actually invest time and resources in professional development and opportunities for collaboration (within a clearly defined framework of standards that teachers have helped develop themselves), so that teachers are provided with the means to improve over time. Capacity-building means helping teachers and communities to be able to respond effectively to changes that come their way and to improve continuously as a lifelong obligation so that standards will keep rising all the time. Compliance is about putting out fires (sometimes ones that governments have lit themselves). Capacity-building is about preventing fires occurring in the first place. No complex social reform has ever worked without investing in local capacity-building. If you want to spread and sustain good ideas, you have to spread the conditions that make good ideas effective, not just the ideas alone. These conditions pertain to local context, local relationships and local capacity.

5. *Deal with the Demographics*

Look at the age profile of the teaching force where, almost everywhere, huge cohorts of teachers are heading for retirement in the coming years and a massive renewal of the teaching force will be needed. You cannot attract high calibre people to a profession which has been subjected to unabated denigration and demoralization. Aside from early childhood development, the next best investment that governments can make is to use the next decade to help redefine and reinvigorate the teaching profession. Few policy initiatives will have greater long-term payoff than redesigning teacher education from the beginning to the end of the career (along with reculturing schools and their communities). (Hargreaves & Fullan, 1998, pp. 121–123)

It is evident, however, that these general guidelines are not sufficient. They are not compelling and powerful enough to cause new action. Rather, success for a government requires:

- ensuring sufficient resources and investment; revenue and capital;
- ensuring steady (and where necessary steadily growing) resources so that schools can plan improvement for the medium and long term;
- generating the public will which helps schools improve and sustains the willingness of people to pay the taxes necessary for high quality public education;
- providing a sense of direction, a set of priorities and a strategy
- creating the frameworks for the accountability of public services including education;

- placing education at the heart of a wider approach to social and economic renewal;
- implementing reform well and creating the capacity for deep and lasting change (M. Barber, personal communication).

What is needed now, I think, is a two-phased process that starts with accountability and incentives as phase one, and adds capacity-building in phase two. The criterion of success is *large-scale reform*, which makes a *deep difference*. Because of the forces of inertia in complex bureaucracies such as the public school system, assertive, intensive action by governments is needed up front. The reason that capacity-building strategies do not work in phase one is that you need capacity to build capacity; that is, if many schools and districts do not have capacity to begin with, capacity-building invitations will not, cannot, be taken up. To state it another way, let us say you are a leader in a government agency and you sincerely believe that professional learning communities are the answer, but you observe that not many schools are this good. The phase one conclusion, then, is that a more tightly controlled accountability/incentives set of strategies is needed to get the majority of schools on the move in dealing with urgent learning problems. The NLNS case in England—1998–2000 actions—is a strong example of this approach.

Phase one strategies are time-limited because you cannot get the deeper commitment and day-to-day creativity of teachers and others through tightly orchestrated centrally driven strategies, no matter how sensitive they become. Thus, as phase one becomes successful within its own terms, you have to build in more and more structures that work on capacity-building. In order to do this you need a very sophisticated conceptualization of how complex systems best solve problems—and this conceptualization must have practical, actionable steps associated with it.

Elmore's (2000) argument for building a new structure for school leadership is similar. In complex systems, he claims you need standards: a set of expectations for what students should know and be able to do, and a teaching force held accountable for its contribution to student learning. *But*, Elmore says, as I have been, that solving problems in complex systems is not accomplished by having great standards, but has to be addressed everyday as a continuous learning proposition:

> Instructional improvement requires continuous learning: Learning is both individual and a social activity. Therefore, collective learning demands an environment that guides and directs the acquisition of new knowledge about instruction. (Elmore, 2000, p. 20)

Capacity-building at its heart is a system of guiding and directing people's work, which is carried out in a highly interactive professional learning setting. All else is clutter. Policies need to be aligned to minimize distractions, and mobilize resources for continuous improvement. This is obviously a tall order, but failure to do it means that we will continue to have small-scale successes that even in the best cases have little likelihood of lasting.

A major part of this tall order is figuring out how to attract, prepare, and nurture the education force that can work in this new way. The preceding chapters have set the stage that will enable us to tackle this question more productively—the subject of Chapters 14 and 15.

CHAPTER 14

Professional Preparation of Teachers

The fact is that our primary value concerns our need to help ourselves change and learn, for us to feel that we are growing in our understanding of where we have been, where we are, and what we are about, and that we are enjoying what we are doing. . . . To help others to change without this being preceded and accompanied by an exquisite awareness of the process in ourselves is "delivering a product or service" which truly has little or no significance for our personal or intellectual growth.

—Sarason (1982, p. 122)

We have another 25%/75% problem. Twenty-five percent of the solution is attracting good people to the profession and providing them with the best possible initial preparation. This would be no mean feat, as solid teacher preparation programs are in the minority; 75% of the solution is ensuring that they have a place to work that enables them to learn on the job. This is a crucial and not very well understood distinction. Most macro strategies to improve the profession are *individualistic* in the sense that they try to generate more and more people with the skills, knowledge, and dispositions to do the things we have been talking about in this book. These strategies by themselves will never work.

Let us start with the five strategies for policymakers set out by the Education Commission of the States (ECS) in their new report *In Pursuit of Quality Teaching* (ECS, 2000):

Strategy 1

Ensure a diverse and high-quality approach to teacher preparation that involves solid K–12/postsecondary partnerships, strong field experience and good support for new teachers.

Strategy 2

Ensure that teacher recruitment and retention policies target the areas of greatest need and the teachers most likely to staff them successfully in the long run.

Strategy 3

Ensure that all teachers are able to participate in high-quality professional development so they can improve their practice and enhance student learning.

Strategy 4

Redesign teacher accountability systems to ensure that all teachers possess the skills and knowledge they need to improve student learning.

Strategy 5

Develop and support strong school and district leadership statewide focused on enhancing the quality of student learning and instruction. (ECS, 2000)

This is laudable, but it is not going to happen because the strategies won't produce what they set out to produce. It is not that the strategies are misguided but rather that they are under-guided. All five strategies focus on improving the skills, knowledge, and dispositions of individuals—teachers and leaders alike. What they don't do is address the core of school capacity—the reculturing we saw in a minority of schools in Chapters 7 and 8.

Elmore (2000) identifies the fatal flaw in these strategies:

Many well-intentioned reformers argue that large-scale improvement of schools can be accomplished by recruiting, rewarding, and retaining good people and releasing them from the bonds of bureaucracy to do what they know how to do ... What's missing in this view is any recognition that improvement is more a function of learning to *do the right thing in the setting where you work* than it is of what you know when you start to do the work. Improvement at scale is largely a *property of organizations*, not of the preexisting traits of the individuals who work in them.

Organizations that improve do so because they create and nurture agreement on what is worth achieving, and they set in motion the internal processes by which people progressively learn how to do what they need to do in order to achieve what is worthwhile. (Elmore, 2000, p. 25, emphasis in original, emphasis added for "in the setting where you work")

This is a very powerful insight and we need to be crystal clear about what it means. The logic goes like this:

1. We are trying to accomplish deeper learning in the new pedagogies of constructivism.
2. Students' and others' motivation depends on the quality of local context.
3. Problems are so complex and context-dependent to solve that they must be worked on all the time—this is fundamentally what is meant (but not understood except as a cliché) by the learning organization. Learning on the job is the sine qua non of improvement.
4. Better recruitment strategies and better ongoing professional development will *temporarily* increase motivation, but it will soon dissipate in the face of underdeveloped learning communities.
5. The more that people realize number four, the less likely they will be attracted in the first place, even though new policies offer incentives to enter teaching.

I am not saying don't pursue the five ECS strategies; I am saying they represent only about 25% of the solution, and the harder work is to change schools into learning *organizations*; that is, the policy considerations in Chapters 14 and 15 must be integrated with the strategies contained in previous chapters, especially Chapters 7–12.

With this in mind we can now delve into the problem and recent promise of the preparation, hiring, and induction of teachers.

THE PREPARATION OF TEACHERS

We did a review for the Ford Foundation of the Holmes Group, and more broadly teacher education covering the 1986–1996 decade. We entitled our report, not facetiously, *The Rise & Stall of Reform in Teacher Education* (Fullan, Galluzzo, Morris, & Watson, 1998). The 1986–1996 decade started with great fanfare. In 1986 the Holmes Group—an alliance of 100 major research universities dedicated to joining with schools in order to produce deep improvements in the education of teachers—produced its first book, *Tomorrow's Teachers.* The Carnegie Forum released its report at the same time— *A Nation Prepared: Teachers for the 21st Century* (Carnegie Forum, 1986). In that very year, Sarason and his colleagues published a second edition of their 1962 book, *The Preparation of Teachers: An Unstudied Problem in Education* (Sarason, Davidson, & Blatt, 1986), noting that the relationship between the preparation of teachers and the realities they experience in their careers is a question "as unstudied today—as superficially discussed today—as in previous decades" (p. xiv).

Especially for the Holmes Group, the next 5 years following 1986 was a period of great excitement, considerable debate, and activity concerning the reform of teacher education. This period encompassed the release of *Tomorrow's Schools* (Holmes Group, 1990), the second in the Holmes Group trilogy. Over the next 4 or 5 years, however, the intensity of the debate began to wane. The energy and enthusiasm of those working on the complex problems of implementing reform on behalf of the group had been heavily taxed. During these years, the Holmes Group collective entered a phase of soul-searching, realizing that it was losing ground. In particular, the period 1993–1995 was one where we witnessed the loss of momentum. It was a time when the Holmes Group faced the question of what must be done to recapture and revitalize an agenda that had barely begun. By the time the third monograph— *Tomorrow's Schools of Education*—was released in 1995, the initial momentum for reform had become more diffuse.

Why do even the best attempts fail? It is a big problem primarily related to the fact that most societies do not treat teacher education as a serious endeavor. As we said in *Rise & Stall*, society has failed its teachers in two senses: it gives teachers failing grades for not producing better results; at the same time, it does not help improve the conditions that would make success possible.

Despite the rhetoric about teacher education in today's society, there does not seem to be a real belief or confidence that investing in teacher education will yield results. Perhaps deep down many leaders believe that teaching is not all that difficult. After all, most leaders have spent thousands of hours in the classroom and are at least armchair experts. And they know that scores of unqualified teachers are placed in classrooms every year and required to learn on the job. In addition, investing in teacher education is not a short-term strategy. With all the problems facing us demanding immediate solutions, it is easy to overlook a preventative strategy that would take several years to have an impact. When a crisis occurs, you have to deal with it. A course of action that is aimed at preventing a crisis, despite being much less expensive in the mid to long term, is much harder to come by.

The problem begins with teacher preparation programs. Howey and Zimpher's (1989) detailed case studies of six universities in the United States enabled them to generate key attributes that would be necessary for program coherence, which they find lacking in existing programs, factors such as:

- Programs based on clear conceptions of teaching and schooling;
- Programs that have clear thematic qualities;
- Faculty coalescing around experimental or alternative programs that have distinctive qualities;
- Working with student cohort groups;
- Adequate curriculum materials and a well-conceived laboratory component;
- Articulation between on-campus programming and field-based student teaching;
- Direct linkage to research and development knowledge bases;
- Regular program evaluation.

Goodlad and his associates (1990) are even more damning in their comprehensive investigation of 29 universities. Among their main findings:

1. The preparation programs in our sample made relatively little use of the peer socialization process employed in some other fields of professional preparation. There were few efforts to organize incoming candidates into cohort groups or to do so at some later stage. Consequently, students' interactions about their experiences were confined for the most part to formal classes (where the teaching is heavily didactic). The social, intellectual, and professional isolation of teachers, so well described by Dan Lortie, begins in teacher education. This relatively isolated individualism in preparation seems ill-suited to developing the collegiality that will be demanded later in site-based school renewal.

2. The rapid expansion of higher education, together with unprecedented changes in academic life, have left professors confused over the mission of higher education and uncertain of their role in it. Although the effects of these changes in academic life transcend schools and departments, the decline of teaching in favor of research in most institutions of higher education has helped lower the status of teacher education. In regional public universities, once normal schools and teachers colleges, the situation has become so bad that covering up their historic focus on teacher education is virtually an institutional rite of passage. Teaching in the schools and teacher education seem unable to shake their condition of status deprivation.

3. There are serious disjunctures in teacher education programs: between the arts and sciences portion and that conducted in the school or department of education, from component to component of the so-called professional sequence, and between the campus-based portion and the school-based portion. . . . It is also clear from our data that the preparation underway in the programs we have studied focused on *classrooms* but scarcely at all on *schools*.

4. Courses in the history, philosophy, and social foundation of education . . . have been seriously eroded (pp. 700–701).

As the momentum for reform in teacher education receded in the mid-1990s, along came the National Commission on Teaching and America's Future (NCTAF, 1996). The commission found:

- In recent years, more than 50,000 people who lack the training required for their jobs have entered teaching annually on emergency or substandard licenses. [In 1990–1991, 27.4 percent of all newly hired teachers in the nation had no or substandard emergency licenses.]

- Nearly one-fourth (23 percent) of all secondary teachers do not have even a college minor in their main teaching field. This is true for more than 30 percent of mathematics teachers.
- Among teachers who teach a second subject, 36 percent are unlicensed in the field and 50 percent lack a minor.
- 56 percent of high school students taking physical science are taught by out-of-field teachers, as are 27 percent of those taking mathematics and 21 percent of those taking English. The proportions are much higher in high-poverty schools and in lower track classes.
- In schools with the highest minority enrollments, students have less than a 50 percent chance of getting a science or mathematics teacher who holds a license and a degree in the field he or she teaches. (1996, pp. 15–16)

The litany of problems, although familiar, is dramatically disturbing:

1. Low expectations for student performance;
2. Unenforced standards for teachers;
3. Major flaws in teacher preparation;
4. Painfully slipshod teacher recruitment;
5. Inadequate induction for beginning teachers;
6. Lack of professional development and rewards for knowledge and skills;
7. Schools that are structured for failure rather than success .(NCTAF, 1996, p. 24)

All this from a commission friendly to the teaching profession! When John Goodlad read the draft of *The Rise & Stall*, he was aware of the new momentum from NCTAF and his own National Network of Educational Renewal. He thought perhaps the title should be altered to "The Rise, Stall, and Rerise of Teacher Education Reform." There is some truth to this, but we prefer to leave the jury out until we see how the 1996–2006 decade plays itself out. Society has never yet sustained an interest in teacher education reform, and until it does there is no chance for meaningful education improvement.

But where are we in the year 2000? Recall the starting point. Most teacher education programs are not coherent within the university campus let alone between the university and the school. Even in content terms the teacher education contains huge gaps—

how to work with parents, assessment literacy vis-à-vis the standards movement, constructivists' pedagogies, understanding diversity, learning to be collaborative—the very things needed to work in professional learning communities.

Recently research and program development (still in the minority of cases) are providing pressure and positive role models for the future. I start with the case for teacher expertise:

> Teacher expertise—what teachers know and can do—affects all the core tasks of teaching. What teachers understand about content and students, for example, shapes how judiciously they select from texts and other materials and how effectively they present material in class. Teachers' skill in assessing their students' progress also depends on how deeply teachers know the content and how well they understand and interpret student [work]. Nothing can fully compensate for the weakness of a teacher who lacks the knowledge and skills needed to help students master the curriculum. (Darling-Hammond & Ball, 1999, pp. 1–2)

NCTAF reviewed all the studies they could find on the relationship between teacher qualification and student learning. Two studies in particular provide a good summary of these results. First, Ferguson (1991) found that teacher expertise (as measured by teacher education, licensing, examination scores, and experience) accounted for a large variation in student achievement (over 40%). Second, Greenwald, Hedges, and Laine (1996) reviewed over 60 studies and found that teacher education and teacher ability, along with small schools and lower teacher-pupil ratios, are associated with significant increases in student achievement. In investment terms, the authors display achievement gains by type of investment, finding that "increasing teacher education" is a major component.

Pushing further, Darling-Hammond and Ball (1999) found that "teacher knowledge of subject matter, student learning and development, and teaching methods are all important elements of teacher effectiveness" (p. 3); and that, "teachers who are fully prepared and certified in both their discipline and in education are more highly rated and more successful with students than are teachers without preparation, and those with greater training are found to be more effective than those with less" (pp. 3–4). With respect to the latter, the commission's review found that "graduates of five or six year programs that include an extended internship tied to coursework are more successful and more likely to enter and remain in teaching than graduates of traditional undergraduate programs" (p. 4).

What should a strong teacher education program look like? Darling-Hammond and her colleagues identified and conducted case studies of seven exemplary teacher education programs—defined as programs that have a consistently high reputation among those hiring their graduates (Darling-Hammond, 2000b, c, d). The following quotes capture the reputation:

> When I hire a Trinity graduate I know [he or she] will become a school leader. These people are smart about curriculum, they're innovative. They have the torch (principal);
>
> I'd grab all the Trinity graduates for jobs [if I could]. They have both a depth of content knowledge and the ability to continue to learn (superintendent);
>
> Integrating new teachers into the staff from Alverno is so much easier, because of their high ability to be self-reflective, their personally wide experiences with performance assessment . . . and their ability to apply critical research bases to their classroom experiences (principal);
>
> They are highly collegial, unafraid to seek out all they need to know from mentors and staff around them (principal);
>
> I had a very challenging classroom with many diverse needs in my first year of teaching. I feel that because of my education at Wheelock, I was able to be successful (graduate).

Darling-Hammond (2000b) concluded that all seven programs, while different in number of design ways, had six common features:

- a common, clear vision of good teaching that is apparent in all coursework and clinical experiences;
- well-defined standards of practice and performance that are used to guide and evaluate coursework and clinical work;
- a curriculum grounded in substantial knowledge of child and adolescent development, learning theory, cognition, mo-

tivation, and subject matter pedagogy, taught in the context of practice;

- extended clinical experiences (at least 30 weeks) which are carefully chosen to support the ideas and practices presented in simultaneous, closely interwoven coursework;
- strong relationships, common knowledge, and shared beliefs among school- and university-based faculty; and
- extensive use of case study methods, teacher research, performance assessments, and portfolio evaluation to ensure that learning is applied to real problems of practice. (p. x)

These components are congruent with our own redesign of teacher preparation at the University of Toronto. The traditional 5th-year program (8 months, September to April) on top of a 4-year bachelor of arts degree has consistently been evaluated as inadequate. We have now replaced this program with two streams: one is an extended 1-year program (September to June, including a new 6-week internship); the other is a 2-year masters of teaching program, which includes a major internship in the 2nd year. An evaluation of a 2-year pilot program with 100 students in comparison to the 1-year program showed that student teachers in the 2-year program felt significantly more prepared in their 1st year of teaching and were judged by employers as more prepared. We are now following these teachers in their first years of teaching to see how they fare.

In addition to the intellectual component of teacher education, we and others have also focused on "the moral purpose" of teaching, as well as on the kinds of partnerships that will interrelate teacher education and school improvement. Teachers are "moral change agents" in the sense that they are committed to making a difference in the life chances of students, and making a difference means being effective at bring about change (Fullan, 1993; see also Cochran-Smith, 1998; Smylie, Bay, & Tozer, 1999).

The design features of how to organize teacher education programs are also critical. Much work needs to be done on linking Arts and Science to Teacher Education (Goodlad, 1994). At the University of Toronto we have been especially interested in integrating university work with schoolwork. As much as possible, we prefer to work with cohorts of students (30 to 60), teams of instructors (university- and school-based leaders), and clusters of partner schools. We prefer the term "partner schools" to "professional development schools" (PDSs) because the latter are too few in number to help with large-scale reform. The best way of characterizing the school-university partnerships is to say that in these arrangements, schools become just as committed to teacher education as to school improvement; and universities become just as committed to school improvement as they are to teacher education. If a whole district is using teacher education as a strategy for reform, it can make a substantial difference.

Backing up all this work in several states, provinces, and countries is the expansion of standards requirements. There are three sets of *interrelated* standards that are being developed—those pertaining to teacher education programs, to the licensing of new teachers, and to the continuous professional development of teachers (a fourth set, as we will see in Chapter 15, applies to school principals and other leaders).

We need to get ahead of ourselves here in order to frame these developments. In the United States, the National Board for Professional Teaching Standards (NBPTS), which we will discuss in Chapter 15, was the catalyst for focusing on ongoing professional development, and for backward mapping in turn, to frame requirements for beginning teachers and for teacher education programs. The assessment of what "teachers need to know and be able to do" involves a variety of methods to profile teachers' work with students, knowledge of subject, expertise in student assessment, and their own professional development. NCTAF had argued that:

> Standards for teaching are the lynchpin for transforming current systems of preparation, licensing, certification, and ongoing development so that they better support student learning. [Such standards] can bring clarity and focus to a set of activities that are currently poorly connected and often badly organized. . . . Clearly, if students are to achieve high standards, we can expect no less from their teachers and from other educators. Of greatest priority is reaching agreement on what teachers should know

and be able to do to teach to high standards. (NCTAF, 1996, p. 67)

The NBPTS has organized its assessment around five major propositions:

1. Teachers are committed to students and their learning;
2. Teachers know the subject they teach and how to teach those subjects to students;
3. Teachers are responsible for managing and monitoring students' learning;
4. Teachers think systematically about their practice and learn from experience;
5. Teachers are members of learning communities. (NBPTS, 1993)

The new Standards of Practice from the Ontario College of Teachers is similar; it is organized around five components:

1. Commitment to students and learning;
2. Professional knowledge;
3. Teaching practice;
4. Leadership and community;
5. Ongoing professional development.

Of course, these are just words, and we will get to their implementation import later. In the meantime, there is policy pressure on schools of education, and better frameworks of assessment to guide their work. I cannot say that there is a great deal of *capacity-building* going on beyond the minority of universities that are taking special initiatives (much the same problem, as I observed earlier, occurs when only a minority of schools and districts are engaged in substantial reform—it is an infrastructure problem).

To understand the themes of the previous chapters is to understand that revamping initial teacher preparation is part and parcel of any solution. You cannot develop professional learning communities if you have a weak foundation to begin with. It is easy to see why one might be tempted to give up on initial teacher education. The cultures of universities represent huge barriers to reform (for positive examples, see Thiessen & Howey, 1998); and more elementary and secondary schools than not are powerful but *negative* socializing agents in this equation.

The biggest barrier, however, is that initial teacher education is always an afterthought in any reform effort. The critical shortage of teachers and the growing research knowledge base that having "three good teachers in a row" can determine a student's life is causing new (and nervous) attention to be paid to the whole area of teacher education reform. We could even safely observe that we are witnessing a "rise, stall, and rerise" phenomenon. It won't go anywhere this time either unless it receives intensive development work in its own right, and unless it is closely integrated with and congruent with other parts of the solution, like how to hire and support beginning teachers.

HIRING AND INDUCTION

It should be abundantly clear by now that learning to teach effectively takes time, and the way in which one gets started on the job dramatically effects the rest of one's career, including driving out potentially good teachers in the early years.

The issues for policymakers are substantive and costly, as the following examples illustrate:

Of 600 students who enter a large four-year teacher education program early in their college years, only 180 complete the program, and only 72 actually get placed in teaching jobs. Of these, about 30 or 40 remain in the profession several years later. (NCTAF, 1996, p. 34)

Darling-Hammond (1999) has gathered a considerable amount of data from across the United States on the attrition rates for beginning teachers. She concludes that at least 30% of new teachers leave within 5 years of entry. The rate is considerably higher for teachers in disadvantaged districts. The rate is also higher where there are no supports—orientation or induction programs—in place for beginning teachers.

Hiring practices themselves, combined with the presence or absence of induction programs, is an indication, usually negative, of whether teaching is a worthwhile, developmental profession. New York City is one of the large cities where hiring practices bring a high proportion of unqualified teachers into the system. In 1992, only one third of new teachers hired in New York were fully qualified. Yet the problem in New York had less to do with a lack of supply, and more to do with poor hiring procedures; a study by the New York Education Priorities Panel discovered that a substantial number of well-qualified new recruits were dissuaded from looking for work in New York City by excessively bureaucratic application procedures, inability to get information, inability to speak to hiring officers, and long delays.

New York has taken these criticisms to heart, and has changed hiring processes. Darling-Hammond (1999) reports that the city has undertaken the following initiatives to improve their hiring practices:

- bring city recruiters directly to students in local preparation programs each spring;
- offer interviews and tests on-site at college campuses;
- recruit teachers in high-need areas like bilingual and special education through scholarships, forgivable loans, and strategically located recruitment fairs;
- work with universities and local districts to bring well-trained prospective teachers into hard-to-staff schools as student teachers, interns, and visitors;
- make offers to well-qualified candidates much earlier in the year;
- streamline the exchange of information and the processing of applications. (Darling-Hammond, 1999, p. 21)

The result of these initiatives is that by 1997, two thirds of new teachers had full qualifications when they were hired; in absolute terms, this is still a poor record, but the improvement from 1992 is significant.

The value of improving hiring and support practices is evident in New Haven, Connecticut, a school district that has made a remarkable turnaround in the last 2 decades. The district has brought about dramatic improvements by focusing on improving the quality of their teachers through a combination of recruitment, standards, development, and school organization. A key element in this strategy has been the development of recruitment strategies that target good teachers, and which uses a process of support and assessment to work with beginning teachers over the first 2 years of their careers, to ease them into the profession, and to provide support for their development. The district's recruitment strategy is to catch the interest of exceptional teachers, and then invest in resources to hire and keep such people in the system:

> New Haven does not have large-scale recruitment crises annually because of the low attrition rate in their new and experienced teachers. . . . Clearly, one of the major recruitment efforts is the district's internship program; 38 of 80 [newly hired teachers] had worked as part-time interns in the district internship program. (Snyder, 1999, p. 13)

Darling-Hammond (1999) also reports that a number of districts (Cincinnati, Columbus, and Toledo, Ohio; and Rochester, New York) "have reduced attrition rates of beginning teachers by more than two-thirds (often from levels exceeding 30% to rates of under 5%) by providing expert mentors with release time to coach beginners in their first year on the job. These young teachers not only stay in the profession at higher rates, but become competent more quickly than those who must learn by trial and error" (p. 20).

In California, the state has introduced a Beginning Teacher Support and Assessment program (BTSA) to support teachers in the first 2 years of their careers. A formative assessment program has been designed as a structure for a beginning teacher to work with a mentor over his or her first 2 years. This structure includes mechanisms such as classroom observations, portfolios, and self-assessment. It integrates a process of assessment throughout the 2-year induction period, in tandem with the state's system of teacher evaluation. This program was implemented in 1998, so it is too early to evaluate its impact; that said, preliminary responses from participants are very positive.

As in California, more and more jurisdictions are developing standards of practice for beginning teachers. The National Board standards referred to above have been "backward mapped" to guide the work of the Interstate New Teacher Assessment and Support Consortium (INTASC):

> [INTASC is] a consortium of 33 states working together on "National Board-compatible" licensing standards and assessments for beginning teachers both before they enter teaching and during their first two years on the job. This effort, in time, has informed the work of the National Council for Accreditation of Teacher Education (NCATE) which has recently incorporated the performance standards developed by INTASC for judging preservice teacher education programs. (Darling-Hammond, 2000b, p. 10)

All in all promising, but one can see how very far we have to go. If most schools and districts are not good learning organizations (or good professional learning communities) this means they are not good employers. They are especially not good employers for teachers who want to make a difference. In sheer quantitative terms, having a 30% or more attrition rate in the first 5 years, when by changing practices you could reduce it to 5%, doesn't make good business sense. In quality terms, if you want improvement you have to attract talented people, and then foster their collective development on the job from day one. Indeed, if you do the latter you are more likely to attract good people in the first place.

Better teacher preparation, hiring, and induction is not a set of structural reforms. We are talking about reculturing the teaching profession as a whole. Thus, the ideas in this chapter must not stand alone. They must flow with continuous professional development throughout the career, which turns out to have more to it than we thought.

CHAPTER 15

Professional Development of Educators

A profession is not created by certificates and censures but by the existence of a substantive body of professional knowledge, as well as a mechanism for improving it, and by a genuine desire of the profession's members to improve their practice.
—Stigler and Hiebert (1999)

Let's get one thing straight from the start. Professional development is not about workshops and courses; rather, it is at its heart the development of habits of learning that are far more likely to be powerful if they present themselves day after day. To define the problem we need to return to the themes we pursued in earlier chapters. In their observations of the Chicago Public Schools (CPS), Smylie and colleagues (1999) remind us:

> Only about one-third of teachers in the system engage in regular dialogue about instruction. One-quarter work in schools where teachers and administrators disagree about school goals and norms of practice. Half fail to see any real coherence and continuity across programs in their schools. Most believe that their schools have so many programs coming and going that they cannot keep track of them all.
>
> Given these situations, it is not surprising that approaches to improvement in many schools lack coherence. In the early 1990s, 31 to 39 percent of CPS elementary schools had unfocused approaches to school improvement. Another 20 to 35 percent had more coherent approaches but these could not be considered systemic. More recent evidence of fragmentation has been found

in a study of the Chicago Annenberg Challenge. Among the major challenges to school improvement reported by principals and external partners was the lack of coherence among multiple programs and innovations at their schools. These data indicate that multiple programs often compete for teachers' time and attention, pull faculties in different directions, and limit teachers' ability to fully participate in any program. (p. 39)

The question, then, is what set of policies and practices stand a chance of changing this deeply ingrained dysfunctional culture. The answer is that it will take a set of policies based on standards of new practice, combined with opportunities to learn new ways of working together. In arguing for a set of standards that would provide guidance and direction, Elmore (2000) makes this key observation:

People make these fundamental transitions by having *many* opportunities to be exposed to the ideas, to argue them into their own normative belief systems, to practice the behaviors that go with these values, to observe others practicing those behaviors, and, most importantly, to be successful at practicing in the presence of others (that is, to be seen to be successful). In the panoply of rewards and sanctions that attach to accountability systems, the most powerful incentives reside in the face to face relationships among people in the organization, not in external systems. (p. 31)

We must also realize that it is not collaboration per se that counts. Collaboration is powerful, which means that people can do powerfully wrong things together. McLaughlin and Talbert (2001), it will be recalled, found that some strong high school communities reinforced traditional teaching and ended up failing large proportions of students. Collaboration only makes a difference when it is focused on student performance for all, and the associated innovative practices that can make improvement happen for previously disengaged students.

We can now take a closer look at where we should be going. First, we will need to build on the valuable work already underway, which formulates new standards of practice and provides corresponding development mechanisms. Second, we need to embed strategies in the day-to-day work of teachers. Third, we need to identify, nurture, and support school leadership that focuses on the first two requirements. In short, we need to reculture the entire teaching profession.

STANDARDS OF PRACTICE

Most professional development experiences for teachers fail to make an impact. Over 20 years ago I conducted a review of "in-service," as it was then called, and concluded that one-shot workshops were ineffective, topics were selected by people other than those receiving the in-service, and follow-up support for implementation was rare (Fullan, 1979). Almost 15 years later, Little (1993) drew the same conclusion, adding that "the dominant training model of teachers' professional development—a model [at best] focused . . . on expanding an individual repertoire . . . of skills—is not adequate to the ambitious visions of teaching and schooling embedded in present reform initiatives" (p. 129). Reform initiatives, as I concluded earlier, are even more ambitious now, both in depth and in terms of being large scale.

Enter new standards of practice, themselves more ambitious. I referred in the previous chapter to the work in the United States of the National Board of Professional Teacher Standards (NBPTS). NBPTS has developed standards and assessment procedures in 30 subject matter disciplines, organized around five major propositions. The five domains, stated here in full, are:

1. *Teachers are committed to students and their learning*
   National-Board certified teachers are dedicated to making knowledge accessible to all students. They treat students equitably, recognizing individual differences. They adjust their practice based on observations and knowledge of their students' interests, abilities, skills, knowledge, family circumstances, and peer relationships. They understand how students develop and learn. They are aware of the influence of context and culture on behavior. They develop students' cognitive capacity and their respect for learning. Equally important, they foster students' self-esteem, motivation, character, civic responsibility and their respect for individual, cultural, religious and racial differences.

2. *Teachers know the subject they teach and how to teach those subjects to students*

   National-Board certified teachers have a rich understanding of the subject(s) they teach and appreciate how knowledge in their subject is created, organized linked to other disciplines and applied to real world settings. Accomplished teachers command specialized knowledge of how to convey and reveal subject matter to students. They are aware of the preconceptions and background knowledge that students typically bring to each subject and of strategies and instructional materials that can be of assistance. Their instructional repertoire allows them to create multiple tasks with knowledge, and they are adept at teaching students how to pose and solve their own problems.

3. *Teachers are responsible for managing and monitoring students learning*

   National-Board certified teachers create instructional settings to capture and sustain the interest of their students and to make the most effective use of time. Accomplished teachers command a range of instructional techniques, know when each is appropriate, and can implement them as needed. They know how to motivate and engage groups of students to ensure a purposeful learning environment, and how to organize instruction to allow the schools' goals for students to be met. They understand how to motivate students to learn and how to maintain their interests even in the face of temporary failure. Board certified teachers regularly assess the progress of individual students as well as that of the class as a whole. They employ multiple methods for measuring student growth and understanding and can clearly explain student performance to parents.

4. *Teachers think systematically about their practice and learn from experience*

   National-Board certified teachers exemplify the virtues they seek to inspire in students—curiosity, tolerance, honesty, fairness, respect for diversity and appreciation of cultural differences— and the capacities that are prerequisites for intellectual growth: the ability to reason and take multiple perspectives, to be creative and take risks, and to adopt an experimental and problem-solving orientation. Striving to strengthen their teaching, Board certified teachers critically examine their practice, seek the advice of others, and draw on educational research and scholarship to expand their repertoire, deepen their knowledge, sharpen their judgement and adapt their teaching to new findings, ideas and theories.

5. *Teachers are members of learning communities*
National-Board certified teachers contribute to the effectiveness of
the school by working collaboratively with other professionals on
instructional policy, curriculum development and staff development. They can evaluate school progress and the allocation of
school resources in light of their understanding of state and local
educational objectives. They are knowledgeable about specialized
school and communities resources that can be engaged for their
students' benefit, and are skilled at employing such resources as
needed. Accomplished teachers find ways to work collaboratively
and creatively with parents, engaging them productively in the
work of the school. (NBPTS, 1993)

By the end of 2000, NBPTS had certified over 5,000 teachers with
over 100,000 more expected in the next decade. Because the program is at the early stages, the research base is not yet developed.
What is available is encouraging:

Teachers report that the process of analyzing their own and their
students' work in light of standards enhances their abilities to
assess student learning and to evaluate the effects of their own
actions. (Darling-Hammond, forthcoming, p. 15)

In an early pilot study of the portfolio in the Stanford Teacher
Assessment Project, "teachers reported that they improved their practice as they pushed themselves to meet specific standards that had
previously had little place in their teaching" (Darling-Hammond,
forthcoming, 15). In a more detailed study, Bond, Smith, Baker, and
Hattie (2000) found that NBPTS-certified teachers were more expert
than non-certified teachers, and that they were "producing students
who differ in profound and important ways from those taught by
less proficient [non-Board-certified] teachers" (p. x).
The NBPTS standards are being used in more and more states.
Seventeen states have agreed to accept National Board certification
as the basis for granting a license to out-of-state teachers or as a
basis for the "recertification" of experienced teachers. Moreover,

Eight [states] have agreed to offer higher salaries to teachers
successful in achieving certification. School districts like Cincinnati, Ohio and Rochester, New York have incorporated standards
into teacher evaluation criteria, using it as one basis for recogni-

tion as "leader teachers" who mentor others and as a basis for salary increments in a performance-based compensation schedule. (Darling-Hammond, forthcoming, p. 22)

Similar developments are underway in England, Canada, and other jurisdictions. What these systems do is to make standards explicit and then enable teachers to develop a portfolio of evidence based on their professional knowledge and practice both inside and outside of the classroom. The portfolios are then assessed by trained experts according to a set of standards. These schemes are by and large voluntary, although increasingly they are becoming requirements (for beginning teachers, for example) and are being heavily encouraged through the use of incentives and expectations that all teachers should move toward advanced certification.

All of this leads to the thorny area of recertification, performance-based compensation, and the like. Certainly individual merit pay, career ladders, and similar schemes have failed miserably. Odden (1996) cites research from a wide variety of American sources, describing the unsuccessful efforts throughout the 20th century to implement these mechanisms. He concludes that such attempts, designed for manufacturing industries, were inappropriate for a system that does not produce discrete products. He recommends that a new system of rewards and career paths be designed to meet the needs of the education system as it exists today.

We believe that the emerging evidence points to building a system of standards-based assessment for beginning teachers as well as standards of practice to guide continuous learning throughout their careers. Forms of teacher compensation would be linked to the scheme. For example, beginning teachers would be awarded their license to teach; threshold teachers should receive an increase in salary (as in the British plan, and in some jurisdictions, for the NBPTS system); more experienced teachers could receive professional development monies, stipends, and release time for mentoring and other leadership roles, and so on. Even performance pay for school improvement could be considered, if carefully developed, and indeed is in place in some jurisdictions (see, for example, Odden, 2000; Urbanski & Erskine, 2000).

In a similar vein, Odden (2000) lays out a framework for teacher compensation focusing on "tools for assessing the knowledge and skills" of (1) beginning teachers, (2) mid-career teachers, and (3) experienced teachers, with corresponding forms of compensation.

Without a doubt, standards of practice policies are providing a powerful avenue for the professional development of teachers; but alas, at best they promote the skills, knowledge, and dispositions of *individuals*. We also need to work on the much harder task of reculturing schools as professional learning *organizations*.

RECULTURING SCHOOLS

To be effective, even the best set of "standards of practice" must be evident in the daily organization and culture of schools. We now have a good idea of what this means. Elmore and Burney (1999) describe successful professional development as

- Focusing on concrete classroom applications of general ideas;
- Exposing teachers to actual practice rather than descriptions;
- Providing opportunities for group support and collaboration; and
- Involving deliberate evaluation and feedback by skilled practitioners.

In a later work, Elmore (2000) notes:

Experimentation and discovery can be harnessed to social learning by connecting people with new ideas to each other in an environment in which the ideas are subjected to scrutiny, measured against the collective purposes of the organization, and tested by the history of what has already been learned and is known. (p. 25)

Similarly, Ball and Cohen (1999) lay out a set of principles and strategies for a "practice-based theory of professional education," as does Ingvarson (1998). McLaughlin and Talbert (2001) also conclude that new policies are required to provide focused occasions for on-the-job dialogue about specific practices.

Stigler and Hiebert (1999) drew the same conclusion after their video analysis of German, Japanese, and American teachers. Compared to Japanese teachers, American teachers do not have habits of learning from each other's practice by continuously improving what they know and can do:

> To do more than improve teaching in their own classrooms, to raise the standard of good teaching within the profession—this demands that teachers work together, sharing what they learn in their classrooms to help one another learn even more. It demands that they assume responsibility for building the professional knowledge base. (Stigler & Hiebert, 1999, p. 146)

It is easy to err in one or another direction—either to assume that accountability standards will solve the problem of poor teaching; or to argue for teacher networks as the route to improvement. The two must be organically integrated. School systems that improve do just that:

> [These systems] have succeeded in getting people to *internalize* the expectations of standards-based accountability systems, and they have managed this internalization largely through modeling commitment and focus using face to face interactions, not bureaucratic controls. (Elmore, 2000, p. 31)

In sum, new policies that promulgate high standards of practice for all teachers invite the possibility of large-scale reform. A corresponding set of policies are required to create many opportunities, in fact requirements, for people to examine together their day-to-day practice. It is through local problem-solving with expanded horizons that new solutions can get identified and implemented. This represents a huge cultural change for schools and as such it is going to require sophisticated new leadership.

THE ROLE OF LEADERSHIP

A front page article in the January 12 issue of *Education Week* is headlined, "Policy Focus Converges on Leadership." Its first two paragraphs commence:

> After years of work on structural changes—standards and testing and ways of holding students and schools accountable—the education policy world has turned its attention to the people charged with making the system work.

> Nowhere is the focus on the human element more prevalent than in the recent recognition of the importance of strong and effective leadership. (Policy Focus Converges on Leadership, 2000, p. 1)

The article quoted above goes on to observe, "Principals Wanted: Apply Just About Anywhere." The same could be said about the superintendency. Leadership has become a thankless and undoable task under present circumstances. If we want effective school leaders we must make it possible for them to develop the capacities to do the job, and to align other policies to make the job possible and rewarding. We do know that individual principals are often the key agents of school success, that there is little direct preparation for the role or systematic professional development on the job, and that there is no research evidence that links particular professional development to success on the job. It seems obvious, however, that systems parallel to teacher development must be developed for school leaders. In other words, standards for school principals and related assessment and development should be pursued. In the United States, there is such a system being developed. The Interstate Leaders Licensure Consortium (ISLLC) has established a comprehensive set of standards for principals, and roughly 200 indicators that help define those standards. Their six standards are as follows (Murphy, Yff, & Shipman, in press):

1. A school administrator is an educational leader who promotes the success of all students by facilitating the development, articulation, implementation, and stewardship of a vision of learning that is shared and supported by the school community;
2. A school administrator is an educational leader who promotes the success of all students by advocating, nurturing, and sustaining a school culture and instructional program conducive to student learning and staff professional growth;
3. A school administrator is an educational leader who promotes the success of all students by ensuring management of the organization, operations, and resources for a safe, efficient and effective learning environment;

4. A school administrator is an educational leader who promotes the success of all students by collaborating with families and community members, responding to diverse community interests and needs, and mobilizing community
   resources;
5. A school administrator is an educational leader who promotes the success of all students by acting with integrity,
   fairness and in an ethical manner;
6. A school administrator is an educational leader who promotes the success of all students by understanding, responding to, and influencing the larger political, social, economic,
   legal and cultural context. (Murphy et al., in press, pp. 7–8).

The consortium has linked these standards to professional development and training, licensure, and assessment for school leaders. So far, this program has been adopted by 16 states, either in
full or in part, and it is under consideration in another 18 states.
There is no evidence yet of the effects of this initiative, but a program
focusing on standards of practice for leaders shows promise for
the future.

Similarly, in England the success of the large-scale reform literacy, numeracy, and other dimensions that we analyzed in Chapter
13 is seen to depend on the strengthening of school leadership.
Barber (2000) summarizes the strategy:

> The framework for school improvement, with its emphasis on
> schools themselves taking responsibility for their own destiny,
> puts a high premium on leadership. It may be a simplification
> to say that the difference between success and failure is the
> quality of the principal but it is not far from the truth. In the
> turnaround of failing schools for example a change of principal
> has been necessary in around 75 per cent of cases. The systemic
> problem is clear. The people currently in, or on the brink of
> leadership positions, have been promoted expecting to adminis-
> ter the traditional education system. Only to reach the top and
> find it in a process of radical transformation. Their careers have
> prepared them to manage a system which no longer exists. In-
> stead of managing stability they have to lead change. In place of
> an emphasis on smooth administration, they find an unrelenting
> focus on pupil outcomes.

Our tasks as a government are to attract and develop a new generation of school leaders and to enable the present generation to adapt to this radically new and demanding world.

To do so we have:

- created a new qualification for aspiring principals (the National Professional Qualification for Headship) which sets new standards and combines workplace learning with scholarship;
- provided all newly appointed headteachers with a £2000 voucher to spend on professional development, invited them every year to a spectacular conference in London and linked them to an online learning community in which they can debate among themselves and with internationally-known education experts;
- established a new qualification for mid-career principals (the Leadership Programme for Serving Heads) which requires them to engage in vigorous, externally validated self-assessment;
- announced the intention to establish a new National College for School Leadership which will become operational later this year, have a new state of the art building on a university campus, develop an online as well as traditional presence, and will link our school principals to leaders in other sectors and their peers in other countries;
- worked with business to provide business mentors for thousands of school principals;
- improved principals' pay and capacity to earn performance bonuses;
- created a new leadership tier in each school;
- established a £50 million fund to enable the removal or a retirement of principals who are not ready for the new challenge. (pp. 15–16; see also the Department for Education and Employment, 1999; Watkin, 2000)

To use the language of Chapter 13, we are almost at prephase one when it comes to school leadership. I noted that we need accountability, incentives, and capacity-building, and that phase one success (which combines accountability and incentives) can achieve some valuable but still relatively superficial results. Phase two work is capacity-building *on the job* and as such requires highly interactive, purposeful, well-led sets of activities. Elmore and Burney's description of District 2 strategies provides a good example:

In District 2 [there] is heavy reliance on peer networks and visits to other sites, inside and outside the district, designed to bring teachers and principals into contact with exemplary practices. Intervisitation, as it is called in the district, and peer consultations are routine parts of the district's daily life. Teachers often visit other classrooms in conjunction with consultants' visits, either to observe one of their peers teaching a lesson or a consultant teaching a demonstration lesson. And groups of teachers often visit another school, inside or outside the district, in preparation for the development of a new set of instructional practices. Usually principals initiate these outside visits and travel with teachers.

In addition principals engage in intervisitations with peers in other schools. New principals are paired with "buddies," who are usually more senior administrators, and they often spend a day or two each month in their first two years in their buddy's school. Groups of teachers and principals working on district initiatives travel to other districts inside and outside the city to observe specific instructional practices. And monthly district-wide principals' meetings are held on site in schools, and often principals observe individual teachers in their peers' schools as part of a structured agenda for discussing some aspect of instructional improvement. Principals are encouraged to use visits and peer advising as management strategies for teachers within their buildings. (Elmore & Burney, 1999, p. 276)

They return to the underlying principle:

Leadership must create conditions that value learning as both an individual and collective good. Leaders must create environments in which individuals expect to have their personal ideas and practices subjected to the scrutiny of their colleagues, and in which groups expect to have their shared conceptions of practice subjected to the scrutiny of individuals. Privacy of practice produces isolation; isolation is the enemy of improvement. (Elmore & Burney, 1999, p. 20)

Let us not be misled by this renewed focus on the principal. We are really talking about teacher leadership in two senses. First, if teachers are not learning to be collaborative from day one in their careers, there won't be enough qualified candidates for the principalship as just described. Second, and more fundamentally, just as policymakers can't solve day-to-day problems, superinten-

dents or principals cannot really "solve" specific instructional problems:

> The closer policy gets to the instructional core—how teachers
> and students interact around content—the more that policymak-
> ers . . . become dependent on the knowledge and skills of prac-
> titioners to mold and shape the instructional core. (Elmore, 2000,
> p. 26)

TO RECREATE A PROFESSION

If you read this book carefully, the biggest revolution I am talking
about is *changing the teaching profession*. If you examine the underlying message of even the most supportive government commissions
on teaching, you are compelled to conclude that teaching as a
profession has not yet come of age. It needs reform in recruitment,
selection, status and reward, redesign of initial teacher education
and induction into the profession, continuous professional development, standards and incentives for professional work, and (most
important of all, perhaps) changes in the daily working conditions
of teachers. Yet there appears to be little political will to launch
sustained reforms in teacher development and in the organization
of the teaching profession more widely.

As teachers work more and more with people beyond their
own schools, a whole gamut of new skills, relationships, and orientations are fundamentally changing the essence of their professionalism. This new professionalism is collaborative, not autonomous;
open rather than closed; outward-looking rather than insular; and
authoritative but not controlling.

More than anything, the new professionalism makes huge demands on teachers' own learning—learning how to keep modifying
and extending their teaching as research discovers more and more
about children's learning styles, multiple intelligences and ways
of understanding; learning how to integrate new technologies into
their classrooms; and learning how to interact effectively with
adults "out there" to deepen their understandings of and get more
support for the students they teach. Some of this learning will need
to be undertaken in preservice teacher education, when teachers

first learn to teach. But in a complex environment, where demands change relentlessly and teachers may work for 30 or 40 years beyond their preservice training, the learning can't stop there. Nor can the learning be "packaged" into brief workshops and structured courses.

Teachers of today and tomorrow need to do much more learning on the job, or in parallel with it—where they can constantly test out, refine, and get feedback on the improvements they make. They need access to other colleagues in order to learn from them. Schools are poorly designed for integrating learning and teaching on the job. The teaching profession must become a better learning profession—not just incidentally, at teachers' own individual initiatives, but also in the very way the job is designed.

The problem is that it is easy to miss how very deep this change is in the culture of teaching. In recognizing that standards (for teacher education programs, for beginning and continuing teachers, for administrators) are needed, it is tempting to make them the solution. There is too much to know and to keep knowing for external standards to carry the day.

It is also tempting under the pressure of shortage to have high standards but to relax their implementation, ending up with the most disadvantaged students having uncredentialled, ill-prepared teachers. Policies do make a difference but only when they are well implemented, as Darling-Hammond (2000a) and her colleagues document so well.

Finally, I hope it is obvious that leadership must come from many sources. The teacher in a collaborative culture who contributes to the success of peers is a leader; the mentor, the grade-level coordinator, the department head, the local union representative are all leaders if they are working in a professional learning community. Our sixth and last guideline for teachers in *What's Worth Fighting For Out There* is "Help to Recreate Your Profession" (Hargreaves & Fullan, 1998, p. 102). This will become possible only if many teacher-leaders, along with administrators, are backed by (propelled by?) a strong framework of policy and practice standards.

Rise, stall, rise, stall—is this a perpetual cycle or is there something qualitatively different this time?

CHAPTER 16

The Future of Educational Change

The future isn't what it used to be.

—Anonymous

Two ships have been passing in the night, stopping occasionally to do battle, in the dark. One is named Accountability, the other Professional Learning Community. Both have evil twins. One is called Name and Shame and the other Navel Gazing. The future of educational change is very much a matter of whether these two ships will learn to work through the discomfort of each other's presence until they come to respect and draw on each other's essential resources.

Both accountability (standards-based reform) and professional learning communities are in their relatively early stages of development. They both need some further refining, but it is more than a linear matter. They must team up—a nonlinear proposition—because they need each other to get the job done. Standards-based reform will never be able to get internal commitment and ingenuity from local educators from a distance. Those committed to learning communities will never evolve if left on their own.

The lessons in this book are contained in each chapter. The invitation for each reader is threefold: (1) get a better understanding of your own role, and be liberated by the insights and possibilities for growth you see in the most successful examples; do not self-limit; (2) work hard at understanding the situation of other roles with which you have the most contact, and alter your approach to them accordingly. Empathy does not mean agreement, but it is an essential component of any strategy that depends on developing the new relationships necessary for success; (3) as difficult as it seems, get a sense of "the big picture." Place your work in the context of society. If there ever was a societal function that has global consequences for humankind, it is the education of us all.

There are six other overall lessons arising from the new ideas of educational change discussed in this book:

Lesson One—Meaning has More Meaning Than We Thought
Lesson Two—You Can't Get There From Here
Lesson Three—Understand the Sequence
Lesson Four—"Learning Organization" is More than a Cliché
Lesson Five—Outward Identity and the Convergence of the Personal and Social
Lesson Six—Learn to Live with Change

Twenty years ago, *The Meaning of Change* had a one-level message: if people don't find meaning in reform it can never have an impact. There is now much more comprehensive confirmation of this stance. Cognitive scientists have made it powerfully clear that learning is meaning-making that requires a radically new way of approaching learning—one that guides the development of individual minds through many minds working together. The theory of change itself has taken on new meaning in what I called the 25/75 rule. Twenty-five percent of the solution is having good directional ideas; 75% is figuring out how to get there in one local context after another.

Just as learning will go nowhere if educators do not have a deep theoretical understanding of the first principles of learning, improvement will not happen if leaders and others do not have a deep theoretical grasp of the first principles of change. Theories of pedagogy and theories of change must be integrated again and again in each action setting.

Lesson two is a warning that existing strategies will not get us to where we need to go, if we want large-scale, lasting reform. In this sense the research can be misleading. If research shows, for example, that successful schools have school principals with "vision," it would be wrong to think that getting more principals with vision is the answer (or if you prefer, it would be wrong to think that you could multiply their numbers). The answer to large-scale reform is not to try to emulate the characteristics of the minority who are getting somewhere *under present conditions*; if the conditions stay the same we will always have only a minority who can persist (for short periods of time) against many odds. Rather, we must change existing conditions so that it is normal and possible for a majority of people to move forward.

Lesson three is, understand the sequence of large-scale reform. Again we can easily be mislead by research findings. To know that standards-based reform combined with incentives increases literacy and numeracy scores is deadly if the conclusion is that we should do more of the same. To know that teachers thrive best in learning communities is also fatal if you pursue a strategy based on that assumption, when the starting point is that only 20% of teachers and principals have the capacity to act that way.

I do think that the sequence, given our starting point of low capacity, and given the urgent problems in schools, is to fast-track phase one by pushing hard on standards, providing quality materials and examples of practice, and aligning the incentive system of accountability and professional development to focus on selected priorities. As phase one begins to get results, it is necessary to shift to what I have called a capacity-building strategy, in which the larger policy system focuses on preparing educators prior to and on the job for context-based solutions, which by definition require local problem-solving. In this sense, phase one is precapacity-building, and phase two builds on this base with different strategies. I do not mean that it is simply linear. There will be phase two people at phase one, and vice versa. And the phases should certainly overlap. But the emphasis that I have placed on the flow of large-scale reform from tighter to looser forms of control (from external to internal commitment) seems more likely to move us forward. In effect, the system shifts from control to direction and guidance (see Elmore, 2000).

Lesson four is that "learning organization" is more than a cliché. The phrase "learning organization" is one of the most used and most superficially understood terms in the change business. How many of us have read a book or article on the learning organization, agreed with everything we read, and then had no clue about what to do? I think here is where the new insights of cognitive scientists and organization theorists converge. Just as the former have discovered that learners must learn in context (because of their individuality and the uniqueness of their situations), the latter have concluded that improvement only occurs in context (again individual and setting uniqueness).

So, what is the real reason why learning organizations are required? The answer is contained in Elmore's (2000, p. 25) phrase, "improvement is . . . a function of learning to do the right thing *in the setting where you work*" (emphasis added). Ultimately, no amount of outside intervention can produce the motivation and specificity of best solutions for every setting. This is confirmed by Nonaka and Takeuchi's (1995) study of successful Japanese companies. They explain that the most successful companies were not successful due to their manufacturing prowess or human resource practices and the like, but rather because of their skills and expertise at "organizational knowledge creation," which they define:

> By organizational knowledge creation we mean the capability of a company as a whole to create new knowledge, disseminate it throughout the organization, and embody it in products, services and systems. (p. 3) (see also Von Krogh, Ichijo, & Nonaka, 2000).

Let us be absolutely clear:

1. People in each and every setting must work together to figure out what is needed as they "set in motion the internal process by which people progressively learn how to do what they need to do in order to achieve what is worthwhile" (Elmore, 2000, p. 25);
2. You cannot get such internal commitment and ingenuity, or more accurately context-specific expertise, from the outside;
3. The only problems worth solving are the ones that exist in each and every organization;
4. These days, organizations are constantly facing internal and external change forces. Put another way, problems don't stay solved, so you have to learn to do the right thing over and over again.
5. Ergo, the learning organization.

The reason that professional learning communities are essential is that they *are* learning organizations, as described in the above five points. They do interact to produce shared commitment and they constantly worry about what is worthwhile and how to get there. Because of their purposeful interactions, they are organically suited to converting tacit knowledge to explicit (shared, definable, learnable) knowledge on an ongoing basis. They are energy and knowledge creators—exactly what a learning organization is, and precisely what is needed to make change meaningful and substantial.

Lesson five raises the question of the collective good. Advocates of school reform cannot be blamed for being impatient with the excruciatingly slow pace of reform. For some the alternative to get action is a market model in which public money is dispensed directly to consumers to purchase education based on their preferences (see Elmore, 2000). This model has some merit; it is efficient; it allows for choice; it generates competition. However, it radically misses two fundamental matters. The first one is that a strong public school system and a strong democracy are closely connected. Education, of all societal functions, has a strong moral component. There are deep theoretical and evolutionary reasons to believe that society will be stronger if education serves to enable people to work together to achieve higher purposes that serve both the individual and the collective good (Fullan, 1999, pp. 11–12). Second, we can only move forward by learning from each other's successes and failures as they occur. Incidentally, this is one of the criticisms of charter schools up to this point. They foster individual success (or failure), but there are no built-in mechanisms for sharing the lessons being learned (in fact, the opposite is encouraged).

Lesson five, then, is that "outward identity" is the route to both personal and social betterment. The line of thinking goes like this:

1. Large-scale change cannot be achieved if teachers identify only with their own classrooms, and are not similarly concerned with the success of other teachers and the whole school.
2. Large-scale change cannot be achieved if principals identify only with their own school, and are not similarly concerned with the success of other principals and schools in the district.

3. Large-scale change cannot be achieved if school districts identify only with their own district, and are not similarly concerned with the success of other districts.
4. Large-scale change cannot be achieved if individual states identify only with their own states, and are not similarly concerned with the success of other states and the country as a whole. And so on.

More than this, small-scale improvement will not last if we do not identify with and help improve the surrounding system. Thus, we have both selfish and altruistic reasons for wanting to see the overall system get better.

Lesson six—learn to live with change—means taking change less and more seriously at the same time. Less, because most change is superficial, more fanfare than substance. We need not worry as much as we do about most change. Taking change more seriously means that we buy into the 25/75 rule. Working through the complexities of change until we get shared meaning and commitment is the only way to get substantial improvement. The best defense against the relentless pace of change is to build professional learning communities that are good at sorting out the worthwhile from the nonworthwhile, and are sources of support and healing when ill-conceived or random change takes its toll.

This book has been a very long journey into complex space. We have seen that there is a deep reciprocity between personal and social (shared) meaning. One contributes to the other, both are weakened in the absence of the other. The ultimate goal of change is when people see themselves as shareholders with a stake in the success of the system as a whole, with the pursuit of meaning as the elusive key.

References

Allison, D. J. (1988). *Ontario directors and American superintendents: A study of contrasting cultures and contexts*. London, Ontario, Canada: Division of Educational Policy Studies, University of Western Ontario.

American Institutes of Research. (1999). *An educators' guide to school-wide reform*. Washington, DC: Author.

Argyris, C. (2000). *Flawed advice and the management trap*. New York: Oxford University Press.

Ashton, P., & Webb, R. (1986). *Making a difference: Teachers' sense of efficacy and student achievement*. New York: Longman.

Baker, P., Curtis, D., & Benenson, W. (1991). *Collaborative opportunities to build better schools*. Bloomington, IL: Illinois Association for Supervision and Curriculum Development.

Ball, D., & Cohen, D. (1999). Developing practice, developing practitioners: Towards a practice-based theory of professional education. In L. Darling-Hammond & G. Sykes (Eds.), *Teaching as the learning profession* (pp. 3–32). San Francisco: Jossey-Bass.

Barber, M. (2000). *High expectations and standards*. Unpublished paper. London: Department for Education and Further Employment.

Bender Sebring, P., & Bryk, A. (2000, February). School leadership and the bottom line in Chicago. *Phi Delta Kappan, 81*(6), 440–443.

Bennett, B., & Rolheiser, C. (2001). *Beyond Monet: The artful science of instructional integration*. Ajax, Ontario, Canada: Bookation Publishers.

Berger, P., & Luckmann, T. (1967). *The social construction of reality*. New York: Anchor Books.

Berman, P. (1980). Thinking about programmed and adaptive implementation: Matching strategies to situations. In H. Ingram & D. Mann (Eds.), *Why policies succeed or fail* (pp. 205–227). Beverly Hills, CA: Sage.

Berman, P., & McLaughlin, M. (1977). *Federal programs supporting educational change: Vol. 7. Factors affecting implementation and continuation*. Santa Monica, CA: Rand Corporation.

Berman, P., & McLaughlin, M., with Pincus, J., Weiler, D., & Williams,

R. (1979). *An exploratory study of school district adaptations*. Santa Monica, CA: Rand Corporation.

Bertelsmann Foundation. (1996). *Innovative school systems in an international comparison*. Gütersloh, Germany: Author.

Block, P. (1987). *The empowered manager*. San Francisco: Jossey-Bass.

Block, P. (1999). *Flawless consulting* (3rd ed.). San Francisco: Jossey-Bass.

Blumberg, A. (1985). *The school superintendent: Living with conflict*. New York: Teachers College Press.

Bodilly, S. (1998). *Lessons from New American Schools' Scale-up phase*. Santa Monica, CA: Rand Corporation.

Bodilly, S., & Berends, M. (1999). *Necessary district support for comprehensive school reform*. Cambridge, MA: Harvard Civil Rights Project.

Bond, L., Smith, T., Baker, W., & Hattie, J. (2000). *The certification system of the National Board for Professional Teaching Standards*. Greensboro: Center for Educational Research and Evaluation, The University of North Carolina at Greensboro.

Bowles, S., & Gintis, H. (1976). *Schooling in capitalist America*. New York: Basic Books.

Boyd, W. (1978). The changing politics of curriculum policy making for American schools. *Review of Educational Research, 48*(4), 577–628.

Boyle, A. (2000). *Turning failing school systems around: Intervention in inverse proportion to success*. London: Leannta Education Associates.

Bransford, T., Brown, A., & Cocking, K. (Eds.). (1999). *How people learn: Bridging research and practice*. Washington, DC: National Academy Press.

Bridge, G. (1976). Parent participation in school innovations. *Teachers College Record, 77*(3), 366–384.

Brighouse, T., & Woods, D. (1999). *How to improve your school*. London: Routledge.

Brown, S., & Eisenhardt, K. (1998). *Competing on the edge*. Boston: Harvard Business School Press.

Bryk, A., Sebring, P., Kerbow, D., Rollow, S., & Easton, J. (1998). *Charting Chicago school reform*. Boulder, CO: Westview Press.

Bussis, A., Chittenden, E., & Amarel, M. (1976). *Beyond surface curriculum*. Boulder, CO: Westview Press.

Carnegie Council on Adolescent Development. (1989). *Turning points: Preparing youth for the 21st century*. New York: Carnegie Corporation of New York.

Carnegie Forum on Education and the Economy. (1986). *A nation prepared: Teachers for the 21st century*. Report of the Task Force on Teaching as a Profession. New York: Author.

Cervone, B., & McDonald, J. (1999). *Preliminary reflections on the Annenberg challenge.* Providence, RI: Brown University Press.

Charters, W., & Jones, J. (1973). *On the neglect of the independent variable in program evaluation.* Unpublished paper. Eugene: University of Oregon.

Clark, D., Lotto, S., & Astuto, T. (1984). Effective schools and school improvement: A comparative analysis of two lines of inquiry. *Educational Administration Quarterly, 20*(3), 41–68.

Cochran-Smith, M. (1998). Teaching for social change: Towards a grounded theory of teacher education. In A. Hargreaves, A. Lieberman, M. Fullan, & D. Hopkins (Eds.), *International handbook of education change* (pp. 895–915). Dondrecht, The Netherlands: Kluwer Academic Publishers.

Cohen, D. (1998). Dewey's problem. *The Elementary School Journal, 98*(5), 427–446.

Coleman, J. (1990). *Foundations of social theory.* Cambridge, MA: Harvard University Press.

Coleman, P. (1998). *Parent, student and teacher collaboration: The power of three.* Thousand Oaks, CA: Corwin Press.

Consortium of Education Change. (2000). *Annual report.* Oakbrook Terrace, CA: Author.

Cowden, P., & Cohen, D. (1979). *Divergent worlds of practice.* Cambridge, MA: Huron Institute.

Daft, R., & Becker, S. (1978). *The innovative organization: Innovation adoption in school organizations.* New York: Elsevier North-Holland.

Danzberger, P., Carol, L., Cunningham, L., Kirst, M., McCloud, B., & Usdan, M. (1987). School boards: The forgotten players on the education team. *Phi Delta Kappan, 68*(1), 53–59.

Darling-Hammond, L. (1999). *Solving the dilemmas of teacher supply, demand, and standards.* New York: Columbia University, National Commission on Teaching and America's Future.

Darling-Hammond, L. (2000a). Teacher quality and student achievement: A review of state policy evidence. *Education Policy Analysis Archives, 8*(1), 1–32.

Darling-Hammond, L. (Ed.). (2000b). *Studies of excellence in teacher education: Preparation in undergraduate years.* Washington, DC: American Association of Colleges of Teacher Education.

Darling-Hammond, L. (Ed.). (2000c). *Studies of excellence in teacher education: Preparation in a five-year program.* Washington, DC: American Association of Colleges of Teacher Education.

Darling-Hammond, L. (Ed.). (2000d). *Studies of excellence in teacher educa-*

tion: Preparation at the graduate level. Washington, DC: American Association of Colleges of Teacher Education.

Darling-Hammond, L. (in press). *Reshaping teaching policy, preparation and practice: Influences of The National Board for Professional Teaching Standards*. Washington, DC: National Partnerships for Excellence and Accountability in Teaching.

Darling-Hammond, L., & Ball, D. (1999). *Teaching for high standards: What policymakers need to know and be able to do*. Philadelphia: CPRE, National Commission on Teaching for America's Future.

Datnow, A. (2000). Implementing an externally developed school restructuring design. *Teaching and Change, 7*(2), 147–171.

Datnow, A., & Stringfield, S. (2000). Working together for reliable school reform. *Journal of Education for Students Placed at Risk, 5*(1 & 2), 183–204.

Dauber, S. L., & Epstein, J. L. (1989, April). *Parents' attitudes and practices of involvement in inner-city elementary and middle schools*. Paper presented at the annual meeting of the American Educational Research Association.

Day, C., Harris, A., Hadfield, M., Toley, H., & Beresford, J. (2000). *Leading schools in times of change*. Buckingham, England: Open University Press.

Department for Education and Employment. (2000). *Leadership programme for serving headteachers*. London: Author.

Dodd, A., & Konzal, J. (1999). *Making our high schools better*. New York: St. Martin's Press.

Dolan, P. (1994). *Restructuring our schools*. Kansas City: Systems and Organizations.

Donaldson, G. (2001). *Cultivating leadership in schools: People, purpose, and practice*. New York: Teachers College Press.

Donovan, M. S., Bransford, J. D., & Pellegrino, W. (Eds.). (1999). *How people learn: Bridging research and practice*. Washington, DC: National Academy Press.

Drucker, P. (1985). *Innovation and entrepreneurship*. New York: Harper & Row.

Dryden, K. (1995). *In school*. Toronto: McClelland Publications.

Duke, D. L. (1988). Why principals consider quitting. *Phi Delta Kappan, 70*(4), 308–313.

Earl, L., & Lee, L. (1999). Learning for change: School improvement as capacity building. *Improving Schools, 3*(1), 30–38.

Earl, L., Fullan, M., Leithwood, K., Watson, N., with Jantzi, D., Levin, B., & Torrance, N. (2000). *Watching & learning: OISE/UT evaluation of the implementation of the National Literacy and Numeracy Strategies*.

London: Report commissioned by the Department for Education and Employment.

Education Commission of the States. (1999). *Comprehensive school reform: Five lessons from the field*. Denver: Author.

Education Commission of the States. (2000). *In pursuit of quality teaching*. Denver: Author.

Education Trust. (1999). *Dispelling the myth: High poverty schools exceeding expectation*. Washington, DC: Author.

Edu-Con. (1984). *The role of the public school principal in the Toronto board of education*. Toronto, Ontario, Canada: Edu-Con of Canada.

Elmore, R. (1995). Getting to scale with good educational practice. *Harvard Educational Review, 66*(1), 1–26.

Elmore, R. (2000). *Building a new structure for school leadership*. Washington, DC: The Albert Shanker Institute.

Elmore, R., & Burney, D. (1999). Investing in teacher learning. In L. Darling-Hammond & G. Sykes (Eds.), *Teaching as the learning profession* (pp. 236–291). San Francisco: Jossey-Bass.

Epstein, J. L. (1986). Parents' reactions to teacher practices of parent involvement. *Elementary School Journal, 86*(3), 277–294.

Epstein, J. L. (1988). Effects on student achievement of teachers' practices for parent involvement. In S. Silvern (Ed.), *Literacy through family, community, and school interaction*. Greenwich, CT: JAI Press.

Epstein, J. (1995). School/family/community partnerships. *Phi Delta Kappan, 76*, 701–712.

Epstein, J., Coates, L., Salinas, K., Sanders, M., & Simon, B. (1997). *School, family and community partnerships: Your handbook for action*. Thousand Oaks, CA: Corwin.

Epstein, J. L., & Dauber. S. L. (1988, April). *Teacher attitudes and practices of parent involvement in inner-city elementary and middle schools*. Paper presented at the annual meeting of the American Sociological Association.

Epstein, J., & Sanders, M. (2000). Connecting home, school and community. In M. Hallinan (Ed.), *Handbook of the sociology of education* (pp. 285–306). New York: Kluwer/Plenum.

Evans, C. (1995). Leaders wanted. *Education Week*.

Ferguson, R. (1991, Summer). Paying for public education: New evidence on how and why money matters. *Harvard Journal on Legislation, 28*, 465–498.

Firestone, W., Rosenblum, S., & Bader, B. (1992). Recent trends in state educational reform. *Teachers College Record, 94*(2), 254–277.

Fullan, M. (1979). *School-focused in-service education in Canada*. Report prepared for the Centre for Educational Research and Innovation (O.E.C.D.), Paris.

Fullan, M. (1985). Change process and strategies at the local level. *The Elementary School Journal, 84*(3), 391–420.

Fullan, M. (1991). *The new meaning of educational change.* New York: Teachers College Press.

Fullan, M. (1993). *Change forces: Probing the depths of educational reform.* London: Falmer Press.

Fullan, M. (1997). *What's worth fighting for in the principalship?* (2nd ed.). Toronto, Ontario, Canada: Elementary Teachers Federation of Ontario; New York: Teachers College Press.

Fullan, M. (1999). *Change forces: The sequel.* Philadelphia: Falmer Press/ Taylor & Francis Inc.

Fullan, M. (2000a). The return of large scale reform. *The Journal of Educational Change, 1*(1), 1–23.

Fullan, M. (2000b, June 23). Infrastructure is all. *London Times Education Supplement, 19,* p. 15.

Fullan, M. (2001). *Leading in a culture of change.* San Francisco: Jossey-Bass.

Fullan, M. (forthcoming). *Change forces with a vengeance.* London: Falmer Press.

Fullan, M., Alberts, B., Lieberman, A., Zywine, J., & Kilcher, A. (1996). *Report of the Country Expert Commission, Canada/United States of America.* Gütersloh, Germany: Carl Bertelsmann Foundation.

Fullan, M., & Eastabrook, G. (1973). *School change project.* Unpublished report, Ontario Institute for Studies in Education, Toronto, Ontario, Canada.

Fullan, M., Eastabrook, G., & Biss, J. (1977). The effects of Ontario teachers' strikes on the attitudes and perceptions of grade 12 and 13 students. In D. Brison (Ed.), *Three studies of the effects of teachers' strikes* (pp. 1–170). Toronto, Ontario, Canada: Ontario Ministry of Education.

Fullan, M., Galluzzo, G., Morris, P., & Watson, N. (1998). *The rise & stall of teacher education reform.* Washington, DC: American Association of Colleges for Teacher Education.

Fullan, M., & Hargreaves, A. (1992). *What's worth fighting for?: Working together for your school.* Toronto, Ontario, Canada: Elementary Teachers Federation of Ontario; New York: Teachers College Press.

Fullan, M., Park, P., Williams, T., Allison, P., Walker, L., & Watson, N. (1987). *Supervisory officers in Ontario: Current practice and recommendations for the future.* Toronto, Ontario, Canada: Ontario Ministry of Education.

Fullan, M., & Pomfret, A. (1977). Research on curriculum and instruction implementation. *Review of Educational Research, 47*(1), 335–397.

Galbraith, J. (1996). *The good society.* Boston: Houghton Mifflin.

Gallimore, R., & Goldenberg, C. (2001, March). Analyzing cultural models and settings to connect minority achievement and school improvement research. *Education Psychologist.*

Gardner, H. (1999). *The disciplined mind.* New York: Simon & Schuster.

Gaynor, A. (1977). A study of change in educational organizations. In L. Cunningham (Ed.), *Educational administration* (pp. 28–40). Berkeley, CA: McCutcham.

Gitlin, A., & Margonis, F. (1995). The political aspect of reform. *The American Journal of Education, 103,* 377–405.

Goertz, M. (2000, April). *Local accountability: The role of the district and school in monitoring policy, practice and achievement.* Paper presented at the annual meeting of the American Educational Research Association.

Gold, B., & Miles, M. (1981). *Whose school is it anyway?: Parent-Teacher conflict over an innovative school.* New York: Praeger.

Goldenberg, C. (in press). *Settings for school change: Improving teaching and learning.* New York: Teachers College Press.

Goldhammer, K. (1977). Role of the American school superintendent. In L. Cunningham et al. (Eds.), *Educational administration* (pp. 147–164). Berkeley, CA: McCutchan.

Goleman, D. (1995). *Emotional intelligence.* New York: Bantam Books.

Goleman, D. (1998). *Working with emotional intelligence.* New York: Bantam Books.

Goleman, D. (2000, March–April). Leadership that gets results. *Harvard Business Review,* 78–90.

Goodlad, J. (1984). *A place called school: Prospects for the future.* New York: McGraw-Hill.

Goodlad, J. I. (1990). *Teachers for our nation's schools.* San Francisco: Jossey-Bass.

Goodlad, J. (1994). *Educational renewal: Better Teachers, better schools.* San Francisco, CA: Jossey Bass.

Goodlad, J., Klein, M., & Associates. (1970). *Behind the classroom door.* Worthington, OH: Charles Jones.

Greenwald, R., Hedges, L., & Laine, R. (1996, Fall). Interpreting research on school resources and student achievement: A rejoinder to Hanushek. *Review of Educational Research, 66*(3), 411–416.

Grissner, D., & Flanagan, A. (1998). *Exploring rapid achievement gains in North Carolina and Texas.* Washington, DC: National Educational Goals Panel.

Gross, N., Giacquinta, J., & Bernstein, M. (1971). *Implementing organiza-*

tional innovations: A sociological analysis of planned educational change. New York: Basic Books.

Grove, A. (1996). *Only the paranoid survive.* New York: Doubleday.

Haney, N. (forthcoming). *Teacher summary on the impact of TAAS test on teaching and learning.* Unpublished analysis, College Center for the Study of Testing, Boston.

Hargreaves, A. (1994). *Changing teachers, changing times: Teachers' work and culture in the postmodern age.* London: Cassell; New York: Teachers College Press.

Hargreaves, A., & Fullan, M. (1998). *What's worth fighting for out there.* New York: Teachers' College Press; Toronto, Ontario, Canada: Elementary School Teachers' Federation; Buckingham, UK: Open University Press.

Hatch, T. (2000). *What happens when multiple improvement initiatives collide.* Menlo Park, CA: Carnegie Foundation for the Advancement of Teaching.

Hay/McBer (2000). *Research into teacher effectiveness.* Report prepared for the Department for Education and Employment, London.

Healey, F., & De Stefano, J. (1997). *Education reform support: A framework for scaling up school reform.* Washington, DC: Abel 2 Clearinghouse for Basic Education.

Heifetz, R. (1994). *Leadership without easy answers.* Cambridge, MA: Harvard University Press.

Henry, M. (1996). *Parent-School collaboration.* Albany: State University of New York Press.

Hess, F. M. (1999). *Spinning wheels: The politics of urban school reform.* Washington, DC: Brookings Institution.

Hill, P., Campbell, C., & Harvey, J. (2000). *It takes a city.* Washington, DC: Brookings Institute.

Hill, P., & Celio, M. (1998). *Fixing urban schools.* Washington, DC: Brookings Institution.

Hill, P., & Crévola, C. (1999). The role of standards in educational reform for the 21st century. In D. Marsh (Ed.), *Preparing our schools for the 21st century* (pp. 117–142). Washington, DC: ASCD Yearbook.

Hodgkinson, H., & Montenegro, Y. (1999). *The U.S. school superintendent.* Washington, DC: Institute for Educational Leadership.

The Holmes Group. (1986). *Tomorrow's teachers.* East Lansing, MI: Author.

The Holmes Group. (1990). *Tomorrow's schools.* East Lansing, MI: Author.

The Holmes Group. (1995). *Tomorrow's schools of education.* East Lansing, MI: Author.

House, E. (1974). *The politics of educational innovation.* Berkeley, CA: McCutchan.

House, G. (2000, April 5). Re-creating a school system: Lessons learned in Memphis about whole-school reform. *Education Week, 19*(30), 38, 41.

Howey, K. R., & Zimpher, N. L. (1989). *Profiles of preservice teacher education, inquiry into the nature of programs*. Albany: State University of New York Press.

Huberman, M. (1983). Recipes for busy kitchens. *Knowledge: Creation, Diffusion, Utilization, 4*, 478–510.

Huberman, M. (1988). Teacher careers and school improvement. *Journal of Curriculum Studies, 20*(2), 119–132.

Huberman, M., & Miles, M. (1984). *Innovation up close*. New York: Plenum.

Ingvarson, L. (1998). Professional development as the pursuit of professional standards. *Teacher and Teacher Education, 14*(1), 127–140.

Jeffrey, B., & Wood, P. (1997). Feeling deprofessionalized. *The Cambridge Journal of Education*, 325–343.

Johnson, S. M. (1996). *Leading to change: The challenge of the new superintendency*. San Francisco, CA: Jossey-Bass.

Katz, E., Lewin, M., & Hamilton, H. (1963). Traditions of research on the diffusion of innovation. *American Sociological Review, 28*(2), 237–252.

Kearns, D., & Harvey, D. (2000). *A legacy of learning*. Washington, DC: The Brookings Institution.

King, M. B., & Newmann, F. M. (2000). Will teacher learning advance school goals? *Phi Delta Kappan, 81*(8), 576–580.

LaRocque, L., & Coleman, P. (1989). Quality control: School accountability and district ethos. In M. Holmes, K. Leithwood, & D. Musella (Eds.), *Educational policy for effective schools* (pp. 168–191). Toronto, Ontario, Canada: OISE Press.

Lasch, C. (1991). *The true and only heaven: Progress and its critics*. New York: W. W. Norton.

Leithwood, K. (Ed.). (2000). *Understanding schools as intelligent systems*. Stamford, CT: JAI Press.

Leithwood, K., Jantzi, D., & Steinback, R. (1999). *Changing leadership for changing times*. Buckingham, UK: Open University Press.

Leithwood, K., Leonard, L., & Sharratt, L. (2000). Conditions fostering organizational learning. In K. Leithwood (Ed.), *Understanding schools as intelligent systems* (pp. 99–124). Stamford, CT: JAI Press.

Lewis, C., Battistich, V., Schaps, E., Solomon, D., & Watson, M. (1998). *School improvement for academic development and resilience: Findings from the Child Development Project*. Oakland, CA: Development Studies Center.

Lighthall, F. (1973, February). Multiple realities and organizational nonsolutions: An essay on anatomy of educational innovation. *School Review*, 255–287.

Lindblom, C. (1959). The science of muddling through. *Public Administration Review, 19*, 155–169.

Little, J. W. (1981). The power of organizational setting. Paper adapted from final report, *School success and staff development.* Washington, DC: National Institute of Education.

Little, J. W. (1990a). The persistence of privacy: Autonomy and initiative in teachers' professional relations. *Teachers College Record, 91*(4), 509–536.

Little, J. W. (1990b). The "mentor" phenomenon and the social organization of teaching. In C. Cazden (Ed.), *Review of Research in Education, 16,* 297–351. Washington, DC: American Educational Research Association.

Little, J., & Dorph, R. (1998). *Lessons about comprehensive school reform.* Berkeley: University of California Press.

Lortie, D. (1975). *School teacher: A sociological study.* Chicago: University of Chicago Press.

Lortie, D. (1987). Built in tendencies toward stabilizing the principal's role. *Journal of Research and Development in Education, 22*(1), 80–90.

Louis, K., & Kruse, S. (Eds.). (1995). *Professionalism and community.* Thousand Oaks, CA: Corwin Press.

Lusi, S. (1997). *The role of the State Department of Education in complex school reform.* New York: Teachers College Press.

McLaughlin, M., & Mitra, D. (2000). Theory-based change and change-based theory: Going deeper, going broader. Unpublished paper, Stanford University, Stanford, CA.

McLaughlin, M., & Talbert, J. (2001). *Professional communities and the work of high school teaching.* Chicago: University of Chicago Press.

McNeil, L. (2000). *Contradictions of school reform.* London: Routledge.

Manno, B., Finn, C., & Vanourek, G. (2000). Beyond the schoolhouse door: How charter schools are transforming U.S. public education. *Phi Delta Kappan, 81*(10), 736–744.

Marris, P. (1975). *Loss and change.* New York: Anchor Press/Doubleday.

Massell, D. (1998). *State strategies for building capacity in education.* Paper presented at the annual meeting of the American Educational Research Association.

Mathews, D. (1996). *Is there a public for public schools?* Dayton, OH: Kettering Foundation Press.

Maurer, R. (1996). *Beyond the wall of resistance.* Austin, TX: Bard Books.

Micklethwait, J., & Wooldridge, A. (1996). *The witch doctors: Making sense of management gurus.* New York: Random House.

Miles, M. (1993). Forty years of change in schools: Some personal reflections. *Educational Administration Quarterly, 29,* 213–248.

Minitrom, M. (2000). *Leveraging local innovation: The case of Michigan's charter schools.* East Lansing, MI: Michigan State University.

Mintzberg, H. (1994). *The rise and fall of strategic planning.* New York: Free Press.

Mintzberg, H., Ahlstrand, B., & Lampei, J. (1998). *Strategy safari: A guided tour through the wilds of strategic management.* New York: Free Press.

Morgan, G. (1989). *Riding the waves of change.* San Francisco: Jossey-Bass.

Mortimore, P., Sammons, P., Stoll, L., Lewis, D., & Ecob, R. (1988). *School matters: The junior years.* Somerset, UK: Open Books.

Murphy, J., Beck, L., Crawford, M., Hodges, A., with McGaughy, C. (in press). *The productive high school.* Buffalo: State University of New York Press.

Murphy, J., Yff, J., & Shipman, N. (in press). Implementation of the interstate school leaders licensure consortium standards. *International Journal of Leadership in Education.*

National Board for Professional Teaching Standards. (1993). *What should teachers know and be able to do?* Detroit, MI: Author.

National Commission on Excellence in Education. (1983). *A nation at risk.* Washington, DC: Author.

National Commission on Teaching and America's Future. (1996). *What matters most: Teaching for America's future.* Washington, DC: Author.

National Research Council. (1999). *Improving student learning.* Washington, DC: National Academy Press.

Newmann, F., King, B., & Youngs, P. (2000). *Professional development that addresses school capacity.* Paper presented at the annual meeting of the American Educational Research Association.

Newmann, F., & Sconzert, K. (2000). *School improvement with external partners.* Chicago: Consortium on Chicago School Research.

Newmann, F., & Wehlage, G. (1995). *Successful school restructuring.* Madison, WI: Center on Organization and Restructuring of Schools.

Noddings, N. (1992). *The challenge to care in schools.* New York: Teachers College Press.

Nonaka, I., & Takeuchi, H. (1995). *The knowledge-creating company.* Oxford, UK: Oxford University Press.

Northwest Regional Education Laboratory. (1993). *Catalogue of school reform models.* Portland, OR: Author.

Oakes, J., Quartz, K., Ryan, S., & Lipton, M. (1999). *Becoming good American schools.* San Francisco, CA: Jossey-Bass.

Odden, A. (1996). Incentives, school organization, and teacher compensation. In S. Fuhrman & J. O'Day (Eds.), *Rewards and reform: Creating educational incentives that work* (pp. 226–256). San Francisco: Jossey-Bass.

Odden, A. (2000). New and better forms of teacher compensation are possible. *Phi Delta Kappan, 8*(5), 361–366.

Ontario College of Teachers. (1999). *Standards of practice*. Toronto, Ontario, Canada: Author.

Peters, T. (1987). *Thriving on chaos: Handbook for a management revolution.* New York: Knopf.

Pincus, J. (1974). Incentives for innovation in public schools. *Review of Educational Research, 44*, 113–144.

Policy focus converges on leadership. (2000, January 12). *Education Week.*

Pressure drives head to drink. (2000, July 14). *The London Times Education Supplement*, p. 5.

Rohlen, T. (1999). Social software for a learning society. In D. Keating & C. Hertzman (Eds.), *Developmental health and the wealth of nations* (pp. 251–273). New York: The Guilford Press.

Rosenblum, S., & Louis, K. (1979). *Stability and change: Innovation in an educational context*. Cambridge, MA: ABT Associates.

Rosenholtz (1989). *Teachers' workplace: The social organization of schools.* New York: Longman.

Ross, S., Wang, L., Sanders, W., Wright, P., & Stringfield, S. (1999). *Two- and three-year achievement results on the Tennessee value-added assessment system for restructuring schools in Memphis*. Unpublished manuscript, University of Memphis, Tennessee.

Rudduck, J., Chaplain, R., & Wallace, G. (1996). *School improvement: What can pupils tells us?* London: David Fulton Publishers.

Sammons, P. (1999). *School effectiveness*. Lisse, The Netherlands: Swetz & Zeitlinger.

Sanders, M., & Epstein, J. (2000). The national network of partnership schools: How research influences educational practice. *Journal of Education for Students Placed at Risk, 5*(1–2), 61–76.

Sarason, S. (1971). *The culture of the school and the problem of change.* Boston: Allyn & Bacon.

Sarason, S. (1982). *The culture of the school and the problem of change* (2nd ed.). Boston: Allyn & Bacon.

Sarason, S. (1990), *The predictable failure of educational reform*. San Francisco: Jossey-Bass.

Sarason, S. B., Davidson, K. S., & Blatt, B. (1986). *The preparation of teachers: An unstudied problem in education* (Rev. ed.). Cambridge, MA: Brookline Books.

Sarason, S. B., & Doris, J. (1979). *Educational handicap, public policy, and social history*. New York: Free Press.

Saul, J. (1995). *The unconscious civilization*. Toronto, Ontario, Canada: Anansi Press.

Schön, D. (1971). *Beyond the stable state*. New York: Norton.

Schorr, L. (1997). *Common purpose: Strengthening families and neighborhoods to rebuild America*. New York: Doubleday.

Scott, C., Stone, B., & Dinham, S. (2000). *International patterns of teacher discontent*. Paper presented at the annual meeting of the American Educational Research Association.

Sebring, P., & Bryk, A. (1998). *School leadership and the bottom line in Chicago*. Chicago: University of Chicago, Consortium on School Research.

Senge, P. (1990). *The fifth discipline*. New York: Doubleday.

Senge, P., Cambron-McCabe, N., Lucas, T., Smith, B., Dutton, J., & Kleiner, A. (2000). *Schools that learn*. New York: Doubleday.

Senge, P., Kleiner, A., Roberts, C., Ross, R., Roth, G., & Smith, B. (1999). *The dance of change*. New York: Doubleday.

Shanker, A. (1990). Staff development and the restructured school. In B. Joyce (Ed.), *Changing school culture through staff development* (pp. 91–103). Alexandria, VA: Association for Supervision and Curriculum Development.

Simms, J. (1978). *The implementation of curriculum innovation*. Unpublished doctoral dissertation, University of Alberta, Edmonton, Canada.

Slavin, R., & Madden, N. (1998). *Disseminating Success for All*. Baltimore: Johns Hopkins University.

Smith, L., & Keith, P. (1971). *Anatomy of educational innovation: An organizational analysis of an elementary school*. New York: Wiley.

Smylie, M., Bay, M., & Tozer, S. (1999). Preparing teachers as agents of change. In G. Griffen (Ed.), *The education of teachers* (pp. 29–62). Chicago: University of Chicago Press.

Snyder, J. (1999). *New Haven unified school district: A teaching quality system for excellence and equity*. New York: Teachers College, Columbia University, National Commission on Teaching and America's Future.

Spillane, J. (1999, April). *The change theories of local change agents: The pedagogy of district policies and programs*. Paper presented at the annual meeting of the American Educational Research Association.

Spillane, J. (2000). Cognition and policy implementation: District policymakers and the reform of mathematics education. *Cognition and Instruction, 18*(2), 141–179.

Spillane, J., & Zeuli, J. (1999). Reform and teaching: Exploring patterns of practice in the context of national and state mathematics reform. *Cognition and Instruction, 21*(1), 1–27.

Stacey, R. (1996a). *Strategic management and organizational dynamics* (2nd ed.). London: Pitman.

Stacey, R. (1996b). *Complexity and creativity in organizations.* San Francisco: Berrett-Koehler.

Steinberg, L. (1996). *Beyond the classroom: Why school reform has failed and what parents need to do.* New York: Simon & Schuster.

Stigler, J., & Hiebert, J. (1999). *The teaching gap.* New York: The Free Press.

Stokes, L., Sato, N., McLaughlin, M., & Talbert, J. (1997). *Theory-based reform and problems of change contexts that matter for teachers' learning and community.* Stanford, CA: Final Report to the Mellon Foundation.

Stoll, L., & Fink, D. (1996). *Changing our schools.* Buckingham, UK: Open University Press.

Storr, A. (1997). *Feet of clay: A study of gurus.* London: HarperCollins.

Thiessen, D., & Howey, K. (Eds.). (1998). *Agents provocateur.* Washington, DC: The American Association of Colleges of Teacher Education.

Times Education Supplement. (1997). *Times Education Supplement Survey.* London: Author.

Urbanski, A., & Erskine, R. (2000). School reform, TURN, and teacher compensation. *Phi Delta Kappan, 81*(5), 367–370.

Von Krogh, G., Ichijo, K., & Nonaka, I. (2000). *Enabling knowledge creation: How to unlock the mystery of tacit knowledge and release the power of innovation.* London: Oxford University Press.

Watkin, C. (2000). The leadership program for serving headteachers. *The Leadership and Organization Development Journal, 21*(1), 13–19.

Werner, W. (1980). *Implementation: The role of belief.* Unpublished paper, Center for Curriculum Studies, University of British Columbia, Vancouver, Canada.

Wigginton, E. (1986). *Sometimes a shining moment: The foxfire experience.* New York: Doubleday.

Wise, A. (1977). Why educational policies often fail: The hyperrationalization hypothesis. *Curriculum Studies, 9*(1), 43–57.

Wise, A. (1988). The two conflicting trends in school reform: Legislative learning revisited. *Phi Delta Kappan, 69*(5), 328–333.

Index

About the Author

Michael Fullan is the Dean of the Ontario Institute for Studies in Education of the University of Toronto. He is recognized as an international authority on educational reform. His ideas for managing change are used in countries around the world and his books have been published in many languages. His *What's Worth Fighting For* trilogy (with Andy Hargreaves) and *Change Forces* trilogy are widely acclaimed.